Everybody's Classroom

Differentiating for the Shared and Unique Needs of Diverse Students

Carol Ann Tomlinson

Foreword by James H. Borland

TEACHERS COLLEGE PRESS

TEACHERS COLLEGE | COLUMBIA UNIVERSITY

NEW YORK AND LONDON

Published by Teachers College Press®, 1234 Amsterdam Avenue, New York, NY 10027

Copyright © 2022 by Teachers College, Columbia University

Front cover art by archideaphoto / iStock by Getty Images.

The "Conclusion" chapter adapts material from *Teaching Reading to Black Adolescent Males: Closing the Achievement Gap*, by Alfred W. Tatum, 2005, Stenhouse. Copyright © 2005. Reproduced with permission of Stenhouse Publishers. www.stenhouse.com.

Library of Congress Cataloging-in-Publication Data is available at loc.gov

ISBN 978-0-8077-6619-4 (paper)
ISBN 978-0-8077-6620-0 (hardcover)
ISBN 978-0-8077-7999-6 (ebook)

Printed on acid-free paper
Manufactured in the United States of America

Contents

Foreword

Mention the word *differentiation* to any educator, and, inevitably, Carol Ann Tomlinson's name will come up. More than any other individual, Professor Tomlinson has made it her life's work to convince teachers and administrators that instructional differentiation is not just a desideratum but a necessity if schools are to truly meet the educational needs of their students, especially in our increasingly diverse classrooms.

The rationale for differentiation is so convincing, thanks in no small part to Professor Tomlinson's tireless and persuasive advocacy, that few in the educational community would advocate "teaching to the middle" or pretending that a class is made up of students whose readiness, aptitudes, and needs are the same in every subject at every time, thereby justifying a reliance on whole-class teaching as one's primary instructional strategy.

However, I visit a number of schools and sit in their classrooms, and you could be forgiven for concluding that differentiation has made relatively fewer inroads into educational practice in this country than one might expect given its necessity. I have visited quite a few school districts where differentiation is the policy. But I have seen very few where it is consistent, quality instructional practice. A policy statement from the superintendent's office or lofty pronouncements from the ivory tower do little to help teachers develop the attitudes and skills needed to make differentiation a reality, not just an empty promise, in American education.

The reason for this, I believe, is that creating a differentiated classroom is no easy undertaking. It takes time, counted in years, not days, to develop the strategies and skills necessary for teaching in a truly differentiated manner. It takes substantial and continuing support from administrators, and an appreciable expenditure of time and resources, to allow teachers to develop into the kind of educators who not only talk the talk but also walk the walk when it comes to differentiation. To address these challenges, Tomlinson offers truly helpful ideas and approaches that will allow readers to experience the kind of success that is both immediately rewarding and also highly motivating to continue to do the needed work as they see students flourish.

Almost 60 years ago, President John F. Kennedy, speaking at Rice University, told Americans that "we choose to go to the Moon in this decade and do the other things, not because they are easy, but because they are hard." Sometimes, as is the case with making our nation's classrooms truly differentiated, we need to seek out the path of most resistance. And there is no one better than Professor Tomlinson to enable us to understand what that path is, how to find an entry point, and how to navigate it.

Professor Tomlinson's preface begins with the following credo: "This book is about Everybody Classrooms—classrooms planned with the belief that every student in the classroom has unique strengths that need to be developed, unique learning needs that vary across time and subjects, and unique patterns of social and affective development." A more succinct, on-target explication of differentiation would be difficult to craft.

As Professor Tomlinson explains, "This book is an invitation to teach hopefully, inclusively, and responsively in ways that stretch us as teachers and that stretch each of the learners in our care" (p. x). Hopeful, inclusive, and responsive teaching—educators who incorporate those qualities into their everyday practice can serve as examples of the heights those who are called to engage in our society's most important profession can reach and inspire their students to reach.

Differentiation *is* difficult, but its importance cannot be gainsaid. I keep returning to the word *hopefully* in the passage above. Hope is a quality that inoculates us against the cynicism that is an ever-present temptation in today's highly charged and sadly politicized schools. With hope, and with the sage guidance of Professor Tomlinson, we can envision schools in which "every student [has] access to classrooms built around meaning-rich curriculum, engaging instruction, positive collaboration, and expectations that indicate a strong belief in each learner's capacity to do important work" (p. ix). I cannot think of a better description of educational excellence. And I cannot think of anyone more qualified to help us reach that level of excellence than Carol Ann Tomlinson.

—James H. Borland
Teachers College, Columbia University

Preface

This book is about *Everybody Classrooms*—classrooms planned with the belief that every student in the classroom has unique strengths that need to be developed, unique learning needs that vary across time and subjects, and unique patterns of social and affective development. These are classrooms whose teachers work with the conviction that every student in their classroom regularly needs the teacher's attention, that no student is an inconvenience, and that no students should feel invisible or inconvenient in classrooms where they spend the preponderance of their waking hours. Those ideas are central to inclusion and differentiation, of course. Everybody Classrooms add additional elements—that every student should have access to classrooms built around meaning-rich curriculum, engaging instruction, positive collaboration, and expectations that indicate a strong belief in each learner's capacity to do important work. These classrooms are invested in equity of opportunity for every student to participate in the best learning experiences a school can provide.

That is not to suggest that inclusion means all students in the same classroom, no matter their needs. There are students whose struggles with learning and/or with life are so great that they require very sheltered support to make their way forward. There are students who are so academically advanced for their age group that public schools lack the human resources necessary to guide their growth. In addition, many teachers will not fare well if their introduction of Everybody Classrooms means their classes will include multiple students with distinct and acute learning needs—especially if those teachers have limited or no experience with differentiating in classrooms with students who bring a more restricted range of learning needs. The message in this book is twofold. First, we can and should do

a much better job of opening our classroom doors to any students who can benefit from membership in classrooms where teachers understand, embrace, and address the human differences that every one of their students brings to school with them every day. Second, such classrooms and their inhabitants can only flourish if the teacher commits to offering each learner access to the highest-quality learning opportunities our profession knows how to provide.

Everybody Classrooms are *big-tent classrooms* with seats at the center of the action for every learner in them. They are *all-embracing classrooms*, welcoming what every student brings to the classroom every day—eager to work with the student as he or she now is and excited to help the student discover what he or she can become. They are *umbrella classrooms* with a canopy generous enough to shelter students when storms come. They are *all-encompassing classrooms* where the learning environment, curriculum, assessment, instruction, and classroom routines are designed to help each learner take his or her next step(s) in growth every day.

Everybody Classrooms offer all comers equity of access to excellent learning opportunities—and support for success with those opportunities.

Everybody Classrooms build teams of learners whose members come to understand that their similarities bind them together and their differences extend their reach.

Everybody Classrooms do not ask students—or their teachers—to be superhuman but rather to work together, one step at a time, to become the best they can be on any given day and over a year of shared opportunity.

If you thought you were about to read a book on inclusion, I think you will find useful ideas and strategies here. If you thought you were about to read a book on differentiation, I hope your needs will be addressed. If you are looking for ways to better respond to the learning needs of students who have experienced trauma, poverty, bias, culture and language differences, or other factors that challenge learning, you will find a repertoire of approaches that draw on the work of experts in the field as well as my own work, and point readers to additional sources as well. If you are looking for something challenging, I believe you have come to a source that will stretch you as a teacher and as a human being.

Lightly paraphrasing an assertion made by Barbara Boroson, we need classrooms designed for the spectacular variety of young learners who populate those classrooms. Among them are students of diverse races, ethnicities, religions, cultures, nationalities, and orientations. There are students just learning the language of the classroom, students of fluid or transitioning genders, students who need glasses or hearing aids or who use wheelchairs, students who come from peaceful homes, students who come from chaotic or violent homes, students who go home not knowing whether there will be food available when they are hungry. There are students with widely differing academic proficiencies kinds of social skills, sensory reactions, levels of emotional maturity, and behavioral patterns. There are students exuberant with the joy of learning and students who have given up on school—or who are about to do so. There are students who have experienced trauma and are struggling not to give up on life. While these differences are not neutral, they are natural. They are part of the classroom, as they are part of all other aspects of life (Boroson, 2020). We need classrooms that are prepared to welcome, embrace, and effectively teach all of these young people—each of them. We need Everybody Classrooms. We will begin the journey of thinking about Everybody Classrooms in Part I of the book by considering what differentiation is—or what it *should be*, how it can help us build classrooms in

which the one constant is student variance, and how a foundation of effective differentiation prepares us and our students for more inclusive teaching and learning. Part II takes a close look at 10 "categories" of learning needs, some of which are commonly addressed in inclusive classrooms and some that reflect student needs less commonly addressed through what we tend to think of as "inclusion"; nonetheless, those learning needs can result in major roadblocks for learners and significant challenges for teachers who teach and mentor those learners. In addition, Part II of the book provides general background on the 11 categories and delineates specific learning needs that are common (but not by any means universal) among students who are often assigned to a category and makes the case that much of what students with these identified learning needs require for growth and success is common across the "categories" and is foundational to effective differentiation. In other words, it makes the case that differentiation, correctly understood and applied, results in classrooms that are ready to embrace students with these and other learning needs.

The two final chapters in the book propose and illustrate the concept of "teaching up" to all learners in differentiated and inclusive classrooms so that the kind of meaning-rich, complex learning opportunities often reserved for just a few students can be the experience of virtually all learners. Readers will also find in the last chapters opportunities to act as clinical observers in two classrooms and use a suggested framework to guide their thinking about the approaches of two teachers to creating Everybody Classrooms. This book is an invitation to teach hopefully, inclusively, and responsively in ways that stretch us as teachers and that stretch each of the learners in our care. Read along with me. Think along with me. Then look at your students and your roles as a teacher a bit differently.

—Carol Ann Tomlinson

Part I

EXPLORING THE BIG PICTURE OF DIFFERENTIATION

An Introduction to Differentiation

I like this class because there is something different going on in here every day. In my other classes, it's like peanut butter for lunch every single day. In this class, it's like my teacher runs a really good restaurant with a big menu and all.

—From an interview with a middle school girl

Big Idea for Chapter 1: To become a master teacher is to become a master learner.

As teachers, we would have to be beyond asleep at the wheel not to notice the remarkable diversity of students who enter our classrooms, or to remain unaware of the daunting range of strengths, needs, dreams, and fears those young learners bring with them every day. It is likely a little easier to overlook the reality that some of those students are lost to learning on most days because of life conditions and/or because the day's content is out of reach for them academically, socially, or emotionally. It is perhaps easier still to overlook the parallel reality that many of our "excellent" students are making "good grades" without stretching, growing, learning new things, or finding their ceilings of possibility. Perhaps easiest of all is overlooking how many students who appear to be doing fine, or at least fine enough, could be doing much better academically if our expectations and support for them were significantly higher, if we were helping them identify and refine their individual strengths, or if we made it impossible for them to feel invisible even as we feel the pressure to cover what we feel must be covered before "the test." The expectation that teachers must "teach" a prescribed and overpacked curriculum in the same way and in the same time span for all students in preparation for a standardized makes it feel impossible to attend to all the needs students bring to school with them daily. We find ourselves practicing triage teaching—sorting the young people we teach and turning our limited attention to those who appear most in need or at least most likely to benefit from the time we can spare them.

Still, I believe, most teachers genuinely understand that "batch teaching" fails a great many learners. I believe that many teachers seek ways to meet students at their varied entry points into learning, to move each of them ahead as far and efficiently as possible, and to help each of them discover and extend their particular strengths. Differentiation is an instructional framework designed to help teachers plan for those goals and translate the plans into classroom action.

SO, WHAT IS DIFFERENTIATION, REALLY?

Differentiation, as I understand it, is an instructional model designed to make room for the needs of a broad range of learners to be meaningfully addressed in a heterogeneous setting. Differentiation shares the belief of inclusion that diversity in a classroom benefits all learners by, for example:

- providing all learners with a sense of belonging;
- reducing stereotypes;
- enhancing understanding, empathy, and respect among learners;
- modeling a world that makes room for all its citizens;
- preparing students for participation and leadership in that world;

- demonstrating the benefit of drawing on many experiences and perspectives;
- increasing friendships;
- supporting collaboration;
- providing flexible learning opportunities;
- helping students achieve to their fullest potential; and
- creating opportunity for each student to develop areas of strength and shore up areas of weakness (Kids Together, Inc., n.d.; New Brunswick Association for Community Living, n.d.).

Understood accurately, differentiation *is*

- an instructional model that prepares the way for successful inclusion;
- for *every* student in a class;
- understanding and acting on the reality that human beings are individuals and therefore differ as learners in ways that can significantly shape the ways in which they learn;
- seeing and planning for students as individuals (THE student) rather than largely seeing them, speaking about them, and planning for them as a batch (the STUDENTS);
- looking for both similarities and differences in students' learning trajectories and planning around both the common and varied needs of students at a particular time in an instructional cycle;
- a collection of attitudes and skills that teachers learn over time by studying their students, trying different approaches to teaching them, and reflecting on what works, for whom, under what conditions, and why; and
- a way of thinking about and "being" in a classroom.

Differentiation is *not*

- only for students with identified special needs, English learners, and students who are advanced;
- a different lesson plan for every student;
- more work for advanced learners or less work for students who struggle;

- teaching down to some students and teaching up to others;
- any specific set of instructional strategies; or
- grouping students inside a classroom or in a school by what we *perceive* to be their "ability."

Figure 1.1 offers some definitions of differentiation that I have used over the years with my university students and teachers with whom I have worked during that time. Figure 1.2 provides some definitions from other professionals who think about and work with differentiation in varied ways. Take a few minutes to see how they compare with your thinking and to consider ways in which they are making similar points and extending other definitions. In Chapters 3 and 4, we'll look at a couple of additional ways to think about differentiation that are helpful in guiding teacher planning.

On some level, what we have come to call "differentiation" is just common sense. If there are genuinely important things for all students to learn, and if some students are not progressing, it follows that a teacher would figure out how to help the student learn in different ways or with different supports or over a longer period of time. Similarly, it seems logical that when students give evidence that they have already mastered particular knowledge or skill, their teacher would figure out how to extend their learning so they continue to develop academically and intellectually. And why would we not help all students discover and extend their unique strengths and interests, or encourage them to learn and express learning in ways that facilitate their success? Why should we not attend to a student's affective and social development just as we should to their academic or intellectual development?

Common sense, however, can be uncommonly difficult to practice—especially in a room with too many young bodies and minds and in the absence of mental images of how a class might look if students often followed different learning paths rather than nearly always moving as a flock. In addition, few teachers feel solid in their understanding of how to make learning more successful for students who are new to the language of the classroom; students from a range of cultures, languages, and races; students who are homeless; students who have to bear the impact of societal inequities and injustice; students

Figure 1.1. Some Basic Definitions of Differentiation

Differentiation looks eyeball to eyeball with the reality that kids differ and that the most effective teachers do whatever it takes to hook the whole range of kids on learning.

It is a way of thinking about the classroom with the goals of honoring each student's learning needs and maximizing each student's learning capacity while developing a solid community of learners.

Differentiation is shaking up the classroom so there are more ways for students to take in new ideas, make sense of them, and express what they have learned.

Differentiation is planning for the unpredictability of the classroom.

Differentiation is respectful teaching.

Differentiation is teachers seeking to see kids first and teaching based on what they learn.

Differentiation is teaching to ensure the support necessary for equity of access to excellent learning opportunities for each student.

who experience an array of physical and/or cognitive barriers to learning; students who are advanced academically, learners who have experienced childhood trauma, those who march to a different and more creative drummer, those who grapple with sexual identity, those who bring with them two or more exceptionalities to the classroom, and so on. As an anxious teacher once exclaimed in a workshop I was leading, "How can anyone expect us to attend to students' needs when they all have needs!?"

Teachers aren't, and can't be, expert in all those areas. Still, the grand array of students comes into our classrooms daily, and there *are* things we can do to make school much more hospitable and learning much more fruitful for each student. We just need the will to persist over time in developing the knowledge, understanding, and skill necessary to do those things. That is the ticket to success in almost any human endeavor. We ask our students to grapple with holding a pencil, learning math facts, creating the illusion of perspective on a flat piece of paper, strategically kicking a soccer ball,

finding meaning in the unfolding of history, communicating in a language new to them. We don't ask them to master it all on day one. Rather, we do all we can to enlist each student's persistence toward a goal over time, lift them up when they stumble and get discouraged, and then gently insist that they once again focus on their own next step toward the goal and move forward. There's no magic in the process, just determination. The magic happens as the learning does. It's like that, too, in becoming the teacher who is a powerful, positive force in the development of *each* student—rather than generally teaching the class as though all students were a single entity.

CAUTION: CHANGE AHEAD!

Differentiation itself is not as difficult as you might think—especially if you give yourself permission to develop its skills over time. What *is* difficult is the reality that in order to develop those skills, you

Figure 1.2. Some Additional Definitions of Differentiation

Differentiation is making sure that the right students get the right learning tasks at the right time. Once you have a sense of what each student holds as 'given' or 'known' and what he or she needs in order to learn, differentiation is no longer an option; it is an obvious response.

—Lorna Earl (2003), *Assessment as Learning*

Differentiated instruction is a way of taking into account the needs and wants of others without either relinquishing our own needs and wants or dominating and controlling the other person. In that way, differentiated instruction is more than just a method of teaching. It is a way of being human.

—John Stroup, University of Virginia Graduate Student

I think of differentiation in terms of taking into account each individual's unique development, talents, strengths, and interests; becoming aware of each individual's distinct and unique characteristics; and then tailoring educational practice to account for these differences.

—Elliott Seif, author of *Teaching for Lifelong Learning*

Differentiation is ***teaching*** so that "typical" students; students with disabilities; students who are gifted; and students from a range of cultural, ethnic, and language groups can ***learn together, well.***

Not just inclusion, but inclusive teaching.

—J. Michael Peterson & Mishael M. Hitte (2005), *Inclusive Teaching: Creating Effective Schools for All Learners*

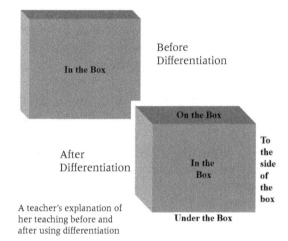

A teacher's explanation of her teaching before and after using differentiation

must give up some habits and practices that may have become "givens" in your classroom. You do not have to relinquish them all at once—it is a stepwise process—but differentiation, practiced in a way that enables you to put students at the center of your work, will lead you to make significant shifts in how you think about, plan for, and enact teaching and learning. For example, differentiation asks teachers to move from thinking about

- able vs. not able in favor of belief in their own capacity and the capacity of their students to learn,
- coverage in favor of student understanding,
- a focus on teaching in favor of a focus on learning,
- the class as a whole to thinking about varied student needs,
- fixed time in favor of fluid and flexible time, and
- assessment as judging in favor of assessment as mentoring.

The changes are not arbitrary. They are necessary for significant differentiation. They are necessary precisely because of what differentiation asks teachers to do. It is not possible to put students at the center of your work if you follow a strict pacing guide. It is not feasible to find time in your schedule to address the varied needs that exist in your classroom if you feel compelled to "cover" the curriculum by a prescribed date. It is not likely that students can grow in social and affective skills if you shy away from students working often in pairs or small groups. A good number of your students will be reluctant to invest heavily in learning if, for example, grades and/or discipline procedures feel punitive or if the environment in the classroom or the absences of images of their lives in curriculum and instruction cause them to feel "less than."

The positive side of change, of course, is that while we humans often resist it mightily, it is necessary for our own growth and development. As you risk small changes that lead you to larger ones, you'll likely find that teaching is more rewarding to you, that your students are responding to you with a greater sense of trust, that you like having more time to connect with and actually teach individual students during a class period or day, and that you feel renewed in your work. Those are comments I hear often from teachers who have made the transition to differentiation. They also nearly always tell me that they can't imagine going back to the way they taught earlier in their careers.

The journey to meaningful change is a long one. I've been at it for over 50 years as I write this sentence. As I look back over that time, I see myself becoming more effective and confident in working with my students throughout that span. I've always liked the answer noted cellist Pablo Casals gave when someone asked him at the age of 83 why he continued to practice several hours every day. "Because," he replied, "I think I am still learning." Me too! And why not? I do not want to go to a doctor who does not feel compelled to improve markedly and continually in her practice. I would be leery of a parent who told me he learned all he needed to know about parenting in his first year or so as a father. The potential to remake, reinvent ourselves is a human gift. It extends us. I hope this book will be an invitation for its readers to opt for that path as well.

A FINAL THOUGHT

A key goal of this book is to help teachers grow a foundational understanding of differentiation, including:

- the realization that part of constructing that foundation is a reasonable awareness of the kinds of needs students bring to the classroom with them,
- how they manifest those needs in the classroom, and
- some fundamental beliefs and practices that help a teacher respond meaningfully to those needs.

Toward that end, the book has two parts. The first five chapters lay out the essentials of quality differentiation. Chapter 6 links those essentials of effective *differentiation* with foundational planning for effective *inclusion*. Part I, then, proposes 12 key principles to guide a teacher's thinking about, planning for, implementing, and reflecting on his or her work in order to benefit each of those learners. These principles serve as a sort of GPS for teachers who want to address learner-specific needs and goals as well as goals for the class.

Part II of the book focuses on clusters or "categories" of learner needs that you will likely see in the classes you teach. What you glean from Part I should plug into Part II so you are prepared to use your expanding knowledge about addressing student variance to support more positive outcomes for a broader range of students—and therefore for you as well—step by step, over time.

The contents of the chapters in Part II are largely a product of my learning—in primary, middle school, high school, and university classrooms over 5 decades—how to be a more effective teacher for each of my students. Like most teachers, I began my career with little clarity about what it meant to teach well. In my early days of teaching, I felt like a failure more often than not. Through most of my 20 years in K–12 classrooms, I was privileged to work with a cadre of teachers who were eager, energetic, innovative, and not easily dissuaded. We met regularly. We shared classroom experiences. We confronted our inadequacies and tried to sort out our confusion. Sometimes we scrapped our ideas and started over. Sometimes we held onto the kernel of an idea and reshaped it. Sometimes we just tweaked. Occasionally, all we needed to do was polish. After nearly 20 years of that collegial process, we understood so many more things about teaching and learning than when we began our work together. We had both greater depth and breadth of knowledge. We were generally invigorated. And still we failed. But because we had grown markedly, we failed better, smarter, and with less discouragement. That's what teaching is about—learning.

From time to time in the book, I'll share with you some of the experiences and insights my colleagues and I shared as we tried to become more effective in our work. These insights and experiences have served me and my students well over a long period of time. Combined with the opportunities I have had as a university professor, in my second life as an educator, to study our field's best understanding of the attributes of effective teaching and learning from both psychology and neuroscience, the depth and breadth of my knowledge are greater still. And I still fail. That's the nature of our profession. For me, it makes pursuing the art of teaching endlessly challenging and rewarding. I hope you feel that way as well.

CHAPTER 2

Flexibility as the Underpinning of Differentiation

Elizabeth Ann fell back on the bench with her mouth open. She felt really dizzy. What crazy things the teacher said! She felt as though she were being pulled limb from limb. "What's the matter?" asked the teacher, seeing her bewildered face. "Why—why," said Elizabeth Ann, "I don't know what I am at all. If I'm second grade arithmetic and seventh grade reading and third grade spelling, what grade am I?" The teacher laughed. "You aren't any grade at all, no matter where you are in school. You're just yourself, aren't you? What difference does it make what grade you're in? And what's the use of reading little baby things too easy for you just because you don't know your multiplication table?"

—Dorothy Canfield Fisher, *Understood Betsy*

> Big Idea for Chapter 2: A classroom cannot work well for any specific kind of learner until it is designed to work well for all kinds of learners.

My first meaningful insight about what we now call differentiation came early in my teaching when a small, fragile-looking boy with large, pleading eyes whispered something to me in the hall during a class change in the third week of school. The hall of our middle school was predictably noisy. He spoke softly and with his hand over his mouth. I had never seen him, but assumed he needed help in opening his locker because that was an endemic problem for students who came to us as middle school ramped up again each year. After three tries, I understood what he was actually trying to tell me. The message was brief and terrifying for both of us. "I can't read," he said, looking at the floor.

He was not 12 or 13 as I had assumed. In fact, he was 15 and entering my class of 12- and 13-year-olds for the first time that day. I instantly realized two things. First, I had no idea how to teach reading, no materials that would help me, and no sense of how to integrate him into the class in ways that would lead to respect and camaraderie among his peers. Second, and far more importantly, I knew I could not let him down. It was an act of great courage and trust that I had seen as first period

shifted to second. I would figure out what to do. I had no choice. And day by day, I did just that—imperfectly every day, but well enough some days so that he made progress and so did I. His name was Golden, and I'll come back to his story shortly.

The word "flexibility" is not exactly a synonym for differentiation, but it certainly reflects a pivotal characteristic of teachers who differentiate robustly and effectively just as it reflects a defining characteristic of an effectively differentiated classroom. Flexibility is necessary in a classroom for the same reason that differentiation is necessary—individuals vary in a myriad of ways that shape their learning. They do not learn in unison or as a pack. Learning is a highly individual proposition. We are led to believe that we teach a class, but that is not correct. We teach young brains that have much in common but that are also wired in ways that result in significant differences, and so we need to teach individual brains. Combine that reality with the vast variety of students' cultures, languages, home experiences, talents, interests, fears, social development, emotional maturity, school experiences, and temperaments, and the idea that we serve students effectively when we favor one-size-fits-all teaching with tight-ship approaches to classroom "management" seems poorly suited to contemporary learners. So, what does flexibility imply, and what does it not suggest?

WHAT FLEXIBILITY IN THE CLASSROOM MEANS, AND WHAT IT DOESN'T MEAN

Let's start with what flexibility doesn't mean. It does *not* mean:

- **Chaos.** The idea of a disorderly, effective classroom is a fiction. Many of us lived with at least some chaos in our earliest years of teaching. It's not something most of us care to revisit. Chaos is disruptive to students—even traumatic for some. It serves both teachers and students quite poorly. In fact, researchers tell us that "flexible-orderly classrooms" are necessary for complex thinking and deep learning because neither of those things is particularly linear and both are somewhat "messy" and unpredictable (Sousa & Tomlinson, 2018). Disarray impairs many of the important academic and social outcomes teachers want for their students. Flexibility supports them.
- **Evidence of weak planning.** In fact, flexibility requires clear, thoughtful planning so that the teacher is always aware of learning intentions, what matters most in curriculum, time constraints, and even philosophical underpinnings that serve as a compass in the classroom. It is precisely that level of care and planning that keeps flexibility from morphing into chaos, allowing learning to work for the class as a whole as well as for the individuals who make up the whole. Young people of all ages can work well in flexible classrooms when we partner with them to establish and clarify routines and teach them systematically how to use the routines to benefit their learning and the learning of their classmates.
- **A lowering of expectations.** In an effectively differentiated classroom, the teacher "teaches up." That is, he or she plans first for learning experiences that will challenge advanced learners and differentiates in order to enable all

students to access those rich experiences. Flexibility enables more students to work at much higher levels of thought and productivity than is possible in more rigid contexts. Teachers who rightly understand differentiation never teach down. Rather, they teach students how to learn so they can achieve more at higher levels of complexity.

Flexibility *does* mean:

- **A teacher who sees that rules and procedures should serve students rather than students being in service of the rules.** That is, the teacher understands that predictability in classroom routines and practices provides a sense of security and safety for students and teacher alike, and simultaneously understands that because human beings vary within and among themselves, the predictability has to combine with a certain amount of malleability to facilitate rather than inhibit the development of some of those variable beings some of the time.
- **A teacher making visible a growth mindset.** That is, the teacher deeply believes that each student has a reservoir of untapped potential and can learn far more than we or they generally believe they can. Flexibility in instruction enables the teacher to demonstrate that belief to students and to work with students in stepwise sequences that prove to each student that with focused persistence and consistent support, they can see their success unfold.
- **Teacher–student partnerships in learning.** Flexibility allows time for a teacher to observe students at work, provide actionable feedback to guide a student's next steps, teach small groups of learners, seek and respond to student voice and input in all aspects of classroom life and work, and guide students in developing increased agency as learners. Those things are difficult to achieve broadly in more scripted, lockstep, and tightly controlled settings.
- **A teacher mindfully using the features of classroom life in varied ways that**

respond to students' varied needs. As often as possible, the teacher's internal question is, "In what way can I use this feature (for example, time, space, materials, schedule) to support student growth and success?" The next section of this chapter provides examples of classroom features that teachers can use flexibly to benefit student development.

WHAT FLEXIBILITY MIGHT LOOK LIKE IN THE CLASSROOM, AND WHY

There are many features or attributes of classroom life and work that a teacher can use flexibly. The goal is not to use them all at once or to use them all flexibly all the time. Rather, the idea is for a teacher to plan and work with the awareness that adapting the right element at the right time can boost learning for a student or group of students. Figure 2.1 presents 10 features a teacher can use flexibly to benefit student learning.

SOME ILLUSTRATIONS OF TEACHER FLEXIBILITY IN DIFFERENTIATED CLASSROOMS

Noah Needs to Move

At 13, Noah was not yet quite 5 feet tall and had the general build of a 4th-grader. He was interested in all sorts of things, resulting at times in a fickle attention span. When he was engaged with what was happening in the classroom, however, he was in the game 100%. One day, a couple of months into the school year, the class was having a weighty discussion about a character in a story we were reading when I noticed that Noah was out of his seat and walking around his desk. I was a young teacher, relatively inexperienced, but I decided to watch him for a bit before I asked him to sit back down. He didn't seem to be distracting anyone. In fact, it appeared that no one even noticed him. So, for the moment, I decided not to intervene. The discussion continued without interruption and several

times Noah contributed to it, pausing beside his desk when he spoke.

As the class ended, I was puzzled, but assumed Noah's wandering was a one-time event and thought little of it for the next couple of days until, once again, he began a slow trek around his desk. This time, I did not watch Noah. I watched the other students in the classroom. My concern was perhaps typical of a novice teacher. I was afraid that if I let Noah get up and wander, other students would want to do it too. Once again, if anyone noticed him, they did not seem to pay much attention.

In time, I came to understand that he moved around his desk when he was thinking hard—when he was particularly absorbed by an idea. In a way, he was serving as a barometer for the degree to which a lesson or conversation was enlisting student attention. From time to time, Noah quietly set out on his slow, circular walks.

As second semester began, Noah's father came to a parent-teacher conference evening. When he walked in the door, I knew instantly who he was because Noah's face reflected his so clearly. I also had an immediate insight into Noah's unusual need to walk. Noah's dad was about 6' 5" tall. Noah was just beginning a major growth spurt and his body ached all the time. He was moving because it hurt not to move and because he had been seated for most of 6 hours before he got to our classroom. Noah grew about 4 inches that semester. He told me later that during his 7th-grade year, his legs and arms ached so much that he almost couldn't think. When he wanted to think deeply, he walked. That let his "brain do its thing." Lesson learned: It's not necessary to be rigid because "if I let one student do something, all the others will want to as well." They will not, and, in fact, they are remarkably aware that different kids have different needs at different times.

Can I Turn in My Project Late?

Students with whom I shared classes often created products or performances as culminating experiences for a unit, a marking period, or even a semester or year. They were opportunities to connect what we had been learning about with their interests, talents, or experiences. They provided us a chance to

Figure 2.1. Some Classroom Features That Can Be Used Flexibly to Benefit Student Learning

Classroom Feature	How It Might be Used Flexibly	Why It Can Support Learning
Time	Some students may need more time to complete work because they work slowly, have learning challenges, or need to explore a topic in greater depth than others.	Flexible use of time helps a student work at an appropriate level of challenge. The goal of student work should be showing understanding, not finishing a race. Some students need more time to learn, at least some of the time.
Space	A room can have spaces that allow for different student configurations and working arrangements or can be set up in different ways as needs arise. There can be space for both individual and group work, for conversation or quiet work. There should also be a space for the teacher to work with individuals and small groups.	Different student work often calls for different uses of space. Centers, stations, conversation areas, and other arrangements allow attention to students' learning needs and preferences. In addition, it is beneficial to give students choices about working arrangements when feasible to support their comfort, voice, ownership, and productivity.
Student Groupings	Students can work in groups with peers who currently have similar readiness needs, students of varied entry points into a lesson or topic, similar or dissimilar interests, similar or dissimilar learning preferences, based on student or teacher choice—or randomly. Also, expert groups can enable students to focus efforts on topics or segments of topics that are interesting or relevant to them.	It is important for students to work in a variety of contexts to hear different voices and perspectives rather than being "categorized" as a particular "kind" of learner. Students bring different strengths to different tasks and benefit from both contributing their strengths and learning from the strengths of others. Flexible grouping promotes respect among students and casts members of the class as part of a learning team to which everyone contributes.
Materials	Students can work with materials at varied reading levels, with or without manipulatives, with print or auditory text, with models or visuals, or with texts in English or another language based on interests, preferences, or needs.	Different sources and types of input can boost student learning at varied points in their growth and also depending on their interests and approaches to learning at a given time. Finding the right sources for a student can support both motivation and achievement.
Working Modes	Students often appreciate having the option for working with a partner, a group, or alone on an assignment. Similarly, it often makes sense to give them choices about how to take in and process what they are learning.	Choice of working modes provides an opportunity for student voice while honoring a student's learning preferences. In many instances, it makes little difference how a student works, and if the goal is accomplishing a task, choice can facilitate that goal.
Student Goals	While there are typically common learning goals for students in a class, Individualized Education Plans can specify alternatives for some or all of the class goals. It can also be helpful for students to have their own personalized goals or to work with goals suggested by the teacher for individuals.	Whole-group goals often do not take into account students' talents, interests, need for advanced work, or need to fill important gaps in background knowledge, understanding, or skill. Student-specific goals can address strengths, needs, and/or interests and can support growth from a student's current development as well as ownership of learning and motivation.
Mode of Expressing Learning	A good assessment (formative or summative) maximizes the opportunity for a student to share all he or she knows about a topic. Often, limiting mode of expression limits that opportunity and thus the effectiveness of the assessment for a student.	Limiting mode of expressing learning can be particularly constricting for English language learners and students with some forms of learning disability. For some students, opening up mode of expression allows them to draw on and develop strengths or talents. Choice of mode of expressing learning also provides opportunity for student voice in and ownership of learning.

(continued)

Figure 2.1. (*continued*)

Classroom Feature	How It Might be Used Flexibly	Why It Can Support Learning
Student Independence	When assignments and products call for student independence, it is important for that work to be presented to a student slightly beyond his or her current level of independence and with support necessary to continue to develop as an independent learner. Students in almost any class vary widely in their degree of independence at a given time.	If student work assumes more independence than a student has, the outcome is likely to be of poor quality as well as a source of frustration and discouragement. When supports help students move through the work with increased competence, not only does the quality of the work improve, but also the student is growing in independence or agency as a learner.
Models of Student Work	Seeing models of previous student work can help current students envision what a quality finished product might look like more effectively than directions or even a rubric can.	Providing a student with models of competent work at a level of sophistication slightly above their current performance level can offer both clarity and an appropriate level of challenge that inspire success.
Reporting Student Progress	To support student motivation, engagement, and persistence, grades are best reported in three categories: performance (what the student currently knows, understands, and can do); process (the degree to which the student's patterns of work contribute to his/her academic growth); and progress (growth evidenced since a prior report card grade) (Guskey, 1994, 2020). Sometimes called 3-P grading, this approach is both more revealing and more encouraging than more traditional grades. The three grades should not be averaged, but rather reported separately. Some reporting systems use 3-P indicators. When that is not the case, a teacher can provide an addendum to the report card, communicate by e-mail, or share the information in a parent or parent/student conference.	Report card grades contribute to a cycle of discouragement for many students who struggle in school. For students whose grades are consistently high, report cards often do more to promote getting more high grades than to promote actual learning and intellectual stretching. A *performance* grade clarifies a student's current status with designated knowledge, understanding, and skill. A *process* grade helps the student and teacher develop a common vocabulary to advance student agency as a learner. A *progress* grade acknowledges growth, which should be a critical indicator of success for every student.

talk about and develop benchmarks for excellence. Students generally took pride in their work and looked forward to sharing what they created with a variety of audiences. There were opportunities for check-ins with and feedback from peers and me as students developed these long-term assignments.

I sometimes felt conflicted as a due date neared. We had worked together to help each learner develop habits of mind and work that should not only enable students to create an end-product they were proud of but should also help them become more confident and skilled as learners. So when a due date was on the horizon and a student asked if he or she could have extra time to complete the work, I was torn. My knee-jerk instinct was to remind the student that following a timeline was an important

skill for success—and besides, they should have had ample time and support to meet the deadline. A more reflective question to myself was whether the quality of a student's work might benefit from an extra day or two, and whether that quality might be more important than my line in the sand. Still, these were young adolescents who just might have wasted time along the way. I wasn't sure that I wanted to enable that behavior.

My compromise was to talk with the students about the conflict I was experiencing. I asked them if any of them had ever squandered time on a piece of work and then panicked when they realized they had too much to accomplish to complete the work before a due date. Nearly all of them laughed. Several shared stories. I shared a couple of my own.

I talked with them about the difference between a student who might want to polish or extend a piece of work that was essentially complete and met the indicators of quality we had established versus a student who "needed" time to compensate for his or her deficits in planning. They understood and felt the first student should be granted additional time while the second one should not.

As the conversation progressed, one student suggested that I might create a form on which a student could request an extension of time. The form would ask for two pieces of information. First, a student would provide a detailed reason for making the request, with evidence that the work was already of high quality based on our class rubric. Second, the student had to describe ways in which the time would be used to extend the depth, breadth, or presentation of the work. The student would complete the form and place it in a "request for extension" box that another student volunteered to make for us. I would read each submission, examine the evidence and plans, and either approve or deny the request, returning the form to its author.

We used that process for years with good results. In addition to enabling students to push for greater scope or quality in their work, it also enabled me to invite students with specific learning needs to use the form. I did that one-on-one—privately. Those students could submit the form to share plans for how additional time and support would help them with reading, researching, writing, organizing ideas, getting additional feedback, and so on. Students who struggled with writing met with me to talk about their request. I am not aware of students who misused the process. The flexibility resulted in better work, less anxiety, and a sense of greater safety in the class—even though the expectations were always high.

Flexible Space in an Inflexible Classroom

Mrs. Schlim was a history teacher whom I often observed and from whom I learned much. She taught in an aging school building with square classrooms and individual student desks. Class sizes were large. There was nothing promising about the space. As the class period was ending on the first day I visited her class, she asked the students to arrange the room in a seminar format on their way out. Every student moved their desk (and occasionally a desk that was unoccupied that day) to a new location. The transition happened so quickly and effortlessly that it seemed like magic to me. Students in the next class knew where to sit as they came into the room and understood generally the kind of work for which they needed to prepare. As that class ended, she asked the students to arrange the desks for learning stations. Once again, student movement was purposeful, quiet, and swift. As the day progressed, students moved the furniture two more times. Each time, I shook my head with some dismay as I asked myself why I had felt it necessary to move all the classroom furniture that needed moving for the past 15 years.

Early in the year, Mrs. Schlim previewed for her students several ideas she had for making the class lively and relevant for them. She asked for their responses to and suggestions for each of the ideas she presented and invited them to offer additional possibilities. As the discussion progressed, she asked the students what she and they would need to do to make the ideas possible in their classroom space. Students quickly realized that much of what they were envisioning could not work with rows of desks facing forward, so they would have to figure out different ways to arrange the desks and would all have to pitch in to move the desks as their work called for different arrangements.

Mrs. Schlim drew four seating charts in addition to the forward-facing-desk configuration and gave each one a name. (The name did not necessarily reflect the nature of work students would do in that arrangement. For example, students did have seminars in the Seminar Format, but other activities that worked well in that arrangement also occurred in that format.) Over the first couple of weeks of school, she and the students rehearsed moving the furniture in a way that would be "efficient without being disruptive." They looked forward to the variety of approaches to learning in that history class and happily contributed to those opportunities in a variety of ways.

Lesson learned: If I mean for the classroom to be "ours" and not "mine," I need to take care to enlist the students as my partners in as many aspects of our shared life as possible. Flexibility requires shared understanding and responsibility.

Learning to Choose Partners Wisely

Ms. Harrold worked consistently with her 1st-graders to help them make thoughtful choices, including in choosing working partners. One day after she had explained an assignment to her students and had made certain they understood the work ahead, she asked them to tell her what skills and strengths the assignment required. They replied that it called for reading, understanding what they read, writing, and using their imaginations.

"I agree," she said. "Now, tap on the side of your head like we do when we are thinking hard, and figure out which of those skills are strong ones for you." After sharing their conclusions with a classmate seated on the floor near them, Ms. Harrold said, "Okay, now tap and think again and this time, think about the skills you would like some help with as you work." Following another brief exchange with a different student, she continued, "Third time. Tap again and think about a student you know who might make a good partner for you because the two of you are strong in different areas."

Next, she watched as students walked around the area and approached a potential partner. In time, she gave them a signal to stop in place and asked the partners to talk about their strengths and their needs for support to be sure they were prepared to help one another do the work really well so they could be proud of what they accomplished. A few students decided to change partners. One group ended up with three members and Ms. Harrold told them she thought that they could make that work just fine.

As the students found spots at tables or on the floor to begin reviewing their task and planning their work, Ms. Harrold walked around the room listening in on their conversations. She also noticed that Seth and Jason had chosen to work together. The two little boys were full of life, not the best at following directions, and neither was yet a confident reader or writer. Kneeling beside the pair, she asked them to remind her what skills the work called for and was pleased that they were accurate in their response. She followed up by asking them to consider their own strengths and needs and, after a pause to allow a moment for thinking, she continued, "So, now tell me, do you think the two of you are a match made in heaven?" Without a pause,

Jason nodded energetically and spoke, "Oh yes, Ms. Harrold, Seth has looks and I've got imagination and we're on the road to success!"

Lesson learned: When teachers prepare students to make good choices, many students do just that much of the time. There are always likely to be a few students, however, who will need more support in choosing thoughtfully. It is counterproductive to scold students of any age for poor decisions. After all, we still make them, too. Sometimes it's wiser to say, "You know, I think I'm going to ask you to try a different path today and we'll see how that goes." Other times it is wise to let those students continue in their chosen route if the stakes are not high. Sometimes they surprise us, and we see them in a different light. Sometimes the experience provides a case in point that can facilitate an instructive conversation between a teacher and the student(s) involved before a next choice. Always, however, we should continue teaching students how to be more aware and mindful in decision-making. It is every bit as important as persistence in teaching reading, math, music, or the skills of soccer. Supporting student self-direction and agency may be the most important learning goal of all—especially for students who do not find the classroom and its demands an easy fit.

Learning from Golden

I had learned a reasonable amount about the dividends of flexibility before Golden further changed my teaching and my life. I began class every day by taking a few minutes to talk about something my students cared about. I used small groups for a variety of purposes. With some regularity, I gave students choices about what to read and how to show what they were learning. I asked for student feedback and altered my plans based on their input. Still, I had a lot to learn.

Golden taught me that I could use different reading materials for different learners and still have all of them explore and talk about the same "big ideas" or concepts. He taught me that sometimes we must take the side of a learner rather than giving our allegiance to what appears to be a sacred and inviolable grading system. Perhaps most importantly, he showed me the truth of the big idea stated at the beginning of this chapter: A classroom cannot work well for any specific kind of learner until it is designed to work well for all kinds of learners.

While I knew early on that I had an impressive range of learners in my classroom, before Golden, I still planned a common lesson, common activities, and common homework for all students on most days, moving among students to provide extra support or to try to extend their thinking. My differentiation was reactive rather than proactive. While responding in the moment to the signals students send to indicate that something in a lesson isn't working for them can be quite useful, that approach is clearly not adequate to help an English language learner master academic vocabulary or to help a student with a significant learning disability plow through dense task directions. Reactive differentiation was clearly not enough to help Golden chart a more promising course as a reader, and so I learned to differentiate proactively as well.

I realized after a few weeks of struggling to find time to work with Golden while I helped the other 35+ students in my class that the way I was framing my teaching plans was anything but flexible. I planned as though I needed to create one plan for the "regular" kids and another one for Golden, who clearly was not a "regular" kid in terms of his current academic needs. There were so many "regular" kids that their work seemed always to fill all the time we had together. It was a struggle to find even a few minutes to spend alone with Golden.

I identified my problem one day when I quickly gave Golden an assignment I had created for him as the "regular" kids were responding to a writing prompt. I had to explain the work to him, of course, because he could not read directions. Although I talked softly to him, another boy seated at his table overheard what I was saying and almost apologetically asked, "Could I please do what he's doing. I think that might help me."

This student was well ahead of Golden as a reader, though he was not close to reading at a 7th-grade level. I knew that, but I had not come to terms with the reality that much of what I asked him to do was so far out of his current league that it made little sense to him. At that moment, I understood that my greatest challenge in terms of flexibility was that many students needed me in quite different ways on any given day. As long as I could escape that reality, I could ask them all to do the same thing in the same way over the same time span with roughly the same support system and feel okay about it. In that moment, on that day, however, I began to grapple with the need to plan proactively with the varied needs of specific learners in mind. It was a game-changer for me.

We'll look in Chapter 4 at a metaphor that can be helpful in thinking about flexible instructional planning. I call the metaphor "Highways and Exit Ramps." It is a way of thinking about planning that consistently takes into account both the shared and variable needs of learners in a class—both needs of "the STUDENTS" and "THE student."

Flexibility in the classroom is no doubt a more natural approach for some teachers than for others. Like the young people we teach, teachers are a varied lot. Those of us who may be more inclined to lead by firm rule can nonetheless learn to employ flexibility and to appreciate it. We are likely to value flexibility in our work as we determine to

- make teaching students our focus rather than covering content;
- get to know our students as individuals so that their individuality is clear to us;
- see, think about, and plan more regularly for THE student rather than only or largely the STUDENTS; and
- teach in ways that help students become increasingly convinced of our belief in and support for their success, increasingly optimistic about their learning prospects, increasingly engaged in their work, and therefore increasingly trustworthy.

A FINAL THOUGHT

For all of our fears that differentiating instruction asks too much of us as teachers, the reality is that differentiation itself is not as difficult as giving up familiar and comfortable ways we currently envision, plan for, and implement teaching. After all, most of us have spent 12 or 13 years as students in classrooms where one-size-fits-all classrooms were the norm, and the images we formed there are deeply embedded in our minds. Then most of us studied in schools of education where we were taught as we had always been taught—more as a flock than as individuals. During that time, most of us had our first consequential teaching experiences in classrooms where our supervising teachers cautioned us to be sure to keep all the students moving together so we could cover the curriculum efficiently. Then, as we moved into our own classrooms and began to establish ourselves as competent professionals, many of us were told by more experienced colleagues that "in this school, all students read the same novel and all students do the same homework." It was not feasible, they told us, to do otherwise. Sometimes, there was an unvoiced subtext that if we elected to "teach against the grain" (Cochran-Smith, 1991, p. 279) we might find that we were outsiders in the faculty.

While I am grateful to live in a time where advances in many fields extend and enrich our lives, I also find myself wishing from time to time that today's novice teachers had the opportunity to intern in the one-room schoolhouses of long ago like the one referenced at the start of this chapter. In those places, there was no master plan to teach all comers alike.

There were 17-year-olds in the room with 6-year-olds, and sometimes the 6-year-old was a more fluent reader than his decade-older classmate. The only approach that made practical sense was to figure out where a student was entering a content area and move the student forward from that point.

The teacher looked for students who had a similar need at a particular time and then organized time, space, and materials so she could work with students in shifts and cycles to be sure every student got the attention needed to continue developing as a reader or a mathematical reasoner. Students regularly helped one another with their classwork. And always there were shared times when the teacher led students in exploring ideas in common.

Those teachers who were the engineers of a literate population a century or half-century ago would be confused by our compulsion to teach everyone alike. And yet, our classroom rosters reflect a greater diversity of readiness, experience, language, culture, handicapping conditions, and economic backgrounds than entered the doors of any one-room school.

One-room schoolhouses still exist in many parts of the world. A few still exist in the United States and still prepare all comers for a complex world. Teachers in those places lack many of the bells and whistles found in contemporary unified or consolidated schools, but spending time in those classrooms and looking at how the teachers there go about purposefully and proactively planning to teach with the needs of individuals in mind would allow us to see flexibility in action and could go a great distance in helping us create "new" images of how we might shift our stubborn paradigm.

Taking Care of the Foundation

I would probably say that reading The Hate You Give *is the best part of the year. The reason is because I finally read a book in my school career that I liked or that relates to me. The book had made a feeling on me that I couldn't explain, and I just wanted to keep reading . . .*

—Excerpt from a high school freshman's English course evaluation

> Big Idea for Chapter 3: Tending to the foundational elements in a classroom may not feel like what you dream of creating with your students there, but ensuring that it is and remains sound frees you to be the architect of a dream more powerful than you had imagined.

During my years in K–12 education and my early years at the university, I thought of differentiation as a set of instructional approaches that encouraged attention to learners' varied needs. That changed in my 3rd year at the University of Virginia, as I had monthly meetings with a teacher who had been hired as a differentiation coach in a school district about an hour away. She was the first person I had known in that role, so I was eager to learn from her experiences. She was the only person in her district with that assigned role, so she was eager to talk with someone who understood what she was hoping to accomplish.

Our first several meetings began in much the same way, although I am not sure she saw the pattern. She would begin by saying, "I don't think I'm doing what I'm supposed to be doing." When I asked why, she said at various points, "Because two of the teachers I'm working with right now don't really seem to like kids or to trust them, and I don't know how to help them with differentiation until we can address that issue at least to some degree first," or "Because several classrooms I'm in are really disorganized and I feel like I have to help the teachers with that before I can do much with differentiation," or "Because the curriculum

in so many classes is deadly boring and it doesn't seem reasonable to try to teach people to differentiate content that is pretty awful to start with." I could never disagree with her line of logic in those moments. Differentiation is, or should be, a way of enhancing or extending the reach of quality teaching. In the end, the more things that are going well in a classroom, the more powerful differentiation is likely to be—and conversely. In other words, successful differentiation is not a practice in isolation from quality teaching. It depends on quality work in each aspect of teaching to be of maximum help to each learner. In turn, quality differentiation extends the power of each classroom element.

I looked forward to our conversations, and I feel certain that I learned more from her than she did from me. But then it's often the case in teaching that the teacher learns more from the student than the other way around.

INVEST IN THE FOUNDATIONAL THINGS

Long before I could think sensibly about buying a house, I knew exactly the one I wanted. It was a small, A-frame chalet on a mountainside that I passed by occasionally. It seemed cozy and inviting and like something I could perhaps afford to furnish. I'm sure I must have commented on more than one occasion that it was cute.

Over a period of a few years as I took the road on which "my house" was located, I noticed that it was for sale often and for significant periods of time. The upper deck began to sag ever so slightly. The wood on the side of the house that received midday sun no longer matched the wood on the rest of the house. I entertained the realities that the unpaved road that led from a secondary road to the house must be a nightmare for most of the winter and that reception for television was probably nonexistent. The rock garden on the side of the house and the carved shutters that had once seemed important to me lost their charm. The devolution of my dream house was a learning experience—a growing-up moment.

My first year of teaching was a lot like that, too. Lacking clarity about the foundational structures and infrastructures of teaching, lacking important knowledge about and understanding of what constitutes worthy teaching, meaningful learning, I invested in carved shutters, rock gardens, and slanty roofs. In other words, I went for cute, entertaining, or clever.

There's nothing wrong with aiming to have students fascinated by a lesson, of course. In fact, there's something wrong when we don't plan teaching and learning with engagement in the foreground of our thinking, but engagement in the absence of substance becomes vapor very quickly, and the classroom becomes a birthday party or a trip to the circus. In my 2nd and 3rd years of teaching, I was forever benefited by the presence in my life of several more experienced teachers whose work consistently reflected both great substance and great joy. They taught me the value and role of both. Among the lessons they taught me through example, conversation, co-planning, and careful questioning were the following:

- Make decisions with a keen awareness of the young people those decisions will impact.
- Understand each student you teach well enough to know how to reach that student.
- Don't start teaching until you can share with precision what is most important for students to know, to understand, and to be able to do as a result of the work you do together.
- If you cannot engage students' minds and imaginations with what you're teaching, they will not learn it in any durable way.

(In regard to this point, one of my colleagues often used a tag line for a current TV commercial as a reminder: Medicine doesn't have to taste bad to be good.)

In the company of extraordinary mentors and committed colleagues, I learned over time to teach from those lessons. They are lessons never fully mastered, but rather become touchstones for continued growth. By the time I was having monthly meetings with the young differentiation coach, I had planned, taught, and reflected based on those lessons for nearly 2 decades. In other words, they were commonplace to me. Still, our conversations disrupted my complacency. I understood on a conscious level for the first time that powerful differentiation was not a thing apart from quality teaching. It was an outgrowth of quality teaching. It was rooted in a solid understanding of the foundational classroom elements and guided by the principles that guided those elements.

To be more specific, learning environment, curriculum, assessment, instruction, and classroom management comprise the structure and infrastructure of impactful teaching. Differentiation is a learner-focused extension of each of those elements and the interaction among those elements. To try to practice differentiation without continual attention to that truth is to make the error I made when I fell in love with the chalet—and when, in my early teaching, I thought cleverness and substance were interchangeable.

So here is the hard truth: To teach in ways that open a promising path forward for all young members of the vast swath of humanity we teach, we have to teach from a firm foundation. That is, we have to seek first, in partnership with our students, to

- create a positive learning environment,
- craft curriculum that opens and extends minds,
- use assessment practices that provide a trusty compass for teaching and learning,
- teach in ways that engage students' energies and help them make sense of what they are learning, and
- orchestrate all of that in effective, efficient, and humanizing ways.

To do those five things well for each learner requires what seems like a contradiction—steadfastly honoring the principles that direct the five elements while simultaneously asking ourselves, "What are all the ways I might think about accomplishing this goal or that one in order to find what works best for this student or for these students?" As in most domains, deep knowledge of the field enables a practitioner to become an artist. Once again, stability frees us up to be flexible. Let's take a brief look at what, based on solid research finding and practical experience, we should like to aim for with each of the five elements.

Learning Environment

To continue the house analogy, learning environment includes most of what turns a house into a home. A learning environment contains both affective and physical elements—both how the residents feel in the house and how use of physical space impacts those people. A student's affective needs are primary. The physical environment in a classroom should be configured to contribute to meeting those needs and to facilitate learning. Figure 3.1 presents affective needs that students of all ages bring into their classrooms—needs that must be adequately met in the classroom to open the way to meaningful learning.

To meet those needs, teachers should begin very early in a school year—perhaps even before day one—to work persistently in three key areas:

- Connecting with each student
- Connecting students with one another
- Modeling and working from a growth mindset

Connecting with each student includes learning each student's name quickly and pronouncing it appropriately, creating opportunities for one-on-one conversations with each student, listening carefully to what students say, and watching their actions and behaviors for clues about their feelings. It means the teacher sharing with the class his or her own stories to open the way for students to share theirs. It means demonstrating unconditional respect and empathy for each learner. It means learning about

Figure 3.1. Affective Needs of Students of All Ages in Their Classrooms

What Students Need in a Learning Environment	Explanation of the Terms
Safety	A student needs to feel physically and affectively safe in order to learn. When those conditions are not met, the brain focuses on protecting its owner and cannot simultaneously focus on learning.
Affirmation	Young people of all ages need clear evidence that they are valued and respected for who they are—that they are seen and seen as worthy.
Connection	Students need to feel that their teachers want to know them, care about them, and are invested in supporting their success. Likewise, they need to feel that classmates are their team members and that all of them work together to support one another's growth and success.
Trust	Being able to trust the teacher and classmates is foundational to take the risk of making mistakes, speaking up, and taking in the varied perspectives that expand learning.
Purpose	Students see a reason for what they are learning and the work they are asked to do. That often means seeing how it is helpful to real people in their everyday lives, how it might/ does work in their neighborhood or school, and/or how it connects to their experiences. A sense of purpose is central to student engagement.
Contribution	Students need to see themselves making a positive difference in the varied aspects of the life and work of the classroom. They need to observe their strengths and ideas benefiting other individuals and the community as a whole.
Challenge	All learners need to feel that the work they are asked to do is a bit beyond their current point of development and to find the support necessary to realize that they are exceeding what they thought they could accomplish.

the cultures of students in the class and integrating perspectives and experiences from many cultures into teaching and learning. It means looking for and building on student strengths and interests. It means making the teacher's support for each student evident throughout every day. Connecting with each student means a teacher doing everything possible to see the classroom and the world through each child's eyes. It means *always* seeking to *dignify* each learner.

Connecting students with one another includes making opportunities for students to get to know one another in the first days of school as well as opportunities to learn more about one another throughout the year, regularly creating student work that promotes student collaboration, teaching students to work together effectively, using flexible student groupings consistently, and seeking and using student feedback on ideas for collaboration and ways to make the collaborations work well.

Modeling and working from a growth mindset is likely not as easy as it sounds, but it is vital to differentiation and to the success of most students in any context. First, it means understanding and genuinely believing that each learner comes to school with only a small portion of his or her possibilities visible and that the chief mission of the teacher is to do as much as possible to help bring the hidden capacity to the surface as well. It means the teacher looks at each student with optimism and interacts with the student in a way that clearly communicates the teacher's firm belief that the student can and will grow consistently and markedly throughout the year. Perhaps most importantly, the teacher plans for the growth and success of each student so that the student sees evidence of that growth on most days. Planning for success means planning work that is appropriately challenging for a student and that builds on the student's strengths. It also means mentoring the student in developing the skills and habit of mind that enable them to increasingly lead their own success.

The physical environment in a classroom involves things like creating spaces that invite both collaboration and independent work and that invite students to stand or sit while they work. It may mean carefully placing supplies and materials for easy student access and asking students to generate ideas that would make the classroom more user-friendly and functional. It may mean creating some quiet spaces as well as some that work well with measured conversation, or some spaces where student work or relevant visuals are posted and others where a wall is blank to help students who are easily distracted to concentrate more readily. In any case, a physical environment that is designed to support learning in many forms and for varied learner needs is an outgrowth of a teacher's determination to make the classroom work well for all sorts of students and to support a dynamic curriculum. It is also a manifestation of instruction that is student-focused, flexible, and collaborative and is evidence of classroom operation that is effective, efficient—and flexible.

A Learning Environment Example

Mr. Santos talks with his students throughout the year about creating a classroom that helps every student learn as much as possible. A theme in the ongoing discussions is the class as a team, each student as a team member who needs to develop his or her strengths to the max and improve weak spots and who contributes to making his or her teammates better as well. The teacher serves as the coach of the team. He uses video examples from several sports to have students look for evidence that the players are pulling together as a team—helping one another "score." He reminds the students that the coach's job is to help each player develop their strengths as much as possible and to keep working on skills that aren't yet fully developed. "But you are the players," he says. "I can help you get ready for the game, and I can make suggestions in time-outs and from the edge of the field, but when the game gets hard, you have to bring out the best that's in you to meet the moment, and you have to be watching your teammates to figure out how to help them make good plays, too. You have to depend on one another."

As students are working on an assignment that is challenging, he may ask a student relevant questions about the work while he moves around the classroom, but he avoids telling or showing the student how to get unstuck. He may say, "Think of things we've worked on recently that you could use here," or "Remember, you can ask teammates for their insights and suggestions." When a student succeeds with a challenge, he does not say, "Great work," or "Congratulations." Rather, he often says to the student, "How do you feel about what you did?" or "I saw you and Javier talking about the problem. How were you able to help one another?" He has a Kudo's Box on his desk in which students can drop notes about a way in which a team member made the day better for the note-writer, for another student, or for a group or the class as a whole. When there is a problem in the class, Mr. Santos may say, "The coach needs a team huddle so we can find a solution to a problem." The students know to go quietly to the area in the class where the bookshelves are located and form a tight cluster so they can talk together about the issue and find a way forward.

Curriculum

Curriculum is not a list of standards, a textbook, or a pacing guide. It is a careful plan to systematically engage students with the most important ideas in a content area and to help each student connect those ideas with the world(s) in which the student lives. Curriculum should feed the minds of

all learners and help them cultivate a taste for the power of learning. Curriculum is dinner. Standards, texts, and pacing guides can be ingredients for dinner, but when we equate the two and serve ingredients rather than dinner, the result is likely to be the malnourishment of most students in both the short- and long-term. The more powerful the curriculum is the better served more students will be. Figure 3.2 lists foundational attributes of dynamic curriculum and briefly explains them.

A Curriculum Example

Mrs. Aimes had taught her 2nd-graders a unit on animal habitats for several years using a "packaged" curriculum purchased by her school. There were visuals for students to examine, activities (often online) to complete, and a great deal of writing practice keyed to Common Core standards. The material was not bad, and students were not generally tuning out, but she felt like the work they completed resulted in a "check-it-off-the-list" kind of unit. "We studied desert habitats and checked that off the

Figure 3.2. Some Attributes of Dynamic Curriculum

Attributes of Dynamic Curriculum	Meaning of the Attributes
It reflects the nature of the discipline.	The curriculum is designed so that students learn to ask the kinds of questions experts in a content area ask, do the kinds of work experts do, create products that reflect the kinds of products experts create, and assess the effectiveness of their work using expert-like criteria.
It is built around clear KUDs known to both teacher and students.	Each segment of the curriculum specifies what students should know (K), understand (U) and be able to do (D) as a result of that segment of learning. The KUDs indicate what is most essential for students to master, and they guide teacher, or teacher and student, in creating the steps and stages of learning in a unit or segment of learning.
It is planned for student engagement.	The curriculum is designed to evoke student curiosity, connect to students' lives and experiences, encourage student questioning, provoke thinking, and make students the chief actors in the classroom.
It is understanding-focused.	The understandings (U) in a unit articulate the big ideas that are at the center of the content's significance and usefulness. The curriculum is designed to keep the understandings in front of the students throughout the unit. The understandings should be written and presented in ways that help students see connections between their own lives and experiences and the understandings.
It is planned to support "teaching up."	The curriculum is designed to challenge advanced learners—to reflect and call for what we often think of as excellence. It will then be taught in ways that support each student in working as we often expect advanced students to work and in accessing and applying the essential knowledge, understanding, and skills. Teaching up is a tool for providing equity of access to excellent learning opportunities for all learners. (See Chapters 17 and 18 for more information on teaching up.)

list so we could move on to aquatic habitats which we then checked off the list so we could move to grassland habitats. We made our way through a lot of material, but I wasn't sure students found much meaning in it."

One year she asked her 2nd-graders how they would like to learn about habitats. After considerable discussion, they said they would like to design a plan for a zoo, and so they did. They worked in various teams on the project as well as completing independent elements. They began by studying their own habitats and making generalizations from what they learned. Then they looked at habitats of animals that were common in their community (e.g., dogs, squirrels, frogs, cows, birds, bears) to see how their habitats were like and unlike those of humans. In the end, the students were able to propose "big ideas" or principles that they felt applied to all animals and their habitats (e.g., to survive, all animals have to live in habitats that can meet their basic needs or adapt to an environment that doesn't.) After some initial study, the students selected animal families representative of five major habitat types. In groups, they researched the habitats and needs of the family they chose and shared information and conclusions with other groups. Along the way, they examined land-use maps to determine possible locations for the zoo in their area, taking care to ensure that a site they chose would be adequate to meet the needs of "their" animals. The unit provided opportunities for students to draw on and contribute through their varied strengths and interests. The work required movement and conversation on a regular basis which was beneficial for many of the 2nd-graders. There were many ways for students to express what they were learning and to contribute to the final class product.

Ultimately, the students presented their proposal for a zoo to a regional planning board complete with a scale model, sketches of the various habitats that included animals who might be housed in a habitat, and recordings of animal sounds for each soundscape. They also provided their best estimates of the kinds and amounts of food that would be necessary on a daily basis for each animal group, amounts of water each group would require daily, and recommendations for ways to make the habitats reflective of the natural surroundings in which an animal

family would normally live. Writing and technology were tools necessary for learning and sharing learning rather than add-ons or gadgets. Student work focused them on all key content, understandings, and skills that were specified in the more traditional unit—and many others across academic, social, and emotional domains. Student ownership of and enthusiasm for the unit was far greater than in the past, and they continued to think about and make connections with the habitat work throughout the rest of the year.

Formative Assessment

In my days as a student—K–12, undergraduate, and graduate—assessment meant tests, which meant grades, which meant tension and often an abiding sense of fear, judgment, and inadequacy. As a new teacher, I saw those same feelings in many of my students. Those who were deemed to be "good students" had a palpable fear of losing that status. Those who were deemed to be "poor students" hurt from continuing reminders that they were still at the bottom of the pack. Students who didn't seem fazed by tests and grades were generally ones who had given up on school and were hanging on because there was no other viable choice—or the few who had decided that school was less interesting than their own agendas and paid only minimal or occasional attention to the classroom-formulated playlist.

My students and I worked diligently and often successfully to create a class environment that was affirming, interesting, collegial, supportive—and challenging. We lost ground every time tests entered the picture, despite efforts to be sure students understood what the learning targets for the test were, how to study effectively, and even how to "be your own best friend" as you were taking a test. The weights some students carried around with them simply became heftier when the tests marked the end of a unit, chapter, or marking period and therefore felt especially consequential and intimidating.

It was a watershed moment for me when I first encountered the idea of "formative assessment." Here was a mechanism to help students learn to do better work and to work more effectively. It was about mentoring rather than judging. Feedback largely replaced grades. There were regular interactions between teacher and student about how the student was faring and next steps in learning. When the summative assessments, which *are* used to judge student performance, rolled around, there were few surprises. Students had identified areas of need, had been supported in attending to those needs, and more clearly understood what mattered in the content, how it made sense, and why it mattered. For the first time, I had a significant sense of my students' individual learning trajectories on an almost daily basis and therefore understood how to help them move forward before it was "too late." Perhaps even more game-changing was the fact that my students began to understand their own learning paths more clearly and to be increasingly in charge of their own learning success. When teachers give it a chance, formative assessment will revolutionize both teaching and learning. Consistent and skilled use of formative assessment is a nonnegotiable for effective differentiation. Figure 3.3 shares some vocabulary and attributes related to formative assessment.

A Formative Assessment Example

Students in Ms. Banerjee's math class are accustomed to a range of formative assessment strategies. One student explained, "It keeps us on our toes. We have to listen carefully and think as we work on an assignment because on different days, she'll ask us to think in different ways."

Sometimes, the teacher works a problem on the whiteboard, giving the students 2 or 3 minutes to examine the problem. At the end of the thinking time, she asks students to hold up their red card if they think her solution is incorrect and to hold up a green card if they think it is correct. With the cards in place, she takes a picture of the class. Her students understand that she will examine the picture later to decided how best to help them continue growing in their work in the days ahead. Next, she sometimes (but not always) asks the students to work with their math squads to share their thinking and ask questions they have. At that point, they go back to their original seats and write a brief explanation of whether their initial thought was

correct and why it was or was not. She can look quickly at the class photo and see whose card was the "wrong" color, and then look quickly at the explanations of those students to see if their thinking seems clearer.

At other times, she will show the students a computation and ask them to solve it more efficiently, or show them a diagram or a picture and ask the students to relate what they have been working on to what they see, or ask them to write a note on an index card to a student who has been absent for several days to give the student a heads-up about the most common errors in thinking about an operation they've been working on while the student was absent. Students often have the option to write explanations on paper, use Flipgrid to show their reasoning, record an oral explanation, or suggest another way to share their thinking. English language learners always have the option of writing or recording in their preferred language first and providing a translation later. Ms. Banerjee says that the variety of assessments keeps the class lively, but that her favorite mode of assessment is walking among students as they work, carrying a clipboard and checklist of learning targets on it, listening to students, looking at their work in progress, or asking them questions as they work, noting both strengths and what she refers to as "potholes" on the checklist. Not only is that method likely to show her things she would not likely have asked on a separate assessment, but, she says, it gives her a chance to make personal contact with students that the other modes do not offer as readily.

Instruction

Instruction is purposefully planning for and directing the learning process. While its goal is student learning, it involves both teaching and learning. If curriculum is a plan for *what* teachers should teach and *what* students should learn, instruction is a plan for *how* the teacher will teach and *how* students will learn. Most of what happens in a classroom likely falls under the umbrella of instruction, and the remaining classroom elements (learning environment, curriculum, assessment, and classroom leadership/management) all exist for the purpose of promoting student learning.

Figure 3.3. Some Attributes of Effective Formative Assessment

Attributes of Effective Formative Assessment	Explanation of the Attributes
Formative assessments are tightly aligned with the unit's KUDs.	The KUDs that establish learning targets for a unit of study specify the essential learning goals. Both formative and summative assessment should be closely aligned with the KUDs so that the intentions of the written unit remain the focus of the unit as students work with it.
Formative assessments help students focus on understanding.	Curriculum should be designed to help students understand what they are learning; therefore, assessments should be monitoring student understanding, not just or largely knowledge and skills.
Pre-assessment helps teachers understand students' varied entry points into content.	Pre-assessments can provide a useful snapshot of student proficiency with both prerequisites for the unit and with the knowledge, understanding, and skill that the unit will ask students to learn. They can also be used to provide insight into student interests that may be relevant to the unit.
Ongoing assessment helps teachers and students follow and address needs and growth.	Careful, ongoing assessment of student work throughout a unit builds teacher and student awareness of strengths, needs, and misunderstandings throughout a unit to support student movement forward.
The teacher nearly always provides students with feedback rather than grades on formative work.	Most student work is practice, and grading practice often causes emotions that detract from learning. Research shows that learning benefits from feedback more than grades or a combination of feedback and grades if the feedback is positive in tone, recognizes what the student has done well, gives specific advice for making improvements, and expresses confidence in the student's ability to achieve at a high level (Guskey, 2019).
Nearly all student work can be assessed formatively.	Formative assessment doesn't have to be a moment where instruction stops so an assessment can be given. Careful observation of students at work can be a powerful way to understand their development and to help students develop agency in their own growth.
Formative assessment can be differentiated.	The only element in a formative assessment that should not be differentiated is the KUDs on which the assessment focuses. Other elements like mode of expression, time for responding, language used to express learning, and degree of complexity can and probably often should be differentiated to ensure that a student can demonstrate learning as fully as possible.
Formative assessment can benefit both teacher and students.	Assessment *for* learning helps a teacher know how to plan and teach more effectively. Assessment *as* learning helps students learn how to learn more effectively. A particular formative assessment can serve either purpose or both.
Formative assessments are snapshots, not detailed paintings.	Formative assessments are quick checks of students' progress. They are not intended to be exhaustive measures and should not require a great deal of either teacher or student time.

The fundamental aim of differentiated instruction is to ensure maximum growth for each learner in a class. Therefore, differentiation calls on teachers to both teach and guide learning in ways that place the individual in the center of thinking and planning rather than only or largely thinking about and planning for the class. For that reason, differentiation guides teachers in getting to know students well enough to

- understand their strengths and needs;
- incorporate their suggestions and choices in instructional planning;
- design instruction at levels of complexity that are appropriate for varied learner needs;
- seek materials that are relevant to learner interests and accessible to students whose primary language is not the language of the classroom;
- place high value on aligning curricular goals with what is relevant to students' experiences, interests, and cultures;
- provide varied ways for students to explore, make sense of, and express learning; and

- make available different ways of working on assignments.

In addition, differentiation commends the importance of helping students develop the habits of mind and work that lead to productivity and success in a full range of pursuits, find and cultivate their own voices and perspectives, and work effectively with others as well as independently. Figure 3.4 displays some attributes of instruction in an effectively differentiated classroom. We will look at some additional ways to think about differentiating instruction in Chapters 4 and 5.

An Instruction Example

In his high school history classes, Mr. Walker divides instructional time between mini-lectures, student investigation, and class discussions. In the mini-lectures, he provides background information and information about critical events and key players in those events. He spotlights important academic vocabulary, which he adds to a large word wall as a unit progresses, and he raises questions he feels important for students to consider in order to understand the meaning of events. Students then work in a variety of groups to explore a network of

Figure 3.4. Key Attributes of Instruction in a Differentiated Classroom

Key Attributes of Instruction	Explanation of the Attributes
The student is at the center of instructional decision-making.	The teacher partners with the STUDENTS and THE student in planning, implementing plans, reflecting on instruction, and adjusting future instruction based on teacher observation and student input.
Instruction is tightly bound with the unit's KUDs.	Teaching and learning are most effective when curriculum establishes clear KUDs, assessment monitors student development with the KUDs, and instruction focuses student work on the KUDs.
Instruction emphasizes understanding of content.	Because understanding happens "in" learners rather than "to" them, instruction in effectively differentiated classes regularly positions students as "doers" vs. largely as "receivers." Students use essential knowledge and skills to act on (analyze, compare, apply, transfer, extend, etc.) essential understandings.
Formative assessment shapes instructional plans to address varied learner needs.	Consistent formative assessment becomes the daily compass for instructional planning.
Instruction frequently responds to student readiness, interests, and approaches to learning.	Readiness, interest, and approach to learning are the three major categories of student variance that impact their learning. Responsive instruction seeks to understand and address those needs to advance learning as effectively and efficiently as possible.
Instructional strategies reflect the needs of learners, the nature of the content, and the principles of how people learn.	Instructional strategies and tools (including use of technology) should be ones most likely to advance student learning, not to be seen or used as novelties.
Tasks are designed to be respectful of all students.	When there is variation in student work, everyone's work should be seen by students as being equally interesting and equally important. It dignifies student capacity.
Flexible student groupings are a consistent feature of the classroom.	Students should work regularly in groups that are both homogeneous and heterogeneous in regard to student readiness, interest, and approach to learning—as well as student-selected groups, teacher-selected groups, and random groupings.
The teacher "teaches up."	The teacher plans first for "high end" challenge, then scaffolds or supports a broad range of learners in accessing and succeeding with complex work that asks students to use key knowledge and skills to act on understandings, reason, solve problems, be self-reflective, and transfer what they have learned to unfamiliar contexts. The goal of teaching up is to enable all students to have equity of access to the most robust curriculum and instruction a school can offer and to succeed with that curriculum.

questions that will cause them to think beyond the text and to raise questions of their own. Class discussions may focus on student questions or student thinking about the questions they are investigating.

In a current unit on World War II, students are beginning to formulate insights into the question, "How do dictatorships evolve in 'free' societies?" At the moment, students are investigating Nazism in "investigation teams." Mr. Walker often provides key questions to guide student explorations, points to vocabulary that is important for their understanding of what they are seeing, and generally makes available graphic organizers that provide structure and direction for student research. Investigation teams stay together throughout a unit and are teacher-selected groups composed of four or five students with different interests and strengths. In addition to investigation teams, students work in "synthesis squads" with about five members. The squads meet about twice a week to respond as a group to a prompt the teacher provides. It calls on students to determine what is of most significance in what they have been learning. Responding to the prompt is timed. All students contribute to dictating a response to a scribe who smooths out what the group says into a cogent paragraph with a response and defense of the response, including evidence. Mr. Walker randomly assigned students to synthesis squads for Week 1 of the unit but then shifted group assignments for about a third of the students in each subsequent week based on his reading of synthesis squad responses. His goal was to ensure that each group had students who represented a range of degrees of understanding of the content as well as at least one student who was a competent writer.

Mr. Walker also periodically sets up learning stations in the classroom by topic, question, or resources. Resources at this point in the unit include podcasts, written and recorded firsthand accounts, virtual tours of the National Holocaust Museum and Auschwitz, texts at varied readability levels, and copies of newspaper reports of key events from both U.S. and German news sources (German articles are translated into English). He also meets with small groups of students at their request and at his request to probe their understanding of what they are encountering and to provide guidance and feedback as they prepare their final products.

Early in this portion of the unit, Mr. Walker provided students with a definition of Nazism and challenged them to extend or revise it in some way as a result of what they learn. He also provided them with several key terms (autocracy, nationalism, authoritarian, militarism, propaganda, xenophobia, anti-Semitism, racism, and scapegoating) that they should be able to explain and apply as they investigate.

An early class discussion centered on ways Hitler seized on current events to make his message compelling and tools he used to communicate his message to German citizens over time. A few minutes before the end of class, Mr. Walker did a "quick check" of student thinking by asking each student to write a two-sentence answer to the question, "How do dictatorships evolve in a free society?" based on what they had learned so far. This formative check helped him plan upcoming mini-lectures and discussions, constitute synthesis squads, suggest resources, and plan small-group instruction.

As a summative assessment, each student will develop and present four brief, first-person accounts—from Hitler's perspective, from a citizen who embraces the Nazi philosophy, from a citizen who accepts what is occurring in his/her country out of fear or a sense of helplessness, and from a resister. The four perspectives singly and as a group should answer the question, "How do dictatorships evolve in a free society?" Students can audio-record themselves presenting the four perspectives, use Flipgrid to create videos of the four presentations, share the four perspectives via annotated storyboards, or write "scripts" of the four first-person accounts. Students work from a common rubric that focuses on goals of the work, quality of research, student habits of mind and work, and general elements of quality presentations. The rubric is applicable to any presentation mode. Mr. Walker provides writing frames for students who are early English language learners and students who find writing to be daunting for a variety of other reasons as well. He tailors the assignment based on the strengths and needs of learners who have specific learning challenges, ensuring that all students work with the essential ideas in the unit in ways that are appropriate for particular students.

Classroom Leadership and Management

Students may have had ample experience in classrooms where the teacher is generally in the front of the room talking to them and where student work is most often completing practice work independently. It may be less clear to them how things should work if students change seats regularly, sometimes reconfigure furniture, get and return resources based on current needs, consult peers for assistance with their work, finish work before many other students do, or turn in work as they complete it rather than at the same time everyone else does. Equally important, students who are accustomed to more teacher-directed and/or one-size-fits-all classrooms may not understand the point of things like varied groupings, selecting from a range of resources, using different room arrangements, and so on.

A goal of "classroom management" in a differentiated classroom is to establish a balance between flexibility and stability or predictability in order to enable students to work in an assortment of ways and with varied tasks, materials, or groups of peers to enable each student to learn as deeply and efficiently as possible. Helping students understand and contribute to an understanding of differentiation and teaching them how to work productively and to help others work productively in a differentiated classroom requires a two-pronged approach to what we generally call "classroom management."

Most young people don't much care for being "managed." Truth be told, neither do teachers! Differentiation suggests that a teacher *lead students* and then work *with* the students to *manage classroom routines*. Figure 3.5 presents a snapshot of what it means for a teacher to lead students and what it means for the teacher and students to work together to manage routines.

Leading is about inspiring people. Managing is about handling routines effectively. It is important to lead first and then work with the people you lead to establish, practice, and refine routines necessary for the success of a shared vision. The general idea with leading and managing in a differentiated classroom is to talk with students about how it feels when you are in a classroom or on a team or participating in an out-of-school activity and everyone else seems to be pretty comfortable with what's going on but

Figure 3.5. A Snapshot of What It Means to Lead Students and Manage Routines Necessary for a Flexible, Orderly Classroom

Leading Students Includes	Managing Routines Includes
• Knowing, valuing, and connecting with each learner	• Planning schedules
• Having a vision for something good—a classroom designed to work well for each student	• Preparing materials
• Having the capacity to share the vision and elicit ideas from the students about making it work and enlist them in working together with one another and the teacher to enact the vision	• Determining and implementing room arrangements
• Working with students to create a team for achieving the vision	• Making plans for things like:
	» Starting and stopping a class/lesson smoothly
• Assessing effectiveness of the teacher's work and team's work regularly, adjusting as needed	» Handing out/collecting materials
	» Moving around a room appropriately
• Renewing the commitment of individuals and the team to the vision over time	» Getting help when the teacher is working with an individual or small group
• Celebrating with individuals and the team	» Where to put completed work
	» How to help peers effectively
	» What to do if you finish work early
	» Getting back together as a whole class as group work or independent work ends
	» Putting things back in place for the next day or next class
	» Handling transitions effectively
	» Adjusting conversations based on the nature of assignments
	• Practicing routines
	• Troubleshooting

you feel lost, or when you are really bored with the activity because there is no challenge in it for you, or you just do not see the point while others seem to think it is interesting and worth their time. You'll see an example of this approach in the next section of this chapter.

Ask for student ideas on how the class might look, what you would need to do to make it work, and what *they* would do to make it work. Over time, ask them to help you create a routine or a process for making a particular strategy or process work, or share with them your idea for a routine and ask them to make suggestions for improvements. Review or practice routines when they begin and debrief after students have carried out the routine. Remind students from time to time—or ask them to remind you—of what the goals of the class are and to talk about what's working well for them and when some adjustments could make things better. Continue that process as you add new routines and throughout the year, with decreasing frequency as students indicate satisfaction with the routines and processes verbally and through effective work with them. If a teacher takes on all the responsibilities implicit in a flexible learning environment, it can be exhausting. When that same teacher has a team of students taking on many responsibilities and "owning" the classroom with the teacher, the result is likely to be fulfilling for the teacher and successful for the students.

Leading/Managing Example

During the first couple of days of school, I often introduced the idea of a differentiated classroom by involving my students in an activity that made visible to them the idea of a classroom designed to meet the needs and address the interests of each student rather than a classroom where students generally did the same work, in the same way, over the same time period, and with the same supports. I used different examples in different years to keep it fresh for me. One of my favorites began by making a trip to the school's lost and found where I would get the biggest jacket or sweater I could find and the smallest.

As students entered the room, I would ask students who were taller than most and who were shorter than most if they would be game for modeling a jacket or sweater for an activity as class began. I assured them it was fine to say no. There were always some students who were happy to participate.

With little introduction, I told the class that two volunteers were going to do some quick fashion modeling for us. First, I would ask the smaller student to put on the larger garment. There was giggling, and then I would ask the student to tell us how it felt to wear the sweater or jacket. Their descriptions were predictable. "I can't find my hands." "It swallows me." "I think this may not be my size."

I would follow the same path with the taller student in the small jacket, again with predictable results. At that point, I would ask each of the students how they would feel about wearing the jacket for the rest of the day. The responses were always a little more serious as the students began to see some costs to that possibility—for example, "I don't think I could eat lunch." "This is so tight I don't know if I could do my work in classes." Finally, I would ask each of them how it would work for them to wear the same jacket every day for the rest of the year. Inevitably at that point, the lightness disappeared from their responses, and they saw that continuing on in the wrong-sized clothes could hamper their growth, change people's opinions of them in negative ways, and even change how they saw themselves. They were clear that a poor fit for a day could be funny or bothersome, but over time, it could have real consequences. The jacket activity took about 10 minutes.

Next, I posed a question to the class that would open the way for a much broader discussion: "Why did I do this activity with you? What does it have to do with our class?" Many students made the connection and shared stories of times when they were lost in a subject, didn't see how what they were learning mattered in their lives, or were being "taught" things they already knew. From there, we talked about what we might do to create a classroom where those things rarely happened, what it would look like for all of us to contribute to creating and sustaining a class like that, how we would know whether our plans were working, and what we would need to do if they were not.

Over the course of the next few weeks, we practiced and tried out routines for several key components of the class, assessed their effectiveness, and tweaked elements of the routines that needed tweaking. Later in the first quarter of the year, we talked about what "fair" would mean in our class and what students might do if something felt unfair to them. A couple of weeks prior to the end of that marking period, we talked about what kind of grading system could accurately reflect our goals for students in the class. Well before the end of October, students worked smoothly with virtually all of the routines we would use that year and could explain how they worked to guests (and subs), talk about why we did what we did in the class, and explain differentiation (although we didn't call it differentiation then) as well as I could to anyone who cared to listen. The class was ours, not mine. We connected as a team.

A FINAL THOUGHT

I feel confident saying that no teacher works perfectly with any of the elements every day. I am pretty sure that even stellar teachers only rarely have a day when every element is planned and working at peak. The goal is not perfection; rather, it is to understand clearly what we are aiming for in our work with each of the elements, and to work persistently to more fully enact that understanding.

It is particularly fruitful to think consistently about how our use of one element in the class can affect all the others, for better or worse. For example, an invitational classroom environment that feels welcoming, supportive, and safe to each student will boost the prospects of students during instruction, even if work sometimes seems disconnected from student lives or is sometimes over- or underchallenging. Because students feel a sense of safety, trust, and collegiality, they are likely to be more willing to continue to engage with instruction, at least for a while, because they feel supported and appreciated. On the other hand, if assessment nearly always feels judgmental to a student and the judgment feels harsh, that reality will undercut potential effectiveness of both the learning environment and instruction for that learner.

Keep learning more about quality teaching and learning. That will keep your work fresh and challenging for you and contribute to the success of a very broad range of learners.

CHAPTER 4

A Closer Look at the Anatomy of Differentiation

Few would argue that opportunity in life is strongly connected with educational opportunity. However, we have often misconstrued the notion of equal access to education to mean that all students should receive precisely the same curriculum, resources, and instruction. The result is a one-size-fits-all education system. Differentiated instruction recognizes that students are not the same and that equal access to an excellent education necessarily means that, given a certain goal, each student should be provided resources, instruction, and support to help them meet that objective.

—From a paper by John Stroup, a University of Virginia student at the time he wrote the paper

> Big Idea of Chapter 4: Understanding the vocabulary and "big ideas" of a model paves the way to success in applying the model.

I was still a relatively new teacher when I began working with young adolescents in what was then called a junior high school, and I was inexperienced enough not to realize for a good while that the composition of my classes was a challenge I was unprepared to meet. It seemed like on most days, in spite of careful planning, a good portion of the class was restless. As I continued to study the students' work, it was first clear that the students entered the year with very different degrees of proficiency in skills like reading, writing, vocabulary, spelling, and listening. It took a bit longer to understand that pattern with enough clarity to make me realize that the way I was teaching was doomed.

For many years, including that first one, about half of my 7th-graders were reading 4 or more years below grade level and about half were reading about 4 or more years above grade level. In between those two extremes, my classes also contained, at best, a smattering of students "in the middle." No wonder a very noticeable group of students was always restless. I had begun the year "teaching to the middle," which was what my experience as a student had led me to believe was what I should do. From the outset,

I was not reaching many students on any given day. Once I saw the disparity in student entry points into the curriculum, I tended to teach some days at a pitch that engaged the 12-year-olds who were functioning like high schoolers if not college students. On those days, the students for whom reading and writing had not yet been demystified were lost. Predictably, those students found it difficult to "get with the program" and sought other ways to occupy their time. When I taught in ways that seemed to me to be promising in helping students who were woefully lacking in skills that my colleagues and I had assumed would enter the classroom with 7th-graders, the students who had mastered those skills years earlier looked like flags at half-mast. In retrospect, all the students were more respectful and patient than I would have been had I been a student in the class instead of the teacher. Nonetheless, it became evident that the teach-to-the-extremes approach was no more fruitful than the teach-to-the-center approach.

Early on, the question my colleagues and I regularly asked ourselves and one another was, "So what can we try next?" Over time, the question became more refined and focused: "How do we organize our time and resources so all of our students could have the opportunity to learn important things together while still having time and support to work on their own needs and interests?"

The answers to that question evolved steadily through trial, error, and nourishing conversations with a group of peers who shared a common vision for our students. This chapter will synthesize some of the beliefs and principles that guided our work, ways we thought about organizing our classes to benefit both the group and the individuals in the group, some vocabulary that proved useful in instructional planning, and some strategies that facilitate attention to students' diverse and common needs.

GUIDING BELIEFS AND PRINCIPLES

My colleagues and I began our journey toward what we now call differentiation with just a couple of guidelines or principles to direct our thinking. The list grew as we grew in our understanding of what it meant to create a classroom that is designed to work well for each learner in it. Here are a dozen of the principles we gleaned over time and that became guides for our work because we continued to feel they were worth our ongoing attention in planning and carrying out plans. They became the "bones" around which we grew the "muscles," "organs," and "systems" that made differentiation a source of life in the classrooms where we taught.

1. The student is at the center of planning, teacher attention, and instruction. (Be there for each student.)
2. The person/people who do the most work in a classroom (that is, those who are on center stage most) are the ones who will learn the most. (That ought *not* to be the teacher.)
3. The class is strongest when its members learn to function as a team in support of one another's success.
4. Every student needs to contribute to and experience the most dynamic curriculum and instruction we can provide and to create thoughtful demonstrations of their learning.
5. Some students have identified learning challenges that require appropriate, more complex modifications and support.

6. Some students who do *not* have identified learning challenges nonetheless struggle with some or many aspects of classroom life and work. These students also need adaptations and support necessary to move forward as efficiently and as far as possible.
7. A key goal in a differentiated classroom is for each student to take his or her own next steps in development every day.
8. Every student needs the full attention and support of the teacher in order to develop as fully as possible academically, emotionally, and socially.
9. When appropriately challenged, every student will need peer and teacher support to meet the challenge.
10. The norm in a differentiated classroom is that there *is* no "normal" work for students. Students regularly do different things in class and at home to take their next step, discover and nurture their strengths and interests, and develop their own voice.
11. Growth matters most. Celebrate it. No student has a good day without making visible progress.
12. Every aspect of every class should be respectful of every student, demonstrate optimism for the capacity of every student, and dignify every student. We respect students when we enable and encourage them to be our full partners in their own success, the success of their classmates, and the success of the class.

Taking time to review these principles as you plan instruction and again as you reflect on how a day or a class period progressed for individual students and for the class will pay significant gains in student motivation, student achievement—and teacher satisfaction and growth. As they become embedded in your thinking, they will also serve as a steady compass for what you say and do in the classroom. Further, understanding the vocabulary of differentiation enables us to think more systematically and clearly about the work we do to ensure that what happens in our classrooms is responsive to the needs of the full spectrum of individuals who come to us to learn.

VOCABULARY THAT REFINES TEACHER THINKING

Language matters on many levels in life and in the classroom. We know, for example, that when a student lacks fundamental academic vocabulary for a subject or topic, that student is unlikely to make sense of, understand, retain, or be able to apply critical content and skills. For a teacher, there is likely to be a strong connection between developing precise vocabulary and associated principles related to differentiating instruction and increased use of effective differentiation in his or her classroom.

There are two sets of terms that can make teacher planning and implementation of plans for differentiation a more precise match for the needs of individual students, small groups of students, and the class as a whole. The first set of terms refers to *categories in which student variance is commonplace*. The categories of student variance are an answer to, "Why do we need to differentiate?" The second set of terms refers to *facets of instruction that a teacher can differentiate*. That set of terms is an answer to, "What do we differentiate?" Teachers who understand both sets of terms and their interrelationships effectively use them as guides for proactively planning instruction that is likely to serve well the full scope of the students they teach.

Student Traits in Which Variance Is Common

Three areas in which student differences are evident in almost any classroom are readiness, interest, and learning preferences. These three categories direct teachers to *why* they would differentiate instruction. They exist in all classrooms all the time, however, they may often go un-named because a teacher has not had the opportunity to learn them and translate them into practice. In that case, differentiation is likely to be more random—less purposeful and focused—than when that vocabulary is present and clear in a teacher's thinking. In other words, using the categories as part of a framework for planning differentiation increases the likelihood that the teacher will proactively plan differentiation rather than differentiating only or largely after he or she sees a problem arise during instruction based on a one-size-fits-all lesson plan. Figure 4.1 defines, explains, and illustrates the three categories

in which student variance is common and helps us answer the question, "Why should we differentiate instruction?"

Teachers who observe their students carefully, including through persistent use of formative assessment, as well as general watchfulness, learn a great deal about students' entry points into curriculum, their interests (including those linked to culture and personal strengths), and modes of learning that seem to result in evident learning in varied contexts. It is also important, of course, to ask students how learning is going for them, to use interest surveys from time to time, and to seek student voice in designing curriculum and instruction.

There is no single right answer on which instructional strategies are best for addressing students' readiness needs, interests, and learning preferences. The good news is that there are many options that can be useful depending on the needs of students and the nature of the content and learning goals at hand.

Facets of Instruction Teachers Can Differentiate

In addition to the three categories of variance that impact student learning—readiness, interests, and learning preferences—there are five facets or aspects of instruction a teacher can differentiate—content, process, product, affect, and learning environment. The five facets, too, exist in all classrooms all the time, and they, too, may also go unnamed because a teacher has not had the opportunity to learn them and learn to use them in instructional planning. In the absence of the vocabulary, here, too, differentiation is likely to be more random—less purposeful and focused—than when that vocabulary is present and clear in a teacher's thinking.

Understanding the terms related to *what* teachers can differentiate, and seeing their possibilities in teaching responsively, makes it more likely that a teacher will regularly consider ways in which each of the aspects can be adapted or sculpted to support learning at a given point in a lesson or unit. In other words, here, too, using the terms as part of a framework for planning differentiation increases the likelihood that the teacher will proactively plan differentiation rather than differentiating only after he or she sees a problem arise during instruction.

Figure 4.1. Categories of Student Variance That Impact Learning—Or Why a Teacher Differentiates

Category of Student Variance	What It Means	What It Does Not Mean	Why It Matters
Readiness	Readiness refers to a student's point of entry into a current lesson or unit. It is fluid—that is, it will be at various points on a continuum depending on the topic or skills being studied. Readiness can be affected by a student's academic, social, and emotional factors, as well as language, culture, and cognitive development.	It is NOT a synonym for ability, IQ, or capacity. It is NOT fixed. Readiness differentiation asks teachers to plan for a student's next steps based on current performance with specific skills or content, and to avoid thinking of students as "low learners," "smart kids," or "just average." This orientation supports a growth mindset.	Research in psychology and neuroscience both clearly indicate that when what we ask students to learn is too demanding for a student's current point of development or provides too little challenge for his or her point of development, achievement suffers. The goal is moderate challenge for a student plus support to make the challenge feasible.
Interest	Interest, in this context, refers to a student's personal interests—something the learner finds engrossing, fulfilling, and engaging.	While it is important for teachers to create lessons that are engaging and interesting, that kind of "interesting" is different from a strong personal interest that feels like an extension of self.	Enabling students to develop their own interests and to connect their interests to classroom content supports motivation to learn, relevance, and often, creativity.
Learning Preferences/ Approaches to Learning	Approach to learning refers to ways in which a student can most effectively and efficiently accomplish the requirements of a particular assignment. Approach to learning is fluid—that is, it changes with time, context, and circumstance.	Approach to learning is NOT fixed. Teachers should not try to determine a student's "learning style" but rather should provide learning options and guide students in understanding how to determine which ones benefit their learning at specific times.	Approach to learning is shaped by culture, gender, personal preferences, and a specific assignment. Providing options for how to take in content, make sense of it, and demonstrate learning supports efficiency and effectiveness of learning.

Figure 4.2 defines and explains the five facets of instruction a teacher can differentiate.

Interrelatedness of the Categories of Student Variance and Facets of Instruction

If the categories of student variance help teachers understand ways in which students vary that significantly impact their learning and thus *why* differentiation matters, and the facets of instruction point to *what* a teacher can differentiate to support the success of a full range of learners, the interrelatedness of the two sets of terms provides part of the answer to, "*How* can we differentiate instruction?"

Each of the facets of instruction can be differentiated in response to each of the categories of student variance. That is, a teacher can differentiate content based on a student's readiness, interests, and/or learning preferences; process based on a student's readiness, interest, and/or learning preferences; product based on a student's readiness, interest, and/or learning profile; and so on. Figure 4.3 provides a few illustrations of how differentiating content, process, and product might look when differentiated based on student readiness, interests, or learning profiles.

As you can see in Figure 4.3, once a teacher decides to differentiate process based on student interests, for example, the next question is, "What strategies or tools can I/we use for this purpose?" The third column of the figure gives some examples of strategies that can be useful in each of the "matches" between the categories of student variance and the

Figure 4.2. Facets of Instruction a Teacher Can Differentiate—or *What* a Teacher Differentiates

Facets of Instruction a Teacher Can Differentiate	What the Facets Mean	How the Facets Might Look in a Classroom
Content	Content is *what* we ask students to learn—or what the teacher teaches. It can also refer to how a student "takes in" information—or how the teacher makes the information available. It is more common to differentiate how a student takes in or accesses content than to differentiate the content itself.	Students often take in content as they listen to a teacher lecture or explain the content. Textbooks, recorded textbooks, supplementary readings, videos, podcasts, pictures/photographs, diagrams, working models, field trips, exhibitions, news sources, and firsthand experiences are other (and often better) ways to take in content.
Process	Because learning happens *in* students and not *to* them, a critical element in learning is processing time. Process is what students do to make sense of what they are learning—to come to "own" it—to make meaning of it—or what the teacher asks students to do for those purposes.	What we ask students to do should be largely focused on sense-making, not just on rote learning. Homework, in-class practice, hands-on activities, small-group or class discussions, and creating concept maps are a few ways students can make sense of what they learn.
Product	A product is something a student produces to demonstrate what he or she knows, understands, and can do relating to group of lessons or a unit—or what teachers ask students to do for this purpose. A daily practice exercise is not a product. Products are generally summative in nature.	A "right-answer" test, an essay test, or a finished piece of writing can be products—so can proposed solutions to complex problems, student-created videos, community projects, portfolio presentations, various forms of art, and so on. The latter examples are often called performance assessments.
Learning Environment— Affective	Learning environment refers to both the physical and affective. Affect relates to student feelings or emotions in relation to instruction and/or to experiences and other influences beyond the classroom.	Because areas in the brain that respond to emotion and those that respond to cognition are both separate and interdependent, learning cannot occur when negative emotions are in play. Teachers look for emotional cues from students and respond in ways that support cognition and learning for individuals and the class.
Learning Environment— Physical	The physical aspect of the learning environment includes things like furniture arrangement, light, sound, walls, and display boards.	The physical environment in a classroom should be designed, as fully as possible, to support a broad range of learner needs and to facilitate flexible teaching and learning.

attributes of instruction. As noted earlier, there is no generically "best" strategy for addressing any of the categories. In general, instructional strategies or tools that invite student-centeredness, teacher flexibility, and student choice and/or voice in learning will invite differentiation. Ensuring student voice and choice in decisions related to content, process, product, affect, and learning environment is important in both student and teacher development. In the end, a good strategy is one that helps a learner or group of learners accomplish worthy learning goals.

Differentiating affect and learning environment based on student readiness, interest, and/or learning profile often calls for nuanced responses by a teacher and/or flexible use of classroom space more than it calls for specific instructional strategies. Often, a combination of teacher sensitivity to student emotional or affective needs in combination with a classroom designed to provide safe spaces for

Figure 4.3. Examples of Differentiating Content, Process, and Product Based on Student Readiness, Interest, and Learning Profile—Part of the Answer to *How* Teachers Can Systematically Differentiate Instruction

	Content	Process	Product
Readiness	• Materials at varied reading levels • Reading/learning partners • Small-group instruction • Recorded text • Culturally relevant issues, topics, and materials • Graphic organizers to support note-taking in reading/lectures • Podcasts with or instead of text • Reading buddies • Graphic novels	• Differentiated homework • Work at learning centers or stations based on students' points of entry • Tiered assignments • Learning contracts, menus • Graphic organizers to guide steps in sense-making • Initial draft in student's first language, then translating • Small-group and individual instruction • Apps that support varied reading levels	• Models of quality student work at different levels of sophistication • Graduated rubrics with personalized student targets • Research/background materials at different levels of complexity • Options for early check-in dates to get feedback before due date • Options for due dates • Scaffolds for independent work
Interests	• Teacher use of content-based examples related to student interests/experiences • Using current media to increase relevance to students • Reading about contributors to the topic from many cultures • Student-choice novels based on topic or genre • Student-choice explorations related to a topic	• Student voice in learning options • Interest centers • Design-a-Day • Expert groups • Enrichment options for all students • Jigsaw • Integration of art, music, and tech into learning • Literature or math circles with student-choice roles	• Independent studies/inquiries/orbitals • Student-designed products with unit KUDs embedded • Student choice of audience for product • Genius Hour or other flex options for student-choice investigation and products • Mentorships • Internships
Learning Preferences	• Teacher/student use of multi-media to take in content • Emphasis on whole-to-part and part-to-whole in reading • Option to listen to music while reading • Option to stand or sit on the floor while reading	• Work alone, work with a partner options • Choice of modes of expression • RAFT options • Option to learn in a quiet area • Option to learn while standing or sitting on a bouncy stool • Competition/collaboration options	• Choice of modes of expression • Student-designed modes of expression • Choice of media for research and/or expressing learning • Varied options for due dates • Varied approaches to organization (outline, storyboard, etc.) in planning • Community-based applications of learning

students works in tandem to defuse a potentially difficult moment. For example:

• A teacher realizes a student is showing anxiety as he often does when he feels he may not be able to complete an assignment on time. The teacher might bend down by the student, ask quietly if something is making him feel anxious, and, after hearing his response, remind him that sometimes it is more important to feel good about your work than it is to turn it in before you have had a chance to do your best work. They then talk about a good target time for him to turn the work in.

• A child comes into the classroom as school begins and pushes a classmate away from a table they share. The teacher says to both students, "You know that we try hard in here to be kind to one another." Then she says to the child who was pushed, "Are you willing to give me a couple of minutes to talk with Brad about what's making him feel bad this morning?' As she talks with Brad, she finds he stayed up very late last night and has not had breakfast. After she gives him something to eat, she asks if he'd like to go sit in the quiet area of the room to eat and to take a few minutes to get himself ready for the day. She also asks if he thinks it would help the day if he apologized to his classmate when he is ready to do that.

- Angelo really likes to share his ideas in class. They are nearly always worth hearing, but if he speaks every time his hand goes up, few other students have opportunity to respond. If he does not get called on frequently, he sometimes blurts out answers or looks sullen. One of several strategies his teacher uses occasionally is to ask Angelo to look for and keep track of a particular kind of response or pattern of responses from his classmates during a discussion, and then to write her a note about what he sees. Today, she asked him to jot down some responses that appear to show an understanding of what they are studying as well as a couple of suggestions of possible areas where student understanding is not yet quite accurate. His answers are useful to her. He provides a second set of eyes and ears in instances like this. He also feels engaged throughout the discussion without the urge to overshare his ideas, and his notes are helpful to the teacher as she plans for the next lesson.

In the end, differentiation, as the quote from John Stroup notes at the beginning of this chapter, is a teacher's realization that to open access to meaningful learning for each student in a classroom will often require different resources, supports, degrees of encouragement, and pathways to learning for different students. A teacher routinely and carefully considering how she might adapt the aspects of instruction that are a part of most classroom moments based on a learner's readiness, needs, interests, and/or learning preferences provides a trustworthy framework for responsive instructional planning and implementation. The next section of this chapter will use a metaphor to explore a helpful way to think about structuring curriculum and instruction to benefit student learning and structuring classroom time to provide predictable opportunities for the class to learn together as well as predictable time to focus on individual and small-group needs.

METAPHORS FOR THINKING ABOUT TEACHING AND TIME IN A DIFFERENTIATED CLASSROOM

Our image of a classroom is often something like a straight chute. Students enter at roughly the same time and more or less proceed through the day together as a group of one. The teacher presents new information or a new skill to the whole class. She demonstrates it for the whole class. Everyone in the class tries it out for the same length of time. Then everyone practices the new skill or knowledge in the same way together and then independently. When they exit the chute, they go home to do more practice—again, the same practice for everyone. They come back to the chute the next day, review homework together, watch together as the teacher teaches or a student demonstrates, and the cycle continues.

This "unitary" classroom rhythm is one of the key reasons it is difficult for teachers to figure out how they could possibly differentiate instruction. Golden needs significant reading support. Javier needs significant vocabulary support and lots of time to talk with classmates in order to learn to navigate a new language. For a variety of reasons, Bianca, Hunter, and Lizzie have difficulty paying attention after just a few minutes of instruction. Sam, Amari, William, and Rosa find the pace of class maddeningly slow—and the list goes on. "When is there time to do anything meaningful for all these students' needs?" the teacher asks. "Besides, I have to cover all this material before the test."

This teacher's dilemma points to two habitual and connected drivers of classroom instruction in many, if not most, classrooms. First, "coverage" of curriculum feels like a non negotiable because of test pressure and habit. Second, we march through the coverage together because . . . well, because it is the most time-efficient way to get the job done . . . and because, well, how else would the day look? Here is a brief response to those two dominant drivers of instructional planning.

In terms of coverage, noted Harvard psychologist Howard Gardner wrote, "Coverage is the enemy of understanding" (in Brandt, 1993, p. 5). With expertise in neuroscience, he fully understood that when coverage is the classroom norm, it is likely that the only person who will remember much of what was taught, have a reasonable sense of how all the content fits together, and be able to use what was covered in novel contexts is the teacher—and sometimes, even that is doubtful.

Races to cover curriculum leave a frightening number of students limping behind in the exhaust fumes (Sousa & Tomlinson, 2018). Consider students with cognitive or emotional challenges, those who are just learning the language of the classroom, those with learning disabilities, autism spectrum disorders, or trauma. Think, too, about students who bear the weight of racial inequity, poverty, hunger, homelessness, abusive homes, and students with developmental delays, who march to a different drummer, who are angry or oppositional. That is just the start of the list of challenges students bring to school each day as they try to engage with learning. Most students in most of those categories are highly unlikely to learn, learn how to learn, or learn to love learning when coverage dominates instructional planning. Add to that list students who are academically advanced, students who are highly creative, and students who learn best by doing and by seeing that their learning benefits others, it is not surprising that after over 25 years of test-driven, coverage-oriented classrooms, high-stakes test scores have risen precious little in most instances and have fallen in some (Tomlinson, 2021). Coverage as an instructional driver flies in the face of nearly everything we know about how people learn. It is not an overstatement to say that coverage does not work! Students would nearly always engage with learning more readily and learn much more effectively if we taught a great deal less a great deal better. Differentiation concurs and calls on teachers to sideline chutes and coverage for more promising ways of thinking about instruction and use of time.

Rather than continuing the race to "cover" a vast expanse of "material" in a school year that is far too brief for curriculum coverage to make sense, differentiation (as well as research in psychology and neuroscience) guides us to determine what is truly essential in a body of content, then to focus on that essential knowledge, understanding, and skill, teaching with an emphasis on students making sense and meaning of those essentials so that they are able to apply and transfer what they learn in meaningful and useful contexts (e.g., Erickson et al. 2017; National Research Council, 2000; Sousa & Tomlinson, 2018; Tomlinson, 2021; Tomlinson & Sousa, 2020; Wiggins & McTighe, 2005). Setting aside devotion to what is often described as curriculum that is a mile wide and an inch deep, teachers can move from a focus on *covering* curriculum to a focus on helping students *uncover* its meaning (Brandt, 1993; National Research Council, 2000; Wiggins & McTighe, 2005).

In terms of time, we could teach much more responsively to the young humans in our classrooms, and much more effectively, if we jettisoned "chutes" and planned instead for "highways" and "exit ramps." That approach to time use signals a teacher's commitment to addressing the shared needs of all students in a class and the particular needs of individual learners.

WHAT'S ON THE MAIN HIGHWAY

There are many things in a classroom that everyone needs to share. Shared time takes place on the highway. The highway acknowledges essential, foundational learning goals that pertain to every student (except, on occasion, students with Individualized Education Plans that indicate otherwise). The highway provides an opportunity for all students to hear from a broad range of peers, learn to appreciate the varied strengths of classmates, make decisions together, share responsibility for effective operation of the class, laugh together, and build the connections and bonds that make the class an "us."

Segments of class that build student-to-student connections should include all members of a class. Exploring new information and ideas that establish a foundation of information essential for learning should belong to all students. All students should learn about and take part in explorations of "big ideas" or the conceptual building blocks of a discipline. Debriefing after significant periods of learning and work is often (but not always) helpful for all students in a class.

WHAT CAN BE BUILT AT EXIT RAMPS

There are also student needs that are, at a specific time, unique to individual learners and/or small subsets of the whole class. Those needs are often (but not always) most effectively addressed on the "exit ramps." Addressing those needs systematically and effectively signals a teacher's commitment to seeing THE student rather than just the STUDENTS and to planning, teaching, and reflecting on student growth for each student as well. Time focused on a range of individual and small group needs requires "exit ramps" from the highway that allow for a variety of student work to occur for a period of time before re-entering the highway for the class to move ahead together again.

Much (but again, not all) differentiation occurs during exit ramp time. A teacher can and absolutely should attend to diverse learner needs while he or she is leading "highway time" (for example, through using visuals or demonstrations, linking content to students' lives, checking for understanding, providing time for students to have a quick chat with a peer, asking questions at a range of complexity, using word walls, and so on). However, close, sustained attention to individual needs, including but not limited to those highlighted in Part II of the book, requires "exit ramp" time. The length of common time on the highway and the duration of exit ramp time is variable depending on the nature of a curricular sequence and the needs of both "THE student" and "the STUDENTS." That variance is another manifestation of flexibility in a differentiated classroom. Figure 4.4 displays some times during an instructional cycle when highway time is generally useful and some during which exit ramp time is valuable.

Formalizing Planning

When it is time to write lesson plans that will frame both instruction and time, consider a simple two-column lesson plan. In some schools, this format will work well for submission to a principal, grade-level leader, department chair, or other individual who keeps an informed eye on what's taking place in each classroom. In other places, there may be a required planning format that is different from the two-column suggestion that follows here. In the latter instance, consider attaching your two-column plan to the required one. Chances are the two-column version may be more informative to you on a daily basis than the required lesson plan format—and perhaps to administrators/leaders as well.

The two-column plan is simply a way to proactively plan for and make clear those elements in a classroom in which all students will take part and those that will be focused on supporting each student in developing essential skills, knowledge, and understanding so that each student will have maximum opportunity to develop the competencies that are necessary for continuing forward progress. In essence, the format tells the story of how a unit will unfold. First, we will do this step as a whole class, then we will do this as a whole class, then we will break out into smaller configurations to address these more specific learner needs, then we will come back together to take this next step, and so on.

In other words, the two-column plan indicates that you have planned for the flow of a unit including both whole-class and key differentiated elements on a step-by-step basis. Many required lesson plan formats have a small section that asks how the teacher will differentiate the lesson(s) but provide neither space nor guidance to make the contents of the space meaningful for supporting rich teacher thinking or useful for implementation. The two-column plan takes care of that deficit. Figure 4.5 shows one page of a two-column lesson plan for a 7th-grade literature unit on ways in which elements in fiction work together to create a theme.

A FINAL THOUGHT

Planning for differentiation in an informed and systematic way is key to effectiveness in addressing the learning needs of all sorts of students. Practice observing students and examining student work to gather insights about their various readiness levels, interests, and approaches to learning. Think about curriculum and instruction in terms of content, process, and product. Consider your own possible responses to students' affective needs, and ways in which you can best utilize the physical space in the classroom you share with them.

Then have a go at creating a lesson plan for just one or two days in which you decide which of the aspects of instruction you can best use to support students who are entering the lesson at different points of readiness, with different interests, and through providing (and/or having students suggest) learning options. Think about the students. In what ways do they manifest affective needs? When you respond effectively, what does that look like? What other responses might you have in reserve? Might you reconfigure the classroom space or materials to benefit different learner needs? The goal is not to

do all of those things in a single day or lesson, of course, but rather to use them as a guide to expand your thinking and to select instructional aspects as they are meaningful options for addressing one or more of the student learning categories.

In adapting curriculum to benefit learners, think hard about stepping aside from curriculum coverage to focus learning on what matters most. Then seek ways to help students learn the essentials in order to uncover meaning and relevance in what they learn. As you free yourself and your students from the race to coverage, begin to ask

Figure 4.4. Some Examples of Highway Time and Exit Ramp Time in Classes

Highways: Times Students Need to be Together as a Class
Checking in at the start of class or start of the day
Planning for class procedures, activities
Introducing new ideas, topics, skills, explorations, products
Exploring, understanding, and applying the "big ideas" of a content area
Mini-lessons, mini-lectures, videos, guest speakers
Discussions around big ideas, issues, problems
Planning for products or performance assessments
Debriefing about a lesson, a class, a day, a unit
Sharing ideas, resources, products
Celebrating successes

Exit Ramps: Times to Focus on Specific Learner Needs
Small-group instruction
Small-group teamwork
Individual practice
Student-teacher conversations, planning, assessment
Independent inquiries, interest-based learning, Genius Hour, etc.
Moving ahead with own next steps in depth and breadth of study
Sharing ideas, resources, products

Source: Tomlinson (2021). *So each may soar: Principles and practices of learner-centered classrooms.* ASCD. Used with permission.

Figure 4.5. A Sample Two-Column Lesson Plan From a Portion of a 7th-Grade English Unit Designed to Help Students Understand and Demonstrate Understanding of Ways in Which Elements of a Short Story Can Interact Around a Theme.

Highway (Whole Class)	Exit Ramps (Focused Differentiation)
Discussion on elements in our lives and how they interact.	
Introduction to unit. Review of elements of literature using matching exercise in which some students have cards with element names, some have definitions, some have examples from stories students have read in common. Discussion of things we analyze in our daily lives and how we go about it—create a set of steps in analysis.	
Students work in quads or triads to analyze a story to identify story elements and analyze how they work together. Group size, story choice, and graphic organizer used to guide work will vary based on pre-assessment results. Teacher will meet with small groups throughout the class period.	
Whole-class review of theme, proposing themes in lives of cartoon characters, then superheroes, then famous people, analyzing how they arrived at those themes.	
	Practice with themes in brief "stories"—stories vary in mode, complexity, and support. Varied organizers will support varied individual and small-group needs for support and extension. "Identify and support your conclusion—Identify and show how the elements contribute to a theme."
	Individually or in teams, students develop a story in which elements interact to point to a theme—differentiation through varied directions, organizers, supports, modes of expression. Teacher observes the working groups/individuals for understanding of key concepts, and will have two 10-minute intensive sessions with English learners and students with reading difficulties.

Source: Tomlinson, C. A. (2021). *So each may soar: Principles and practices of learner-centered classrooms.* ASCD. Used with permission.

yourself which elements of a lesson and unit plan all students will need to experience together (highway time) and when it will benefit students most to work on aspects of the unit they need to master, polish, or extend (exit ramps). Try creating a two-column lesson plan—and after you use it, think about how you might want to recraft it next time based on what you observed as you watched your students at work.

Again, the goal is not instant or even rapid mastery of these approaches, but rather a firm intent to learn, grow, take your own next steps forward, reflect—and try again. The benefits from that approach are abundant.

CHAPTER 5

Laying a Foundation for Teaching All Learners Responsively

Self-awareness is a trait of any good leader. Being a good leader requires being a good observer. Being a good observer is more than just self-awareness. Observing oneself is essential, but observing others provides another angle to absorb. Together, observing self and others creates richer insights to use . . . Being a good observer enables us to take a step back and peer into ourselves and others. Just looking produces nothing. Observing produces insights when we assess for patterns, styles, and results. Why observing matters is centered here—discerning patterns, styles, and results.

—Jon Mertz

> Big Idea for Chapter 5: Teaching and learning that meet students where they are and moves them forward is about much more than differentiated activities.

This chapter builds on the earlier chapters by providing two tools for planning foundational differentiation—that is, differentiation that learner-centered teachers might expect to provide routinely in their classrooms. Foundational differentiation lays the groundwork for more inclusive teaching—that is, differentiation that is required by students who have more complex learning needs than many agemates. Foundational differentiation also includes an important indicator for Everybody Classrooms—that teaching is most likely to serve most students well when it begins with the premise that the vast majority of students in a school should have equity of access to the richest, most engaging curriculum and instruction that a school can offer any learner, coupled with active support to succeed with those elements.

First, this chapter proposes a baker's dozen of "big picture" benchmarks or guidelines for teachers to consider when planning or reflecting on instruction for the diverse students who make up today's classrooms. These benchmarks are not recipes or algorithms, but rather touchstones or heuristics that can inform our decision-making. Following presentation and a discussion of these guidelines, the chapter then provides a more detailed but also more distilled digest of some principles and practices that can make each of the classroom elements (learning environment, curriculum, formative assessment, instruction, and leading students/managing classroom routines) work more effectively to support the diverse needs of learners. Both the general guidelines (found in Figure 5.1) and the more specific digest of teacher actions (found in Figure 5.3 on p. 53) point to *common* needs of the full spectrum of learners.

Part II of the book focuses on the more "specialized" needs of learners with complex challenges that can impede their learning. Addressing those needs in inclusive classrooms requires this solid foundation of differentiation on which the classroom teacher further tailors teaching and learning to support students who need additional scaffolding, different scaffolding, or more intensive scaffolding to grow academically, affectively, and emotionally. In Everybody Classrooms, learning and support for learning work in service of "deep learning" for each student—that is, learning for understanding, for meaning, and for application and transfer into the world beyond the classroom. In this approach,

41

Figure 5.1. Benchmarks for Planning Instruction That Is Responsive to Each Learner's Needs

1. Remember that student needs, even within a "category," are rarely homogeneous.
2. Expect great outcomes from every learner, and "teach up" to support that outcome.
3. Teach with student strengths and interests in the foreground.
4. Set out to study every student every day.
5. Plan for a classroom in which respect is a shared norm.
6. Create a culture of inclusion from day one, or before.
7. Work with your students early and often to create a classroom that works for everyone.
8. Plan and teach to ensure that each student regularly sees him/herself in the content they learn.
9. Establish an ethic of "taking your own next step."
10. Remember that students need to learn how to learn, not just learn content.
11. Be sure each student has ready access to the tools, resources, and technologies necessary to succeed.
12. Ensure that each student sees him/herself in what and how they learn.
13. Use "highways and exit ramps" to ensure time for the class to work as a whole and for students to focus on their needs and strengths.
14. Mind the foundation! (See Chapter 5 and Figure 5.3.)

students continue to work with the basic skills and competencies they need to master, but most often in the context of relevant, engaging, discipline-based work that calls on them to think, problem-solve, collaborate, and develop agency as learners.

The 14 guidelines presented next in this chapter *should* be the "entitlement" of all students who have little choice but to trust us to teach them well. Figure 5.1 lists the benchmarks for quick reference. As you consider the list of guidelines, take time to note which ones are already pivotal in your planning and teaching, which ones you are inclined to disregard, and which ones you already know you want to cultivate. Feel free to add to the list items you believe to be markers of responsive teaching. Following the figure is a brief discussion of each of the 14 benchmarks.

HAVE GREAT EXPECTATIONS FOR EACH LEARNER AND "TEACH UP" TO SUPPORT THAT OUTCOME

It is likely that many teachers "teach down" to students who struggle with school in one way or another. We recognize the stresses these students carry, and we want to help them feel successful—to stay motivated to learn—and so we set a low bar for success. Or perhaps we do not really think some of our students have the capacity to do complex work. While the students may, indeed, face significant barriers to learning, they are not unaware of the world around them by any means. They see in our faces and tones of voice that we view them with reservations. They are absolutely aware, for example, that when we meet with small groups, we are typically assembling students who are doing poorly in their work. When there is tracking or ability grouping in a class or between classes, they fully understand that they are in the "low-hope group" and see that students in other sections of the subject are doing work that is more compelling—work that they are likely to agree is not within their reach because they, too, have concluded that they are not "school material."

There is great truth in a comment made by a young learner who was seen as having "limited capacity" by a previous teacher and who had come to see herself through that lens as well—until she got a teacher who saw her differently. "My new teacher taught me like I was smart," she said. "So I was." Research in both neuroscience and psychology affirm that an individual learns only when that individual must stretch to reach beyond his or her current comfort zone and gets support from peers and/or adults to make the stretch possible. Therefore, we need to ask each of our students to stretch a bit further every day than they believe they can. And we need to support that reach every day.

"Teaching up," a core practice in differentiation, means believing that every student has hidden capacity, that every student can reason, solve problems, and understand big ideas. So a teacher who teaches up plans first to challenge advanced learners appropriately, then asks the question, "Now what can I do to support a broad range of other students not only in having this rich learning experience, but also in succeeding with it?" Teaching up demonstrates to students that success with work they previously felt was out of their reach is, in fact, attainable.

That may mean encouraging some students to draw rather than write an answer, to listen to an assigned reading rather than reading it, to respond to a question first in their home language and then translating the response later, to work with instructions provided in a stepwise way rather than as a whole, to turn in an assignment for feedback prior to submitting it in final form, to use a checklist of steps in an assignment rather than assuming the student is ready to determine the steps unaided, attaching content to their experiences, and so on. There are scores of ways to scaffold student success.

The goal of teaching up is to ensure that every student works with the pivotal big ideas or principles of a content area, uses knowledge and skill to act on those big ideas, is cast as a thinker, makes meaning of ideas, and "gets" why/how the content matters in their lives. Big ideas are universal. They are connective. They make content make meaning. Knowledge and skill should be used in service of big ideas—by everyone. "Teaching up" says to individual students and the class as a whole, "In this class, everyone can do important things, and we work as a team to make that happen."

In an effectively differentiated classroom, there is ongoing time provided (often through exit ramps) for students to tackle knowledge and skills that may be difficult for them to master at this point in their learning journey, but that difficulty should not keep them from having time and opportunity to do meaningful work as well.

TEACH FROM STUDENT STRENGTHS AND INTERESTS

It is devilishly easy to look at students through a deficit lens—focusing on what is "broken" or "wrong" in them. Students who grapple with one or more potential impediments to learning in their lives are nearly always acutely aware of those impediments and frequently feel reduced by them. It is important, then, when we set out to connect with those students and to teach them effectively, to park our deficit thinking by the side of the road and concentrate on learning about the student's strengths—about those things that make him or her feel whole.

A math teacher was aware that one of her students "hated" math and had performed poorly in math for several years. Rather than seeing the student as deficient in attitudes or skills related to math, she chose instead to focus on the girl's love of poetry and occasionally asked her to write a poem about a math problem, a computation they were working with in class, or numbers in general. The poems were sometimes clever, sometimes rich with insight, and sometimes even provided clarity about how and why the content they were studying in class was useful. The teacher shared her pleasure in reading the poems, often asking permission to use them in her classes. Using this and other strength-based approaches to teaching, she found the student first warmed up to her, then began to engage more with lessons, and ultimately told her teacher that math made more sense to her once she began writing about it.

A history teacher taught a number of students who were far from fluent readers and who continually struggled with comprehending complex texts. As often as feasible, he used websites that provided readings at varied levels of complexity so that all of his students could read the same materials at appropriate challenge levels and take part in class discussions. He tended to think of these students as "weak readers"—and it was certainly true that the students resisted reading whenever they could and, when pressed to read, came away from the experience with little evident understanding. After a class discussion on racism one day, one of the "weak readers" asked the teacher if he could get him a copy of *Stamped from the Beginning*, a National Book Award winner about the history of racism in the United States. The teacher was just about to explain to the student that the book was probably too difficult for him to enjoy reading when he realized he needed instead to support the student's desire to try it out. The book was, in fact, challenging for the student, but he was absorbed by each page he read and not only completed the book, but referred to it often in class discussions and assignments. That experience changed how the teacher thought about reluctant students. "My job," he said afterward, "is to find out what really matters to a student and build from there."

Nadia Lopez (in Namahoe, 2020) created curriculum for incarcerated juveniles on entrepreneurship. "It's about survival and economics," she explains. "The kids understand that concept. It's what they have lived." They created entrepreneurial products, met with successful entrepreneurs in their communities, learned how their businesses worked, found mentors to guide their first entrepreneurial ideas, and saw themselves building futures they had assumed did not exist for them. She developed a science and history project for students in an urban high school to examine the idea that all men are created equal through the lens of Hurricane Katrina. It changed the students' lives and trajectories. She took students on field trips to places they didn't know existed to meet successful people who had lived their struggles and had moved on to being successful contributors in a range of endeavors. In one instance, 24 of the 25 students who went on the field trips later went on to 2- and 4-year colleges. The student who did not go to college became a professional soccer player. "Success isn't about magic," Lopez explains. "The only magic I have is believing. There's the magic of power that comes from simply believing."

Almost paralyzed by fears, including but by no means limited to school failures, Charles, one of my middle school students, made eye contact with no one, refused to speak in class or to write, and gave no indication that he understood what was going on in class. One day, I saw several students who sat near him looking slack-jawed at something he seemed to be making with his hands below the top of his desk. Careful not to intrude on the moment, I moved slowly around the room to find an angle that

would let me see what his classmates were clearly engrossed in watching. I am not sure Charles was even fully conscious of what he was doing. For him, I think it was akin to biting fingernails or cracking knuckles—something to do to release tension, to stay in one's skin. He was crafting the most complex Jacob's Ladder (a ladder-like string figure similar to a cat's cradle) that I had ever seen. I asked if anyone would like him to teach them how to make them. He quickly had a long waiting list. He began making eye contact and speaking so he could be their teacher. He began writing so he could share diagrams and directions. It was a small thing. And it was everything.

Catch yourself in midthought when you engage in deficit thinking. Shift quickly to looking for and building on what makes a learner feel whole.

SET OUT TO STUDY EVERY STUDENT EVERY DAY

That goal seems beyond daunting, especially for teachers at the secondary level. There are too many students, short class periods, too little time to "cover the curriculum," and a perpetual overload of papers to grade. "It is," we say, "unrealistic to expect us to know each student!"

It *is* unrealistic to expect a teacher to know each student deeply and broadly, but it is also unrealistic to think we can teach well if we do not know about a student's culture, are not following the student's learning trajectory, or do not attempt to be aware of and build on their interests and strengths and dreams. It is unlikely that we can teach a student well enough if we are unaware of the learning challenges that student faces and the nature of those challenges.

Further, unless we are continually learning about a student, it is likely that the student will conclude that we don't really care to know him or her. We lose student trust in us, or perhaps never gain it at all.

A teacher of middle school students wrote to me recently, "I didn't see any way to get to know that many students, or, for that matter, to differentiate instruction for them. I could see, though, that my students were hungry to succeed and so I gave it a try. What I have learned is that a student-focused classroom provides time for me to walk around and observe as students work, and to sit with individuals and small groups and listen to their thinking. Formative assessment gives me a window every day for seeing how they are understanding, or not understanding, what we are exploring. And, in fact, I have come to understand that everything a student does in class is a kind of formative assessment. I'm learning more about my students in a week than I once would have learned about them in a year. What a difference this is making for all of us!"

As the quote that opens this chapter reminds us, being a good observer allows us to understand ourselves and others more fully. Just "looking" produces nothing. Systematic and "focused observing" produces insights as we assess for patterns, styles, and results. That kind of observing matters because it helps us discern those patterns, styles, and results, both related to a specific learner and across learners. It is discerning those patterns, proclivities, and unfolding results that enables us to understand both how to teach the class as a whole and how to reach individual learners as well—how to teach based both on students' shared and unique needs.

Be an unrelenting student of your students! The benefits for learners are profound and the rewards for a teacher no less so.

PLAN FOR A CLASSROOM IN WHICH RESPECT IS A SHARED NORM

All human beings, I believe, have a need to be respected. Feeling demeaned has a corrosive effect. That effect is clearly visible in the lives of children who are abused and will likely struggle for a lifetime with the conviction that they are shameful, "less than." The first world of children is their family. The absence of respect in that context is scarring. The second world of children and young people is generally their peer group. The absence of respect in that world is also damaging.

Vivian Paley's classroom rule, "You can't say you can't play," was insightful. She saw young children excluding peers from their play and understood that exclusion to be the beginning of a process that she felt hardened children over time, long into adulthood. When Paley (1993) authored a book by that title, she interviewed both children who were excluded and those who did the excluding. The excluded children described a life of loneliness, rejection, and self-doubt. The children doing the excluding concurred that Paley's rule was fair but found it difficult to envision accepting the rule themselves. Excluding and bullying were part of their fun. Both perspectives are sad.

Paley felt it was the responsibility of adults to intervene so that the cruelty and rejection we often feel are inevitable components of children's play do not become inevitable components of adult life. When rejection and exclusion are allowed, even subtly, in classrooms that include students who already struggle with physical differences, emotional challenges, poverty, cultural and/or language differences, racial inequities, gender identity, homelessness, inadequate home support, or many other weights students bring to school with them, the act of learning becomes exponentially more difficult. A colleague of mine once reflected that life gives every one of us a box of rocks we carry on our back at some time on our journey, "but," she continued, "a teacher ought to be helping young people *remove* rocks from their boxes and from one another's boxes. We should not sanction anything that becomes an opportunity for more rocks to be added."

Model respect in your choice of words, tone of voice, eye contact, patience, careful listening, acknowledgment of growth, teaching the skills of respect, and ensuring work that dignifies each learner. Respect speaks of trust. Trust enables a learner to take the considerable risk of learning.

CREATE A CULTURE OF INCLUSION FROM DAY ONE, OR BEFORE

Closely related to respect is a culture of inclusion. Inclusion doesn't just mean that people with varied backgrounds, needs, experiences, and/or learning proclivities occupy a common space. The goal of inclusion is having all those students learn well together, on their own terms, in ways that work for them. That requires respect for varied manifestations of humanity, for perspectives different from our own, and for the contribution each voice adds to our understanding of the world around us.

Inclusion is not about having students with identified exceptionalities join "the rest of us" in the classroom, but rather about having all of us join together as a community of learners in a classroom that is designed for all of us—and for each of us.

Creating a culture of inclusion means that the teacher is a champion of the right of each learner to both belong and achieve, that the teacher is ready to receive and support each young person as he or she is while simultaneously envisioning and supporting who that student might become. It means talking with students about the reality that we have shared *similarities that make us human*—the need to be accepted and valued, the need to grow, the need to laugh with others, the need to contribute to the world we share, and so on. Understanding our shared humanity is key to a workable society.

Inclusion also means talking with students about our differences—in language, body type, talents, experiences, ways of seeing the world. Those *differences make us individuals*. We vary in the amount of food we eat and *what* we like to eat, in the amount of sleep we need. We vary in how well we sit still and for how long, in how fast we run. There will be times when reading or math or art is hard for some of us and easy for others of us—and if class is challenging (as it should be, because a shared human need is the need to stretch, to take on a task we feel pretty sure we can't accomplish and then to feel almost reborn when we do accomplish it), there will be no assupmtion of a one-size-fits-all challenge.

Inclusion calls on us to work with students to set norms for positive interaction and to work diligently to ensure that the norms are in the foreground of our thinking and actions as we share space and time and learning. And inclusion calls on us to use purposeful, flexible student groupings as well as flexible use of time, space, and resources, based on the needs of individuals, the nature of the work we are doing, and the talents and interests each of us brings to that work.

If inclusion seems difficult, it is. Just look at the world we live in. We tend to believe it is our job to mentor young people in becoming better students of history, music, science, literature, and so on—and it is. It is no less important, and arguably more so, that we invest heavily in mentoring better citizens of the world, as well.

WORK WITH YOUR STUDENTS EARLY AND OFTEN TO CREATE A CLASS THAT WORKS FOR EVERYONE

From an early age, children can share stories of times when they tried to do something they were not yet ready to do and how it felt to be in that situation. They can share experiences of being asked to do something a younger brother or sister needed to do and feeling frustrated or angry because of that expectation. They understand with clarity the idea that we are ready to do things like walk or talk at different times and that our teeth do not fall out on the same timetable. And they have many personal experiences with one-size-fits-all assignments, schedules, modes of expressing learning, and so on. They can also talk about interests they have that do not ever seem to intersect with the classroom agenda and about how it would be possible to merge those interests with what we learn in class.

A teacher of elementary students began the year by asking his students to create paper cutouts that represented them. With necessary supplies at hand, he asked them to make the body of the cutout the color of their favorite subject as listed on a key (for example, green for math, yellow for music, orange for reading), to make their hair color their least favorite subject (for example purple for spelling, pink for science, etc.). Their shirt color indicated a talent or interest that was important for them (for example, gray for sports, red for music, white for building things, tan for helping people). If the talent or interest they wanted to spotlight was not on the list, they could choose another color and put a symbol or logo on the shirt that helped others know what the interest or talent was. The teacher asked them to put stripes on their shirt if they really liked to work with others in class, polka dots if they especially liked to work alone, and a different design of their choosing if they liked to work in both those ways. Finally, he asked them to make a hat for their cutout if they liked to learn new things and to design the hat to show some of their personality.

The day after students completed their cutouts, he posted them on a bulletin board, placing a number beneath each figure. He asked that each student spend a little time during the day looking at the board and writing on an index card the numbers under all the cutouts that were just like theirs. Not surprisingly, no student found a single match for the figure they created. That was the start of a year-long conversation. A conversation around student experiences can lead to questions like: "If no two of you are alike, how should I teach?" "Should I plan to teach those of you who love science the same way I plan to teach those of you for whom it's your least favorite subject?" "Should I make sure to connect only the most popular interests with what we do in class?" "Do you think we could create a classroom that works well for everyone here?" "What would the class look like?" "How would it be different from some other classes you've been in?" "What would my roles be?" "What would your roles be?" "Why would it matter to create a class like this?" "Would it be worth the effort?" "How would we know how it was working and for whom?"

In time, there will be a need to have conversations about things like how to get help if you feel stuck with the work you are doing but the teacher is busy working with a small group of students and is not available to help you; how to make sure conversations you are having with classmates about your work do not get loud enough to make it hard for students who are working alone to concentrate on their assignments; how to get and put away materials and supplies smoothly when classmates are using different things to do their work; and where to put completed work and where to find work that has feedback from the teacher on it.

There will need to be conversations about routines—for example, how to complete science labs effectively when groups of students may be doing different labs or using different materials for the labs; ways the teacher can let students know what they need to work with on a given day, including where to sit in the classroom, goals for success, and so on; when there is more than one assignment going on in the classroom; when it is okay to move around the classroom and how to do that so it does not distract others; and how to clean up at the end of a segment of work so the room and its students are ready for what comes next.

For younger students, it is wise to practice a routine before students use it the first time. With older students, reviewing the routine is usually adequate. In both instances, it is important to debrief about the routine after its use to discuss what

worked, what did not, and what can be tweaked or modified the next time students use the routine in order to make it more effective and efficient.

After a few weeks of working with agreed-upon routines and procedures, I found it important to talk with students about what "fair" would mean in our class. We had already agreed implicitly that "fair" wasn't about everyone doing the same thing. It is important for all of us to feel that the place we work is fair. So, what would that term mean in *this* kind of class? A common definition the students suggested early in the year was, "The class will be fair if you like us all alike." Later in the year, the most common response was, "The class is fair if everyone gets what they need to succeed." Both definitions convey significant insight.

Ultimately, I talked with students about how we might best report their status as learners at the ends of marking periods. By the end of the first quarter, they understood the importance of growth or progress as an indicator of learning, and we discussed ways they and I could describe their growth so that it would be part of a reporting process.

When students play a central role in envisioning, planning for, enacting, and refining class goals and structures, the idea of meeting students at their current entry points into the curriculum, following their progress, and planning instruction that addresses their strengths, needs, and interests makes sense to students. Teachers' concerns about student push back on students in the same class sometimes doing different work, the possibility of different timetables for completing work, use of flexible grouping, and so on are rarely realized. In an effectively differentiated and effectively inclusive classroom, it is not just "exceptional students" who, on some occasions, do work that is different from the norm. In fact, in Everybody Classrooms, the norm is all students doing work that helps each of them move ahead. The norm is that there is no "normal" assignment. Further, students come to believe that if they do have questions about how the class is working, it is safe to ask them.

Time spent on co-constructing the class is more than reclaimed through smoothly functioning routines, student comfort with how things work, and a significant increase in positive student behavior. In addition, the process helps forge strong teacher/student connections and student/student connections.

ESTABLISH AN ETHIC OF "TAKING YOUR OWN NEXT STEP"

In classes where teachers plan largely for "the STUDENTS" instead of "THE student," assignments often ask or require all students to take the same "next steps" in learning on a given day. For many students with attention problems, reading difficulties, behavioral challenges, language constraints, persistent anxiety, or other significant learning hurdles, that expectation is likely out of reach. That reality can frustrate, anger, or discourage learners, leading to a mounting trail of failures and commonly to behavior problems as well. Teachers who feel responsible to move all students along as a group also can become frustrated. Learning to plan for THE student as well as the STUDENTS—in other words, learning to differentiate to create Everybody Classrooms— can reduce these frustrations all around.

It is also generally the teacher's responsibility in a differentiated classroom to guide and assist students in working forward from their evolving Zones of Proximal Development (Vygotsky, 1986) and to provide support in a variety of ways that enable a student to succeed with the slightly-too-difficult task. The student's role is to take his or her own next step in a learning progression every day. Those responsibilities are interdependent whether the class is deductive, inductive, or a combination of the two in its approach.

The teacher in a differentiated Everybody Classroom establishes the ethic with students that what matters most is a student's growth. It rarely serves us well to try to achieve someone else's goals or take someone else's next step. Where you begin a learning sequence is not nearly as important as your continued movement in a direction that extends your capacities. Standing still is not acceptable. This applies to every student, including those who seem to be doing "well enough" and students who are top performers. Most of us resist what we feel we cannot accomplish, and most of us *can* accomplish what we resist with the right support.

This mirrors John Hattie's (2012) reflection that in classrooms that effectively mentor the development of each learner, the goal each day is +1 learning—each student moving forward one segment from the day before. The idea of +1 learning is not a precise measure, but rather a depiction of meaningful progress toward an important goal.

REMEMBER THAT STUDENTS NEED TO LEARN HOW TO LEARN, NOT JUST LEARN CONTENT

While some students arrive at school as seasoned, mature learners, many/most do not.

Students who struggle with school often, although certainly not always, arrive in the classroom with gaps in learning proficiencies. Those gaps, of course, are major contributors to the struggles the students experience.

We see it as a given that a contractor must be able to read blueprints, understand and comply with building regulations, use a variety of tools and materials effectively and even creatively, and guide the work of a team of builders in order to build worthy structures. By contrast, we overlook the complexity of skills and attitudes involved in learning and assign low grades when students are not yet able to be architects of their own learning.

It is a mighty contribution to student success when teachers are clear on the skills and habits of mind their students need to develop in order to become efficient and autonomous learners and when teachers take great care to teach those skills and habits of mind, monitor how each student applies the skills, and provide regular mentoring to support student growth in those areas. A key component of the skills and habits of mind necessary for success are those necessary for productive collaboration. Group work often falls short if students in a group do not understand how to mindfully contribute to its success.

Remember, too, that many students who are advanced academically and regularly make "good grades" may never have had to step up to academic challenge, do not know how to do so, and become frightened and even angry in the face of challenges that they have not learned to unlock. If we do not teach learning agency, odds are that the content we feel is important for students to take away from our classes is, at best, inert when our students leave us.

ENSURE THAT EACH STUDENT SEES HIM/ HERSELF IN WHAT AND HOW THEY LEARN

Research from both psychology and neuroscience emphasizes the importance of content relevance to learning. Content is relevant when students see themselves in it. For some students, that may mean seeing people from their culture or people who have encountered challenges similar to their own related to the content in some way. For other students, it may mean reading about or listening to what they are learning in their primary language. Some students will find content relevant when they can relate it to their own lives, families, or neighborhoods. Having opportunity to connect their interests or talents to content is a source of relevance.

Students from the dominant culture in a region or school are likely to see people like themselves in most content much of the time. That is generally not the case for students from non dominant groups unless schools and teachers are purposeful toward that end. Figure 5.2 lists a few categories of students along with areas in which they may, or may not, see people like themselves portrayed at all or in a positive light. There is no single correct response to the prompts provided in the figure. Recall that students within a category will not all experience school in the same way. Still, it can be thought-provoking to consider the questions in a general way as they relate to your work as an educator.

Content relevance links to learning success on several levels. When a content area seems relevant to a student, it is an indicator that the student feels able to make sense of—to relate to, to understand—the content. *Understanding* content, as noted earlier, is a nonnegotiable for meaningful learning. In addition, when a student sees connections between his or her family, neighborhood, aspirations, and content, that student is more likely to identify with the content area than without those links. Further, affiliation with a content area is necessary for a student's continuing interest and investment in that area.

When a student can connect personal interests with a content area, the student is likely to feel more confident in his or her ability to succeed in that area; even if the student often perceives it to be beyond reach, that student is more likely to engage with the content and persist in learning it. For example, researchers (Walkington et al., 2014) divided math students into two groups for a study of the impact of connecting content with students' personal interests. They asked students in half of the group to share their interests with the researchers via a checklist (ranking interest areas on a list of possibilities). Students in that experimental group received math problems on linear equations that were linked to sports, music, art, games, and such, so that all students in that group received the same problems to solve as their peers in the experimental group but with the problems embedded in the student's interest area. Students in the second (control) group solved the problems with no interest-based modification. Students who received the interest-based problems solved them more readily and more accurately than the students in the control group, and students who benefited most from the interest-embedded problems were the students who had previously had the most difficulty with math. It appeared that when a student who was a great fan of music read a problem that dealt with selling tickets to a rock concert, the student felt encouraged. "I know about concerts, so I can solve this!"

While one experience with a problem set that links to your interest or one opportunity to read about someone who has autism spectrum disorder, as you do, and who makes major contributions to science will probably not change the world for either of those two students, it is a great first step. It is a commendation that this content, this subject, learning, making a difference in the world, just might be within your reach.

We are wise to be conscious of ways we can enable the full range of learners in our classes to regularly see how what we teach—what we ask them to learn—makes room for them and their experiences. Likewise, learning is more relevant, inviting, and natural when students have voice and choice in *how* they learn. Approaches to learning are shaped considerably by a person's culture. Gender can impact a person's approaches to learning as well. A myriad of other factors can also influence how a student might work most effectively on a given topic and day (for example, how the student is feeling physically or emotionally; how comfortable the student is with the teacher, peers, and/or content; and/or the student's proficiency with the language of the classroom and with academic vocabulary). Likewise, many factors can influence how a student might best express learning at a particular time and in a particular context. The aim in giving students choices in both areas and encouraging them to propose other options is to enable the student to work more efficiently and effectively than might be the case if choices were not available.

Figure 5.2. Opportunities Students in Various Categories of Exceptionality Have to See People Like Themselves Represented in School Experiences

How often are students in the left-hand column likely to see people "like them" portrayed at all and/or portrayed positively in the areas listed at the top of the other columns? Use the key below to respond.

Key: 1—Often   2—Occasionally   3—Seldom   4—Never/almost never

Exceptionality Category:	Scientists they learn about in school	History they study in school	Students who are academically successful	Art and music they study in school	Literature they read in school	Teachers who teach them	Speakers who come to class	Images of homes and neighborhoods in texts, videos, field trips, etc.	Images of successful people/ contributors to society
Physical disabilities									
Specific learning disorder									
LGBTQ									
Homeless									
Poverty									
African American									
ADHD									
Latinx									
Trauma									
Autism									
Advanced/Gifted									

BE SURE EACH STUDENT HAS READY ACCESS TO THE RESOURCES NECESSARY FOR SUCCESS

As knowledge has become ever more accessible to many of us through technology, it is easy to forget that there are still great swaths of people who do not have that access as readily as we might assume. I have seen excellent teachers assign work that must be word-processed to be acceptable when several students in the class have no access to a computer or printer. When schools have found it necessary to pivot from in-classroom to online teaching, they have seen that significant numbers of students have no Internet access at home and often no access to the technologies that schools rely on for distance learning even if they could connect to the internet.

And technology is not the only area in which students may lack access to what they need to complete an assignment. An art teacher in the middle school where I taught for many years became a hero of mine when she let students know they could come by her classroom to get materials they needed for projects in other classes and could also work there in the afternoons if that would be helpful. She was making it possible for students to succeed with work that teachers who assigned the work had not realized was beyond their reach simply because they had no way to get markers, posterboard, and other supplies that the teachers took for granted were in students' homes.

When some students can access information at the flick of an on button and others lack even a way to get to a library, the playing field is not level. When the parents of some students are on call as soon as their children have a need for their assistance and other students live in a car or a homeless shelter or have one parent who works two jobs and younger siblings to care for, we set those latter students up for failure with assumptions made, not from malice, but from lack of awareness. When we ask students to read complex texts in order to complete assignments without considering that some of our students, through no fault of their own, have never become proficient readers or without realizing that when we ask them to read in a language they do not yet speak, we are asking them to do the impossible, we multiply the anxiety and sense of hopelessness those students experience

regularly in school when we then grade them harshly because they *did* not do what they *could* not do.

Craft assignments so there are multiple ways for students to accomplish them and/or so you become part of the support a student needs to have a good shot at success. Invite students to propose their own ideas about how to best demonstrate what they know, understand, and can do as the result of a segment of learning. This is one of many examples of how our knowledge about and determination to reach each student can be critical to their success.

CREATE INSTRUCTIONAL UNITS AND LESSON PLANS AROUND HIGHWAYS AND EXIT RAMPS

As you begin making specific plans to teach both "the STUDENTS" and "THE student," revisit the metaphor of highways and exit ramps discussed and illustrated in Chapter 4. To make the class work well for a range of learners, you must provide regular and predictable times to work with the whole class and regular and predictable times to focus on the strengths, needs, and interests of individuals and small groups of individuals as well.

This pattern of classroom time in which students come together and break apart, come together and break apart is fundamental to making certain that differentiation is proactively planned rather than happening when you can find a minute here or there. It is primary evidence that this class is about individuals as well as the flock, evidence that it is an Everybody Classroom. Enacting the pattern is a visible signal to students that this class is about supporting the success of each of its members.

MIND THE FOUNDATION!

Remember that effective differentiation is an attribute of effective teaching, not an add-on. Take some time to reflect regularly on how you are thinking about and using the elements of quality instruction presented in Chapter 3.

- To what degree is your classroom consistently inviting to each learner in the class? How connected do you feel to each of your students, and what evidence do you have that they feel connected to you? How well do they work together as a team of learners to support one another's success?

- Do you have knowledge, understanding, and skills goals (KUDs)? KUD is an abbreviation for what is most important for students to Know, Understand, and be able to Do—a skill—as the result of any segment of learning. Regularly ask yourself these questions: Are the KUDs clear to you and to each student throughout a unit? Do you regularly emphasize *understanding* the content you teach versus largely practicing, remembering, and repeating knowledge and skills? Do you design curriculum to engage students' attention, imagination, and wonder? Is your curriculum planned for teaching up? Do you ensure that your students have voice and input in curricular decisions, in how they learn, and in the daily operation of the class?
- Do you carefully align assessments with the unit/curricular KUDs? Do you persistently use formative assessment to help you teach each learner more precisely in the near term? Do you use formative assessment information to help students learn to learn more effectively and efficiently? Do you emphasize feedback more than grades? Do students see that you place great value on their growth over time? Do you think about formative assessment as an ongoing process rather than a sequence of instruments?
- Do you tightly align teaching and learning with the curricular/unit KUDs? Are students active participants in their learning (vs. recipients of teaching)? Do you encourage and facilitate student collaboration as key in learning? Do students have opportunities to connect their interests with content and learning goals? Do you consistently plan for use of flexible grouping and respectful tasks? Do you plan instruction to support teaching up? Do you make regular provisions to address students' varied readiness levels, interests, strengths, and learning preferences? Do both your planned and spontaneous instructional decisions demonstrate flexibility in service of student needs? Do you give students generous opportunity not only to share ideas for instruction but also to give you feedback on how various instructional approaches are working for them?
- Do you *lead* your students to join you in creating a vision for a classroom that works for everyone, both as the school year begins and throughout the year? Do you establish partnerships with students that enable them to co-own the classroom with you and to see that their efforts contribute to the success of their peers? Do students work with you to create, implement, evaluate, and adjust learning and management routines? To what degree does the class consistently reflect a balance of stability and flexibility?

Figure 5.3 provides a second planning and reflection tool. Like the more global benchmarks in Figure 5.1, this tool amplifies some teacher actions that lead to strong, foundational differentiation. This chart examines the actions within each of the five key classroom elements. This second tool is a quick but illustrative guide for planning and reflecting on the impacts of differentiation. You will see references to a number of the actions in Figure 5.3 in chapters that follow as those upcoming chapters reflect the guidance of experts in various exceptionality areas, noting the importance of those actions in supporting growth for students who experience a particular exceptionality.

A FINAL THOUGHT

The remainder of this book, then, provides suggestions for effectively teaching students who often do not find school to be a great fit. The truth is that there may be about as many categories of students who often find themselves a mismatch for what is going on in a classroom as there are students in that classroom. For example, one of the chapters ahead proposes strategies for working with students who have been diagnosed as having specific learning disorder (SLD). You may find students in your classes who have no diagnosis but who appear to function in ways that are much like the students who have

Figure 5.3. Actions Teachers Can Take With the Classroom Elements to Build a Solid Foundation for Learning for All Students

To Build a Solid Foundation for Student Growth

- Examine the degree to which you are aware of and appreciate the diversity of learners you teach.
- Reflect on the degree to which you believe that every student is capable of major growth and success with the right support.
- Think about your readiness to emphasize individual growth vs. competition or a single definition of success.

To Create an Invitational Learning Environment

Goal: To create a learning environment that feels safe, affirming, supportive, communicative, respectful, positive, and hopeful.

- Let each learner know you are happy to see them and eager to work with them on Day One—and on each day that follows.
- Lead and teach from empathy and respect.
- Communicate to the class and to individuals through actions and words that you value diversity in student cultures, experiences, and perspectives.
- Create a culture of inclusion—this is who we are, what we stand for, and how we work in our classroom.
- Make it natural for students to embrace their cultures and languages.
- Make time for sharing good news, making memories, and fun and laughter as a class.
- Consistently represent a growth-mindset orientation.
- Teach students about the importance of a growth mindset, using examples of growth vs. fixed mindset from class and the world at large. Ask students to share examples as well.
- Commend making mistakes as an opportunity to learn. Point out your own mistakes and laugh at them sometimes.
- Find small snippets of time to have brief exchanges with each student each day.
- Regularly ask students how things are going in class and in school and how you can make things better (even if they are going well).
- Be patient and acknowledge increments of growth.
- Take each student and his/her concerns seriously. Make sure each student feels seen and valued.
- Connect with students' parents or guardians/homes as often as possible, emphasizing positive and encouraging messages.
- *To be sure learners connect with their classmates:*
  » Model appreciation for and belief in every student.
  » Help students understand why learning to work productively with classmates is important.
  » Use a variety of student groupings for varied purposes to ensure that they work together with many classmates on a regular basis to explore ideas, solve problems, and learn together.
  » Arrange furniture to invite collaboration and sharing.
  » Teach students how to work successfully in groups and monitor their skills of collaboration as they work together.
  » Make successful collaboration, including helping one another learn, a matter of pride in the classroom.

To Create Curriculum That Supports and Inspires Success

Goal: To provide equity of access to learning experiences that build student capacity to make sense of the world around them, prepare them to be positive contributors to that world, and inspire additional learning.

- *To ensure clarity about learning targets/goals/KUDs:*
  » Using "backward design," indicate clearly what students should know, understand, and be able to do as the result of a unit/inquiry/lesson.
  » Be sure to teach toward essential knowledge, understanding, and skill rather than assuming students can or should master vast amounts of content.
  » Make sure the KUDs are in learner-friendly language.
  » In advance of beginning a unit or inquiry, describe the right-answer and performance-based summative assessments you will use as a measure of student growth and proficiency with the KUDs to ensure alignment between curriculum, assessment, and instruction.
- *To support student engagement and understanding:*
  » Be sure students know the KUDs for each segment of learning.
  » Put understanding at the core of learning for all students.
  » Plan learning experiences that ask all students to use essential knowledge and essential skills to address (expand, take a position on, apply, make connections with . . .) essential understandings.
  » Connect understandings (or concepts and principles) to students' experiences, interests, and cultures.

(continued)

Figure 5.3. (*continued*)

» Connect understandings to students' strengths and interests.
» Whenever possible, teach around concepts such as equity, agency, patterns, environment, change, and responsibility that can extend to student experiences and societal concerns.
• *To Teach Up:*
» Develop learning experiences that tightly align with the unit/inquiry KUDs, emphasizing student understanding and ensuring that students see the alignment.
» Begin by creating learning experiences that would be stimulating for advanced learners, then scaffold the experiences of students who cannot yet succeed independently with those experiences so each student can access important ideas, think analytically, apply what they are learning, and make connections with their own lives.
» In curriculum planning, build in time for students to work on their own skills needs and interest-based applications (exit ramp time) as well as time to work in small groups and with the whole class on understanding and applying KUDs (highway time).
» Practice "attribution of status"—noticing and commenting on significant contributions made to a task or discussion by a student from whom other students might not expect success (Cohen & Lotan, 2014).

To Use Assessment to Advance Your Teaching and Each Student's Learning

Goal: To extend the teacher's competence and confidence in addressing students' varied learning needs and the student's independence/agency as a successful learner.

• Routinely use pre-assessments to get a sense of each student's entry point into an upcoming unit or inquiry and to check for status with prerequisite knowledge and skill.
• Ensure that formative assessments (diagnostic and ongoing) align well with KUDs indicated in the curriculum.
• Use focused observation, student work, and conversations with individual students as well as teacher-created assessments to gain insight into each student's progress in a current learning path (assessment *for* learning).
• Examine pre-assessment information for patterns of similar learning needs among students in the class.
• Use the patterns you see to plan instruction that makes provision (including time, materials, and support) for students to work individually, in small groups, and with the teacher to experience consistent growth toward learning goals (KUDs).
• Provide various ways for students to demonstrate what they know, understand, and can do—and encourage them to propose additional ways to show what they know.
• Provide clear, targeted, actionable feedback on formative assessment to help students understand what they did well, where their work falls short, and steps they can take to move forward in their work.
• Teach students—individually and as a group—the habits of mind and work that are likely to facilitate their success as learners and to help them analyze contributions they make to their own success.
• Provide time and support for students to reflect on their work in relation to goals and feedback and to make plans for next steps in progress.
• Differentiate formative assessments in ways that enable students to clearly determine what they know, understand, and can do. (It is acceptable to modify any attribute of an assessment except the learning targets/KUDs. Even the learning targets can be modified for some students with individual learning plans.)

To Teach Responsively to Student Readiness, Interests, and Approaches to Learning

Goal: To support each student's motivation to learn and their learning success as fully as possible.

• Align instruction with KUDs.
• Teach up.
• Encourage and support student voice and choice in learning when feasible.
• Create respectful tasks when students do different work (assignments that are equally interesting, equally important, and call on all students to be thinkers and problem-solvers).
• Use flexible grouping to enable all students to work with all their classmates. (Avoid "fixed" or "stable" groupings by varying group membership, size, and seating position in the classroom as well as student-choice, teacher-choice, and random groupings.)
• Be attentive to a student's academic, social, and emotional needs as you create student work groups.
• Work with students to continually develop skills of effective collaboration.
• Design the physical environment to support collaboration as well as individual learning.
• Address student readiness needs by adjusting resources/materials for learning, task complexity, length of time for task completion, scaffolding, adult and peer support, and providing time for students to develop knowledge and skills necessary to move ahead.
• Aim for student work that is just a bit ahead of a student's current performance with a support system to enable the student to "bridge the gap"—a necessary component for a student to develop a growth mindset.
• Connect topics, concepts, and skills with areas of significant cultural and/or personal interest to a student or group of students.

Figure 5.3. (*continued*)

- Encourage and support student voice in shaping curriculum and suggesting instructional approaches.
- Be sure students see a wide range of cultures and contributors represented in the content they study.
- Encourage students to link what they are learning with their interests, experiences, communities, and aspirations.
- Encourage interdisciplinary learning whenever possible.
- Help students identify and develop their strengths and talents.
- Encourage students to work in ways that are effective and efficient for them with a given assignment and to know how to find other approaches to succeeding with their work when the one they are using is not productive.
- Be attentive and responsive to a student's need for social and emotional support as well as academic support in the classroom.

To Lead Students and Work With Them to Establish and Manage Classroom Routines

---

Goal: To develop classroom routines that balance predictability and flexibility to ensure opportunity to address both whole-class and individual learning needs.

- *To Lead Students*
  » Engage students in conversations about the possibility of creating a class that is designed to help each learner grow as much as possible rather than assuming all learners need the same work and support all the time.
  » Draw on students' experiences (and/or experiences of siblings and friends) to connect the ideas with their experiences.
  » Ensure that the conversations examine both benefits and challenges of such a classroom.
  » Let the students know the importance of their partnership in creating a classroom that focuses on individual strengths, interests, and needs as well as on the class as a whole and determine whether they are willing to play a variety of roles in making the class work well.
  » As you take early steps in differentiation—and throughout the year—ask the whole class and individual students to reflect on how well the class is working for them and the degree to which classroom routines are operating effectively and efficiently. Request and use suggestions to strengthen the elements of differentiation. (Even if they seem to be going well, they can always be refined in helpful ways.)
- *To Manage Classroom Routines*
  » Work with students to develop or refine general processes:
    ○ starting class
    ○ stopping class
    ○ moving around the room without disturbing other learners
    ○ rearranging furniture in the classroom
    ○ getting materials and supplies
    ○ returning materials and supplies
    ○ monitoring and regulating conversational noise
    ○ how to get help when the teacher is busy
    ○ how to help one another without doing the work *for* a classmate
    ○ where to turn in completed assignments
    ○ how to be sure your work is of good quality
    ○ what to do when you finish an assignment early
  » Work with students to develop routines for specific learning activities they will regularly use in your class:
    ○ learning centers/interest centers
    ○ learning stations
    ○ technology centers or stations
    ○ literature circles (math circles, history circles, etc.)
    ○ collaborative learning teams/problem-solving teams
    ○ gallery walks
    ○ inquiry teams
    ○ science labs
    ○ philosophical chairs
    ○ fishbowls and other class discussion formats
    ○ debates, collaborative controversy
    ○ ETC!!
  » Practice/rehearse a routine before using it.
  » Begin using the routines very early in the year, but in a stepwise fashion that allows students to learn one routine comfortably before adding another.
  » Debrief regularly after use of each new routine, then periodically through the year to reinforce and refine processes and procedures.

---

been diagnosed. In that case, of course, it makes sense to try some of the strategies recommended for students with SLD that seem potentially useful for a student who has not been diagnosed. You may teach a student who has not been identified for additional support in managing his behavior but who, at least for the present, would benefit from strategies proposed for teaching students with a range of named challenges that impact their behavior.

It is nearly always even more nuanced than that. A *boy* with SLD may (or may not) approach learning quite differently than a *girl* who has SLD. An African American male who struggles with large and small injustices every day may (or may not) trust the school to help him overcome his learning disorder and may (or may not) see his learning problems as just another indicator that the world is not fair.

A student whose specific learning disorder is compounded by that student having great difficulty with sequencing in physical space as well as in text will need some different supports in reading than the student whose SLD is complicated by the fact that she is new to the English language. Two students at different points on the autism spectrum may appear more different than alike in the classroom and yet they may both have reading challenges, social difficulties, and manifest some emotional upsets.

Because students and their learning needs are multifaceted, puzzling out how best to teach each of them can feel like planning to solve several dozen Rubik's cubes whose facets move about even as you are planning. Use the contents of the chapters ahead to *frame* your thinking—to help you *begin* planning or to get unstuck when an approach you thought would be helpful turns out not to be helpful at all. Read several chapters about categories or sources of student need—culture, language, poverty, emotional struggles, trauma, race, sexual identity—the list is long, of course, but learning is as important for us as for our students, and you may be surprised how often gaining an insight into one kind of learning need will help you more effectively teach students with another learning need.

Keep being a dedicated student of your students. As you purposely observe a student over time, you will find yourself gaining better traction in helping that student find success. Talk with the student about what he or she finds difficult and ask for advice so you can be a better learning partner for him or her. Talk with specialists in your school who have had opportunity to study in some depth the needs of various categories of learners. Ask parents or caregivers to be your partners by sharing with you approaches that they and other teachers have found successful in supporting their child's success and by working with their child at home to extend your reach. Insight into one kind of learning need will often help you address other learning needs as well.

Remember, too, as you examine the various categories of need in the chapters ahead, that Everybody Classrooms incorporate differentiation to honor the learning needs of a broad range of young people, including (but not limited to) those whose needs are described in the chapters ahead and that teachers in those classrooms practice teaching up as a key component of meeting those needs. Note how frequently the guidance in those chapters, drawn from educators with knowledge about and experience in working effectively with students with complex learning needs, commends high expectations, learning for understanding, and relevant curriculum and instruction as key ingredients in their growth and success.

Kudos for caring about the many ways your students need you, for investing time and energy in being the best possible ally you can be for each student in your care. You are going in a good direction. Keep going! Every step will make you a better teacher for someone who depends on you.

EXPLORING SOME SPECIFICS OF DIFFERENTIATION IN EVERYBODY CLASSROOMS

CHAPTER 6

Building on the Foundation to Support Students With Specific Learning Challenges

Every child deserves a champion—an adult who will never give up on them, who understands the power of connection and insists that they become the best that they can possibly be.

—Rita Pierson

Big Idea for Chapter 6: The best our profession knows to do, we owe to every child—and sometimes, we have to stretch *beyond* our best professional knowledge to help a child learn. In those times, we both grow.

A colleague who studied anthropology in college explained to me in my early years at the university that there were two kinds of anthropologists: "splitters" and "lumpers." Splitters focus almost solely on a distinct culture, learning as much as they can about all of its aspects. Lumpers, on the other hand, look for similarities and differences across many cultures. In that way, splitters become specialists and lumpers become generalists. There's a familiar parallel in medicine where some physicians study to be general practitioners and others to become experts in one domain or cluster of domains. Both approaches are quite important, of course, and interdependent in quality medical practice.

Most teachers are typically "lumpers," generalists, not in terms of their content areas but in terms of specialized knowledge in areas like counseling, special ed, and ELL. Like general practitioners, these teachers need to have solid knowledge of how to understand and respond to a wide range of needs. They also need to know when to call on specialists for additional insight and guidance. This book is intended to help K–12 classroom teachers be more confident and competent generalists. As is the case with general practitioners in medicine, there will absolutely

be times when serving a learner well will require the classroom teacher to consult a specialist, blending the generalist's broad understanding of a student and the specialist's focused understanding of particular aspects of that student. There will also be instances in which teachers in general and disciplinary classrooms, at least for a time, cannot provide the level of support a student needs to thrive, so that the student will need support in an environment that *is* structured to help that student continue to grow. No teacher can be all things to all young people at all stages of their development.

As a generalist, then, a teacher seeks two levels of knowledge and skill: (1) what virtually all learners need to grow and thrive in a classroom and how to lead a classroom to meet those needs, and (2) how to extend or adapt the foundational classroom supports, processes, and practices to a student whose needs, at least at a particular time, call for something different from their classmates to grow and thrive. Said differently, all students, including those with some unique learning challenges, will benefit from an array of practices that are based on our field's current best knowledge of productive teaching and learning, including effectively applying the foundational principles and practices of differentiation.

Think back to Figure 5.3, which provides a matrix of *general*, or foundational, practices that support healthy learning and, in *general*, lead to healthy learners. These practices contribute greatly to the success of a very wide variety of young people, and in the absence of those practices, a wide variety of learners is likely to fare less well than they could and should.

LOOKING AHEAD

The remaining chapters in the book provide guidance related to particular needs that students less commonly (but not uncommonly) bring to a classroom. Those needs call on teachers to build on or otherwise adapt the quality foundational practices already in place. The more proficient a teacher is in establishing and developing a *baseline* of quality practice, the greater the proportion of students who will learn and grow robustly under the leadership of that teacher.

Chapter 4 makes a case that differentiation is not something other than or additional to quality teaching but rather is an extension of quality classroom practices that stem from our current best research evidence and classroom experience. Here is a short review:

- The learning environment in a classroom is the "incubator" from which everything else in the learning process draws oxygen.
- Curriculum is nourishment for the mind.
- Formative assessment is an information source that signals the need for academic differentiation.
- Differentiation is the road map for addressing both individual and group needs.
- Classroom leadership of students and management of routines enable teachers to orchestrate teaching and learning to balance the needs of the class and of individual learners.

When one of those elements is out of sync with the others or when one of them is "low on power," all the elements suffer as a result. More to the point, so do learners. Thus, each learner, including those spotlighted as the book continues, needs

- a learning environment that feels invitational;
- curriculum that feels relevant and meaningful, fueling their thinking, imagination, and motivation to learn;

- formative assessment that helps teachers understand their learning progressions while also helping the student develop increasing agency as a learner;
- instruction that attends to their readiness needs, interests, and approaches to learning; and
- classroom routines and processes that balance predictability and flexibility so that each student can be part of the group as a whole while having consistent opportunity and support to take their own next steps academically, socially, and emotionally.

Figure 6.1 provides a visual metaphor for the role of each of these five elements in making the classroom work effectively for virtually all students. The graphic reinforces the idea that the five elements work in tandem with one another.

After viewing and thinking about Figure 6.1, you may wonder which of the five elements associates with the largest of the four inner cogs in the design—and which with the smallest. The answer to that question, it seems, would indicate which of the elements is most critical for a teacher's attention and which is least essential. That is a little like trying to decide whether it is most important to maintain the soundness of the roof of your house or of its heating and cooling system. Both play pivotal

Figure 6.1. A Visual Metaphor for the Interdependence of the Five Classroom Elements

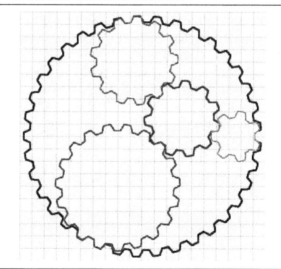

roles in the safety of your home and comfort of the humans who live there. In general, your attention to the soundness of one of those features should not diminish your attention to the soundness of the other.

At a particular time, however, you may realize that both elements need extra upkeep and simultaneously realize you do not have the resources to repair or replace both at once. Let's say you decide to put a new roof on the house and take extra care to ensure that minimal strain is put on the heating and cooling system so it can last a little longer. Once the new roof is in place, the heating and cooling system will, for a while, be in the forefront of your thinking—even as you take care of kitchen appliances, a front door that sticks when the weather gets hot, and the grass and flowers in the yard. In other words, the heating and cooling system now is the largest one of the cogs once the roof has been replaced—but still you pay attention to the other aspects of home upkeep as well.

The graphic in Figure 6.1 should convey a similar message. All five classroom elements are essential to the upkeep of student learning. All five cogs need to turn together every day. As you are trying something new and challenging with your curriculum, however, curriculum is likely to be the element in the forefront of your thinking. Still, the fact that the new curriculum is taking up a good bit of your mental real estate does not mean it is okay to let the other four cogs slide. Actually, once you understand how one element affects each other element in terms of student learning, it becomes natural to think of them in integrative ways. In the figure, however, it is likely that the large outer circle will always represent teacher leadership of students and management of classroom routines. That is the case because it is a teacher's positive connection with each learner and with the class as a whole, linked with effectively implementing pliable instructional routines, that allows the other four cogs to function in ways that address both individual and group needs. The remainder of the book focuses on ways in which teachers can build upon or adapt the principles and practices of differentiation, unpacked up to this point and distilled in Figure 6.1, to address some unique needs of a few students who, at least for a time, appear to require additional attention and support.

A FINAL THOUGHT

My great challenge in writing Part II of this book has been to balance a teacher's need for practical guidance in working effectively with English learners, or students with specific learning disorder, students who have experienced trauma, and so on, without appearing to say, "Do this for all English learners," or "Do that for all students who currently struggle with reading," or "All students who have experienced trauma are essentially the same."

That is a challenge similar to one we fight against daily in the classroom if we regularly plan instruction that is differentiated. We struggle to avoid the seductive nature of labels like "7th-grader," or "French I," or "struggling learner," by persistently asking ourselves, "What does *this* learner have in common with *these* learners at *this* point in our work together, and in what ways do their needs *differ* at this moment? What are reasonable next steps to respond to both their similarities and their differences?" In other words, we look for patterns in student needs and plan from there rather than depending on labels to guide our planning.

I have used categories or labels in the remaining chapters because, after trying several other approaches, the labels seemed to be the most practical way to ensure that students who face some mighty obstacles to learning will have their needs recognized and addressed by thoughtful teachers who care to make a positive difference in their lives. I have used the categories, however, to indicate clusters of learning needs, not to label the learner. I trust that teachers who read the book thoughtfully will be able to make the use of categories more redemptive than destructive.

The upcoming chapters provide reminders to focus on understanding and responding to a student's specific needs and strengths rather than generalizing to a category of learners or seeing the label as an indicator of inability to learn and to thrive.

As you read, keep in mind that the categories in the chapter titles are not precise and cannot be. Avoid pigeonholing or stereotyping students in terms of category. If you read through all the remaining chapters rather than consulting them one at a time as you have a specific need for them, you will see that there is great overlap or "bleed" in them. It is likely, for example, that some students represented in the chapter on LBGTQ needs would benefit from your studying the chapter on trauma. Some students whose needs are explored in the chapter on English learners would find it helpful if you consulted the chapter on students with specific learning disorder, or the one on attention deficit disorder, or the one on teaching advanced and advancing learners. At best, the categories are separated from one another with screens or maybe picket fences—never with walls. Every student is an individual. No student is a representative of a category of needs or of a group of students. Most students have multi faceted strengths and multi faceted needs as well. Keep that thought firmly in mind as you read on.

It is also wise to recall again that you likely teach a good number of students who have *not* been identified as belonging to any category but who nonetheless grapple with mastering reading skills, or communicating with peers, or anxiety and depression, or racial inequities, or tensions related to sexual identity—or some combination of stressors to learning. Further, a student who has been identified as experiencing one exceptionality may, in fact, struggle in other domains that have not been identified as areas of need. In addition, students in any category will vary widely in their strengths, interests, and approaches to learning, and those factors are frequently pathways—or at least door openers—to success.

So, as you look for guidance within a learner classification, remember that you might benefit students by looking across categories as well. The questions you're seeking to answer about a particular student are, first, "What indicators do I see in *this* student at *this* point that suggest a bumpy road to learning?" and "What might I do, working in partnership with this learner, to smooth the way ahead?" Then, as you plan, look across categories for shared needs as well. For example, two students with autism, a student with a learning disability, and three who are new to learning English might all benefit from use of visual prompts to facilitate reading, writing, or vocabulary development in science, for example. A key aspect of planning for differentiation involves both understanding individual needs and looking for patterns of shared needs across students to make your plans and your students' work both efficient and effective.

As you read the next section of the book, you will note that I occasionally use the term *general education classroom* to include classrooms at all grade levels and in all content areas that are not specifically designated as self-contained special education classrooms. The terms general education classroom and general education teacher are used in this way in key education law and policy documents.

CHAPTER 7

Teaching Students Who Are Learning English

Do you know what a foreign accent is? It's a sign of bravery.

—Amy Chua

INTRODUCTION

Approximately 10% of students in U.S. classrooms are learning English as they try also to learn academic content. That number is growing and will likely continue to do so.

- Some of these young people will have been learning English for several years before they arrive in your classroom, and some will speak their first English words, phrases, and sentences in your class.
- Some of them come to the United States from war-torn countries and may never have been to school in their native land.
- Some are children of doctors, lawyers, engineers, professors, and scientists who have come to the United States for a broad range of reasons and whose children have had rich learning opportunities in the country of their birth.
- Some have been learning English for only a few days, weeks, or months—some for years. Some are young children, some adolescents.
- Some English learners will have specific learning challenges that may or may not have been diagnosed.
- Some will be quite advanced in their thinking even as they are at the starting gate with learning English.
- Some will have experienced trauma.
- Some will be the object of bullying, derision, and even violence.

- Some will be gregarious and confident in their new setting.
- Some will be weighted with self-doubt.
- Their strengths and dreams will differ markedly and, as with most young people, will change over a school year.

This population of learners is absolutely *not* homogeneous. Nor is it a population we should see as limited in their capacity to learn, or inconvenient. They bring rich experiences, a broader view of culture than many of their teachers have had the opportunity to develop, and courage—for goodness sake, they are learning to make their way in the world by speaking at least two languages. In every case, their experiences in your classroom will expand or constrict the opportunities that lie ahead for them and their capacities to engage with those opportunities to build the lives they and their parents hope for. They need your respect, trust, focus, and partnership as they learn to live successfully and confidently in two worlds. They need you to teach up to them.

Below are some guides for understanding, planning for, and responding to the varied needs of students who learn English as they simultaneously learn academic content and a new culture. The goal is not to use all these strategies, of course, but to understand them as a repertoire from which you can consider options that seem likely to benefit a given learner at a particular time, in a specific context. Be sure also to look at websites that provide resources and guidance for teachers of English learners (ELs) and their families, for example: Colorín

Colorado, FluentU, Literacy Center Education Network, NIH Kids' Page, Reading Is Fundamental, Starfall, and UsingEnglish.com. Some of those resources are targeted at specific age groups, and some provide support for a broad range of grade levels.

SOME PRINCIPLES AND PRACTICES FOR TEACHING ENGLISH LEARNERS

To Ensure Your Readiness to Teach English Learners Effectively

- Think carefully and in detail about how you would feel (or have felt) if you were suddenly living in a country where almost no one speaks your language, understands your customs, is familiar with your favorite foods—where you don't know how to get from Point A to Point B and can't even read the street signs (if there are any). You can't understand television programs or read the books they give you in school. You know no one outside your immediate family. What would you need? What would be helpful to you?
- Examine the degree to which you see diversity as an asset rather than a problem in the classroom.
- Reflect on your mindset so you are confident in your belief that students who are learning English in your classroom are capable of major growth and success with the right support—that you don't equate early language development with low ability.
- Understand that bilingualism is an asset, not a problem or a barrier.
- Begin learning about the cultures that your English learners represent, including languages, religions, places they have lived, and celebrations.
- Know that trying simultaneously to learn complex content and the language in which that content is communicated is incredibly difficult. Understand that developing proficiency in a second language takes between 4 and 10 years to accomplish, depending on the age of the student,

previous school experiences, and adult support both in and out of school. Work for the long term.
- Be aware that some/many of your English learners are, at least for a time, lost in a new place. Not only do they not understand the language, culture, food, geography, or how to get around, but many of them have come from places that are unsafe and bring those stresses and fears to the classroom. Many come from families with economic vulnerability. Sadly, many of them become targets of peer derision, bullying, and even violence. Every one of them brings great hopes and great possibilities to class as well. Be there for them. Listen to them carefully. Support them. Be their champion in class, in the school, and in the community.

To Create a Safe, Inviting Learning Environment for English Learners

- Work with the whole class to create a culture of inclusion in which safety is a non-negotiable, diversity is a value, empathy is a way of relating, and varied perspectives enrich every member of the group. (This is who we are. This is what we do.)
- View your English learners with "unconditional positive regard." That term, proposed by noted psychologist Carl Rogers, refers to a belief that the young person is valuable and worthy of your care, just as the student is—with nothing to prove or accomplish to merit your respect (in Gobir, 2021).
- Ensure that your facial expression, body language, tone of voice, and vocabulary reflect acceptance, caring, and respect.
- Learn as much as you can about each English learner you teach. In addition to learning about their cultural backgrounds, find out about their prior school experiences, level of English proficiency, interests, things they are proud of, and how they like to learn. Begin the process before the school year begins. Continue it throughout the year.

- Make sure you know how to pronounce the students' names correctly to signal respect for them and for their language.
- Appoint a "buddy" or "colleague" for a newcomer to English to provide varied kinds of support as the English learner begins the difficult work of acclimating to a wholly new world.
- Find some time every day to share stories, to do something fun or unexpected, to laugh, and to make shared memories.
- Learn a few words and phrases in the student's primary language and use them when possible. From time to time, ask a student to teach you and members of the class some words and phrases in his/her primary language.
- Create opportunities for students to share their home language vocabulary for items in the classroom, numbers, names of everyday objects, important terms in content, and so on. Post English labels on classroom elements along with terms from other languages spoken by students in your class. Encourage English-speaking students in your class to learn words and phrases from other languages.
- Build trust with the student from your first meeting with them. They need to know you care about them, value them as they are, have high expectations for them, will support them as they learn, and will be their champion. Then honor the trust!
- Check in with the student every day to have brief exchanges.
- Use icons with labels on objects around the classroom to help English learners learn common and immediately useful vocabulary.
- Ask students to share information about their cultures as a way to help all students understand both similarities and differences across cultures.
- Encourage students to use their home language as a learning tool in your class. This not only facilitates learning but also helps students maintain pride in their home culture as they learn to appreciate their new culture as well.

- Know that many English learners will need opportunity and support to learn fundamental and communication skills to navigate school and community as well as foundational knowledge and skills in one or more content areas. It is important to address both needs.
- Make sure all students see themselves in print, digital, and visual materials from varied cultures that you make available as resources for learning; in art and music you use in the classroom; in authors, scientists, creators, and leaders you discuss in the subject(s) you teach; and in student work you post in the classroom.
- Work with all students in the class to find ways to communicate effectively with students who are learning the language of the classroom. Use pantomime, objects, content-specific vocabulary charts that include images, and other tools for ensuring that English learners are included in classroom dialogue.
- Make it safe to make mistakes—to risk speaking while you are learning English. Be sure students see your mistakes. Make it clear that making mistakes is the way we learn new things.
- Be patient. Acknowledge increments of growth and help English learners do that as well.
- Develop positive connections with students' families and spend time in their communities as often as possible.
- Offer support to parents or caregivers who are also trying to learn a new language and find their roles in a new culture. Use translation apps like TalkingPoints to facilitate communication about a student's goals and growth as well as ways the student's adults can support that growth at home.
- Invite the student to spend extra time with you in the classroom when the schedule makes that possible (for example, at lunch, upon arrival at school, while waiting for buses to arrive in the afternoon). Use that time to learn about the student, provide learning support, or help the student find resources related to their interests.

- Own the success of your English learners rather than counting on specialists to "fix them."
- Consult and co-teach with specialists as a way of expanding your confidence and competence in teaching students who are learning English.
- Be an advocate for English learners in your school and community.

To Create Curriculum That Supports and Inspires Success

- Create curriculum that has mirrors, windows, and doors. Mirrors help student think about and understand themselves and their cultures more fully. Windows help them learn about other cultures and places beyond the ones they have personally experienced—help them understand the wider world a little more fully. Doors give them opportunity to connect with, understand, and contribute to the community.
- Connect understandings (or concepts and principles) to students' cultures, strengths, experiences, and interests (for example, move from discussing ideas, concepts, and issues in current content to their context in society as a whole—for example: equity, agency, patterns, environment, change, courage, responsibility, etc., across times, cultures, and disciplines).
- Build into the curriculum opportunities for students to learn about the long struggles of various populations in the United States and around the world to achieve equity and justice. Be sure students have opportunities to extend their understanding of that history in their home country and in the United States. Help them learn the skills of advocacy that will be important in contributing in positive ways to bettering their own lives, the lives of their families, and the communities in which they live.
- Take care to specify what is *essential* for students to know, understand, and be able to do as the result of any segment of learning. Ensure that English learners are aware of

and understand the learning goals for the work they do and how that work relates to those learning goals. Check regularly for their understanding of the learning targets and their progress toward those learning targets.
- Create opportunities for students to learn vocabulary and communication skills necessary to communicate in the classroom and the knowledge, understandings, and skills necessary for success in a specific content area so that language development is integral to development in content proficiency.
- Put *understanding* content at the core of learning for English learners, just as for other students. Balance student need for foundational work and meaningful work.
- Develop learning experiences that enable students to practice and use foundational vocabulary and skills in the context of the subject the class is learning and in the context of their lives in school and community.
- Within your curriculum, plan instructional time for students to work on their own skills needs and interest-based applications (exit ramp time) as well as time to work in pairs, small groups, and with the whole class to understand and apply KUDs (highway time). It is unlikely that English learners (as many others) can flourish in a "curriculum of coverage" in which there is little or no time to address individual strengths, needs, and interests or to make meaning of content.

To Use Assessment to Improve Teaching and Learning

- Ensure that formative and summative assessments align tightly with designated KUDs.
- Formatively assess English learners regularly (through observation and conversation as well as written/drawn/spoken responses on assessments) to understand how each student is developing in both foundational skills of literacy and in content areas.

- Avoid heavy reliance on paper-and-pencil assessments. They often make it difficult for an English learner to share all or most of what he or she knows, understands, and can do. Also use strategies like drawings, sentence-starters, role-play, products, performances, pictures/photos, student read-alouds to the teacher (or recorded), and conversations between teacher and student to assess English learners.
- Consider having the student keep a portfolio of work over the course of the year to help both of you trace progress and areas that continue to need work.
- Use performance assessments as often as possible to summatively assess what English learners know, understand, and can do. They provide many more options for learners of English to demonstrate learning than do right-answer/single-answer assessments or options that require extended writing.
- Try 15-second videos as a way for new learners of English to demonstrate their growing abilities to communicate. A student combines new words with images and sentences to share an idea (Ferlazzo & Sypnieski, 2018).
- For students new to English, consider encouraging them to speak, write, or label assessment responses in their primary language, then translate or work with a peer or teacher to translate the responses into English. Consider also allowing students additional time to complete assessments.
- Ensure that assessments call on English learners to reveal and apply understandings as well as knowledge and skill.
- Work with English learners to co-create classroom work/activities that will help them move forward in knowledge, understanding, and/or skill.
- Work with English learners to co-create personal success criteria for their work in both foundational and content-related goals.
- Emphasize individual growth versus competition among students for all learners in your class.

- Be sure students understand success criteria established for the class as well as personal success criteria and that they understand how to examine their work in relation to those benchmarks.
- Give students focused feedback about what they are doing well (which targets they are meeting/approaching), areas in which they are not yet demonstrating proficiency, and steps they might take to continue to develop in those areas. It is important that English learners and their teachers have a clear sense of their successes rather than focusing only on what is not yet mastered.
- Avoid the urge to mark all errors in a piece of work. Respond to the most important areas for growth at a given time by giving clear feedback that helps the learner know what steps to take next.
- Teach students to give one another useful, reliable feedback.
- Assist English learners in analyzing feedback to understand how their work habits support, or could support, their success (for example, being sure they know the learning targets for a lesson, group of lessons, or unit/inquiry; asking questions when they aren't sure they understand or know how to do a task; monitoring their work for accuracy; using a rubric to guide their work, studying effectively; etc.). Using formative assessment in this way is central in helping students become metacognitive (self-aware of their thinking and able to adapt how they are working in ways that facilitate greater success).
- When students work on long-term projects or performances, establish check-in dates along the way to give students feedback about the direction and quality of their work that will help them move forward effectively, without unnecessary and discouraging missteps.
- Use both formal and informal assessment to learn about student interests, and use what you learn to link important content to those interests.
- Ask students regularly, formally and informally, how class is working for them

and how you can work together to make it a better fit (even if it is working well).

- Remember that assessment is a process, not an instrument or moment. It provides the information stream a teacher needs in order to understand and respond to a learner's development. Each insight we gain from reflecting on a student's work prepares us to teach more effectively—and prepares us for the next insight.

To Provide Instruction That Is Responsive to Student Needs

- Use what you learn from formative assessment to design work for learners that calls on them to use developmentally appropriate, foundational literacy skills and skills of a discipline to communicate targeted information and understandings necessary for growth.
- Teach up to ELs. Expect them to make meaning, think about important ideas, make connections, and so on. Use exit ramp time to work intensely on the skills of literacy, but do not restrict the learning of ELs to skills-based work. Plan for high ceilings of expectation and high support to enable the students to grow intellectually as they grow in language competence. Mindless busywork does not build the kinds of knowledge, understanding, and skill that ELLs need in order to develop as they should.
- Build your instructional schedule around both highway and exit ramp time to allow attention to whole-class, small-group, and individual learning interests and needs.
- Work to extend student interests and strengths as you help the student develop new language skills.
- Provide peer and teacher support for a student or group of students based on what you learn from a formative assessment about the next steps the student(s) needs to take in the learning process.
- Design your class to ensure that English learners have many opportunities to talk and collaborate throughout the day. Decrease teacher talk; increase student

dialogue. There is a strong relationship between opportunity to speak a new language and rate of gaining fluency in that language.

- Use small-group and whole-class brainstorming groups to help English learners (and others) hear ideas that may be helpful in writing about or understanding what they are learning. Encourage students to borrow one another's ideas in those sessions, explaining that teachers borrow one another's ideas frequently to do more effective work (Ferlazzo, 2017).
- Use Read/Think/Talk/Write (RTTW) cycles to help students clarify and flesh out ideas they are building (Ferlazzo, 2017).
- Build a culture of doing to help students make meaning of what they learn.
- Add engaging books in the languages of English learners to your classroom library and encourage the school media specialist to add multi-language books to the library as well.
- Encourage every student to read something they are interested in reading any time that is possible. When you can, read the students segments of something you are enjoying reading and talk about why you like the piece. Finding pleasure in reading is essential to a learner's motivation to do the hard work of learning to read.
- Use verbal cues, repetition of key elements, wait time, and rewording to scaffold understanding and participation of new learners of English.
- Avoid jargon, idioms, sarcasm, and an abundance of "ten-dollar words" as you talk with and teach the class.
- Use gestures, pictures, icons, objects, facial expressions, charade-like actions, modeling, and demonstrating when you are presenting to the class or a small group to communicate effectively with a wide variety of learners, including some English learners.
- For early English learners, provide word cards with key terms or phrases on one side and a translation and related image on the other. Encourage the student and his or her classmates to add cards that would be

useful to the English learner. These anchor words connect new learning with a student's home language and experiences, providing a context for new learning.

- Consider front-loading *vocabulary* that is key to a new topic that will begin in a day or two for English learners and others who may need additional support in building vocabulary. The teacher selects no more than 5–7 words that are fundamental to understanding the new area of study; meets with a small group of students during exit ramp time; and introduces the words, their meanings, and their pronunciation to build familiarity and confidence for the student before the new unit or topic begins. Significant in this process is connecting the words with a student's home language vocabulary and experiences.
- Consider front-loading *a unit* for English learners and other students who may have difficulty making meaning of new content for a variety of reasons. The teacher meets with the students during exit ramp time and shares an overview of what is coming up in the next unit or inquiry. It is helpful if the overview is in story form. (The content of all disciplines can be shared in story form.) Front-loading a unit is much like showing someone a trailer for a movie in that both activate prior knowledge and experience, provide a big-picture sense of the content, and build student interest in finding out more.
- Support use of a student's primary language to facilitate learning by providing reading materials in that language; bilingual dictionaries; translation apps (for example, Google Translate); and a language buddy/partner who can clarify directions, respond to questions, and perhaps translate when appropriate. Using a primary language is helpful in developing skills in a new language.
- Steer clear of everyone-reads-the-same-materials approaches whenever possible. When that is not possible, teach students who need support in reading the text how to unlock text meaning—including

studying its organization, using sticky notes to summarize key passages and to pose questions about the text, and practicing think-alouds.

- Incorporate a wide range of genres and formats into student reading, enabling learners to make choices about their reading and to extend their proficiency with reading a range of literary forms.
- Be sure materials you provide for groupwork are appropriate for use by all members of that group. Assigning students to varied groups and then giving all groups the same materials to use is not likely to be effective.
- Move from read-alouds to shared reading, to guided reading, to independent reading as a student is ready to move through that sequence. The sequence is not always linear, of course. A student may be ready for independent reading in a topic that is of high interest to the student but still need shared or guided reading related to complex and/or unfamiliar content.
- To support vocabulary development, use a variety of instructional materials, including websites that offer both fiction and nonfiction reading materials at different levels of reading complexity (for example, Newsela; the Smithsonian's Teen Tribune, Tween Tribune, TT Jr., and TT Español; Storyworld; and Common Lit), illustrated books, graphic novels, picture books, recorded materials, websites (for example, Fluent U) that offer real-life videos that allow English learners to learn from popular culture, websites that support students in learning English (for example, Duolingo, No Red Ink, SpeakingPal, The British Council's LearnEnglish Kids), highlighted texts, and peer-recorded reading of important materials. For teachers who work with English learners, Larry Ferlazzo's blog is a practical and informed treasure chest of resources and classroom applications.
- Partner with community groups (for example, the International Children's Library) to provide ELs with resources they can access from home.

- Give an English learner a heads-up that you will be calling on him or her in a few minutes to answer a question, telling the student what the question will be so there's time for the student to develop an answer before having to speak. In fact, it is helpful for you to provide opportunity for many English learners to practice, whenever possible, before you expect them to "perform."

- When a student new to English will need to present to or perform for a group, begin with student-selected groups or small groups of students with whom that student has worked several times prior to the presentation or performance.

- Preview text with ELLs, and others who would benefit, by looking at the table of contents, headings and sub headings, graphics, index, and so on. Model and teach students how to skim text.

- Provide graphic organizers, outlines, content digests, highlighted texts, and sentence or paragraph frames to scaffold both English and discipline-specific growth in early to mid-range English learners. For early learners, it can be useful to provide an organizer that is partially completed, asking the student to add the missing parts—in other words, to further scaffold the scaffolding.

- When English learners read text that is complex for them, use strategies that help them read for meaning rather than simply calling words as they go. Select text that is manageable in length, vocabulary complexity, and content so the students can succeed with support. Ferlazzo and Sypnieski (2018) recommend segments of no more than two pages for secondary students.

- Before students read, preview the structure of the text with them and establish a purpose for reading.

- As they read, it is often useful for you to read the text aloud to the students, modeling pronunciation, voice inflection, and rate of reading. Occasionally stop and ask students to work with a partner so that one of the pair reads a sentence you designated and the other writes the sentence on a white board or erasable desk surface. That approach builds students' listening and speaking skills. Think-alouds, annotating text in the margins, and using graphic organizers are helpful for engaging students and supporting comprehension of what they are reading.

- After reading, strategies like summarizing, paraphrasing, and quoting also support engagement and comprehension. At least initially, it is important for you to guide the students' thinking and/or model the practice for them. Working in pairs to apply the strategies provides opportunity for conversation as well as two heads to make sense of the work.

- To support English learners in understanding assignment directions, video yourself explaining a key process, giving directions for an assignment or performance assessment, posing thought questions that can lead to student understanding, or presenting a mini-lesson or mini-lecture. Encourage students to use the recordings to support their learning and to help them assess their current level of knowledge and understanding of a topic. If students need to use these materials at home, be sure they have access to the technology necessary to support the use.

- Consider using schedule charts or assignment boards to easily connect students with varied assignments that occur simultaneously in the classroom. Students "read" the chart to learn what they will be working with during a part of a class or week, who they will be working with, and where they will work in the room. The teacher can vary the tasks, who will work with the tasks at a given time, and the nature of the tasks students will find when they go to an assigned place in the room. Students often, but not always, move to a different assignment each day. It is generally not the case that all students will do all tasks in the span of time covered by the schedule chart or that the nature of a task will be the same for students who work with it on different days. Schedule charts and work boards allow a teacher to match an assignment to the needs or interests of a broad range of learners. For example, all students in the class may work as "vocabulary detectives" one day during the week, but the vocabulary sets and assignments may vary at that location each day to enable students to do work they need in order to grow in content-related and/or English vocabulary.

- To engage English learners in communicating with peers about important content while developing language skills, use instructional strategies like jigsaw, expert groups, collaborative teams, problem-solving teams, text-analysis teams, literature circles, book clubs, and reciprocal teaching.

- To scaffold student development in writing and mathematical thinking/problem solving, use strategies like writing workshops and math workshops (which also support peer connections and oral language development).

- To tailor assignments to current learning needs, strengths, and interests of individuals or small groups of students, use contracts and contract-like strategies (for example, learning menus, learning agendas, think-tac-toes, bingo, learning tickets, hyperdocs, choice boards, and playlists). These strategies allow attention to student variance even though all students are working with the same topic and same KUDs.

- To support students in thinking about, writing about, and applying content, use instructional strategies like RAFTs, Six Word Memoirs, Headlines, or structured paragraph frames such as Cloze writing.

- Use layered questions when interacting with students individually, in small groups, and with the whole class. In this approach, the teacher asks varied questions that can be answered with different levels of language proficiency. For example, one question might be, "Can you point to . . . ?" Another might require a yes or no answer. Still another might require a

sentence to describe the object or event. Layered questions allow all students to be successful in answering questions and also model increasingly complex communication structures.

- To enable students to practice specific skills that are important in taking their next steps in language development (for example, focus on everyday English vocabulary in context, content vocabulary in context, sentence or paragraph construction, oral production, text analysis), use learning centers or learning stations. Student work at a station or center will vary to align with the needs of students who will work there during an indicated time.

- To enable students to work with topics of personal interest or to choose among subtopics in a content area about which they would like to learn more, use interest centers. Encourage students to suggest topics for that work or to work with you to create an assignment or investigation for an interest center.

- To encourage students to learn about their talents and/or areas of personal interest, use independent investigations. These investigations are also quite useful in helping students learn to develop important questions, find and use a range of resources (print, tech, human), establish timelines for various components of their work, develop criteria for quality work, assess their work according to those criteria, and present their findings to meaningful individuals or groups. The investigations can vary in length of time for completion, organizers, access to resources, peer and teacher support, mode of expressing learning, personal goals, and so on.

- Teach and practice skills like asking good questions, making predictions, visualizing what they are reading, finding a main idea, summarizing, making connections, evaluating sources/arguments, and inferring as students are ready for these steps.

- Integrate social and emotional skills into all aspects of classroom life, being sure to teach the skills rather than assuming students know them or will learn them as they go along.

- Keep learning from and about English learners and refining your understanding of their strengths and needs as well as avenues through which you can support their growth. (Take a look at Chapter 15 on supporting students from varied cultures.)

English learners vary considerably in their proficiency with English. Some are fluent, some just beginning to acquire new words. They come to school in any case with problem-solving skills, a culture, and a raft of experiences, talents, and determination. Tap into those strengths to support their learning. Help them realize the dreams that brought their families to an unfamiliar place that represents hope to many.

NOTE

The following sources were consulted for this chapter. Full citations appear in the References section. Breiseth, n.d.; Cole, 1995; Coulombe & Marquez, 2020; Ferlazzo, 2016, 2020, 2021a; Ferlazzo & Sypnieski, 2018; Gobir, 2021; Gonzalez, 2014; E. Kaplan, 2019; Ottow, 2021; Rojas, 2007; Witt & Soet, 2020.

CHAPTER 8

Teaching Students Who Have Experienced Trauma

There are wounds that never show on the body that are deeper and more hurtful than anything that bleeds.

—Laurell K. Hamilton, *Mistral's Kiss*

INTRODUCTION

Trauma is prevalent in our society. Many educators may be surprised to learn that approximately 47 percent of the nation's students have experienced one or more types of trauma (Zacarian et al., 2020). The word *trauma* is used to describe negative events that are so emotionally painful that they overwhelm a person's ability to cope. Traumatic events are frightening, dangerous, and/or violent when they happen to a child. When a child witnesses a traumatic event that threatens the life or physical security of someone close to the child, that can be traumatic as well. Such events can evoke emotions and physical reactions so strong that they persist long after the event itself is over and can profoundly affect the child emotionally and physically, producing social and academic consequences as well.

When a child (or adult) experiences or is exposed to trauma, that activates biological stress responses. Most of us experience stress or trauma occasionally, but when the stress response happens frequently, adrenaline and cortisol are produced in amounts that affect the brain, cognition, emotions, hormonal systems, immune systems, and even how our DNA is read and transcribed. Often, those changes are long-term and lead to increased risk of health problems throughout life. For example, in adulthood, children in this category are at risk for higher rates of alcohol and substance abuse, depression, lung cancer, heart disease, suicide attempts, and early death. There is also a strong relationship between trauma and the onset of learning and behavioral issues in children. Because of the widespread prevalence of trauma and its impact on those who experience it, we should count trauma as one of the top human rights issues of our time. Most trauma is a result of human action and is therefore alterable through human intervention.

Traumatic events that negatively impact young people are often called "adverse childhood experiences," or ACEs. Having even one adverse childhood experience can have a significant and lasting impact on a child. The more ACEs a child experiences, the greater the likelihood of behavior or learning problems. For example, 51% of children with four or more ACEs have behavior or learning problems that negatively impact their development (Merrill, 2020). While trauma can certainly stem from a single incident (for example, the sudden death of a parent), in other cases, it stems from persistent traumatizing conditions (for example, repeated sexual abuse by a trusted adult, generational racial discrimination and inequity, or persistent economic deprivation). Either can be debilitating, but conditions that persist through much of a child's growing up years can multiply a young person's feelings of distrust, hopelessness, and alienation.

Sources and Symptoms of Childhood Trauma

There are many sources of childhood trauma or ACEs; among them, but not all of them, are the following:

- Physical, verbal, sexual, or emotional abuse.
- Physical or emotional neglect.
- Parental separation or divorce.

- Living with a family member who has mental illness, engages in substance abuse, or is involved with criminal activity.
- Violence among members in the child's household, gun violence, gang violence, war, refugee experiences, or physical bullying.
- Growing up in poverty.
- Continuing exposure to discrimination, injustice, and/or inequity.
- The death of a person to whom the child feels a strong bond.
- Natural disasters, particularly ones that expose a child to danger and/or cause the child to feel powerless and vulnerable.
- Moving, especially when it involves leaving close friends behind, a new school and/or new culture, and when the child is shy or lacks self-confidence. Young people often have no voice over whether a move takes place and can feel powerless as a result.
- Military family-related stressors (for example, deployment, parental loss, or injury).
- A medical crisis, including a serious accident, a long hospital stay, surgery, extended pain, and so on.
- Adoption when it involves leaving caregivers who were important to the child; unfamiliar surroundings, culture, and/or routines; loss of friends, and so on.

It is important for teachers and other educators to understand that trauma itself is often hidden deep inside the young people with whom they work and to understand also that behavior is communication. Persistent or repeated physical symptoms such as headaches or nausea can also signal a traumatic response. Childhood trauma results in fear, anxiety, confusion, and a deep sense of shame. Those emotions manifest through troubling or problematic behaviors and symptoms such as those listed below. Students who experience trauma will display varying degrees of its impact and through different behaviors and symptoms. No student will display all these symptoms.

- Over- or under-reacting to stimuli
- Recreating traumatic events (through "playing out" or stories)

- Rapid changes in extreme emotions
- Language development delays and challenges
- Excessive crying or irritation in younger children
- Regression—returning to behaviors they have outgrown (like bed-wetting)
- Excessive worry, sadness, depression, and fears
- Aggression—yelling, hitting, destroying objects
- Controlling behaviors
- Hypervigilance
- Hiding
- Running away
- Unresponsiveness, disengaging from activities
- Unhealthy eating or sleeping habits
- Irritability, negativity, and acting-out behaviors in teens
- Difficulty with attention and concentration, learning, and applying learning
- Avoidance of activities enjoyed in the past
- Unexplained headaches or body pain
- Use of alcohol, tobacco, or other drugs

This wide array of behaviors that can stem from trauma are not willful acts on the part of children or young people. They do not seek to appear disinterested in learning or to be disruptive, or to disrespect people or norms. Rather, what adults may label as "misbehaviors" are actually involuntary responses to events that were so frightening, disorienting, or demeaning that they changed the child's biology. Therefore, that child is exhibiting fear-invoked rather than reason-invoked behaviors and needs teachers who respond with reason rather than emotion in virtually all highly charged situations. A young person whose brain is filled with shame, anxiety, and fear simply cannot learn. The first role of the brain is to protect its owner from harm. The limbic system, which is the chief protector, often blocks access to the cerebrum, the part of the brain which functions as chief learner and thinker, when it perceives that its owner is in danger—thus impeding learning (Sousa & Tomlinson, 2018).

Below are some guidelines for working effectively with students who have experienced trauma. The guidelines are heuristics, not algorithms—principles, not guarantees. Students who have experienced trauma vary from one another in significant ways and will not exhibit all the same behaviors or to the same degrees. Likewise, they will not all respond to a teacher's actions in the same way. Look at the guidelines that follow as informed suggestions. Modify the list as you learn. Add to it as you discover new actions that support student success.

SOME PRINCIPLES AND PRACTICES FOR EFFECTIVELY TEACHING STUDENTS WHO EXPERIENCE TRAUMA

The Role of the School in Responding to Trauma

Before looking at ways in which teachers can be a positive and healing force in the lives of students who have experienced or are experiencing trauma, it is wise to look briefly at ways in which schoolwide practices and policies can either mediate the impact of trauma on students' well-being or contribute to the trauma. The concept of a trauma-sensitive or trauma-informed school has received much attention in recent years, and many schools have invested time and attention in becoming more trauma-sensitive. The change process in a school, however, is nearly always slow and too often becomes moribund after a short time precisely because real change is exhaustive, exhausting, time-intensive, and uncomfortable. It is likely, then, that many schools that see themselves as trauma-informed are actually contributors to student trauma.

In such schools, policies and processes can actually contribute to trauma for students who enter each day with other challenges to learning. For example, in schools in which bullying (in-person or on the Internet) is a regular feature, vulnerable students often become objects of derision, meanness, and even physical violence. Schools in which students with special learning needs are isolated from mainstream students for much of the day and in which those students are perceived as "less than," or incapable, and where they are teased or bullied on the school bus or in the cafeteria can experience trauma as a result. Where students who identify as lesbian, gay, bisexual, transgender, queer, or questioning (LGBTQ) are forced to use bathrooms that do not match their gender identity, where they are the subject of jokes or hatred, and where they are referred to by pronouns that do not match their gender identity, they may experience repeated trauma.

When African American students and other students of color are called names, streamed largely into low-level classes, taught that the dialects of their neighborhoods are unacceptable or that traditional hairstyles are grounds for being barred from school or from athletic events, and are largely absent from or misrepresented in the content they study, these students often experience sustained trauma. Likewise, Islamophobia, taunts aimed at Asian or Asian American learners, administrative rules that cause embarrassment for students who qualify for free or reduced meals or that result in their going hungry rather than being embarrassed, and adults turning away from language and physical acts that can frighten and demean girls and young women are all evidence of a school that is, in fact, not trauma-sensitive.

Schools that create and apply long lists of automatic punishments for specified infractions, using punitive rather than restorative disciplinary practices, are likely contributing to student trauma as well. While schools certainly need policies that support safety and smooth operation, science suggests that those should center on approaches like in-school suspension, restorative justice, and time, space, and opportunity to de escalate so the school is working with rather than against the child's biology.

Individual teachers can make a great contribution to restoring a sense of safety and efficacy to young people who experience trauma, but their job is lonelier, feels riskier, and is likely to be diminished if the school in which they work is less than truly trauma-sensitive. Therefore, a significant contribution of teachers to their students is speaking out for the need to ensure that their school becomes trauma-informed and trauma-sensitive, and active and vigilant in doing the work necessary to extinguish attitudes and behaviors that threaten student well-being.

Even in schools that are trauma-sensitive, teachers cannot be the *primary* source of support for students who have experienced and perhaps continue to experience trauma. Students will often need care from medical professionals and/or emergency care providers to begin and continue the healing process. Still, teachers can play a significant and healing role in the lives of children and teens who live with the effects of trauma. Educators can deliver the daily doses of healing interactions that truly are the antidote to toxic stress. And just as the science shows us that it is the cumulative dose of early adversity that is most harmful, it also shows that the cumulative dose of nurturing interactions is the most healing. Consistent buffering care literally helps release healthy hormones into the bloodstream, calming and interrupting the biological stress response (Merrill, 2020).

Following are some guidelines for working effectively with students who experience trauma. Here are some guides for teachers that are helpful in both proactive and reactive contexts. The goal is not to use all of these strategies, of course, but rather to understand them as a repertoire from which you can consider options that seem likely to benefit a given learner at a particular time, in a specific context.

To Create a Safe, Inviting Learning Environment for Students Who Experience Trauma

- Develop and nurture a stable and trustworthy relationship with the student.
- Create a classroom culture of acceptance, empathy, and respect that begins with your beliefs, thoughts, communications, and actions—and extends to all members of the class as you model, teach, and support those values.
- Make it a high priority to become aware of a student's strengths and interests and to draw on those strengths and interests as pathways to academic and social growth.
- Help students identify their strengths and learn to draw on those strengths as bridges to academic and social growth.
- Refuse to think of the young person as a problem or as deficient.
- Speak to the student (and all students) with "unconditional positive regard." In other words, accept and "own" the student for who he or she is, not for what the student does or does not do.
- Be present through regular communication and emotional support so the student sees you as caring and trustworthy.

- Don't feel that you need to talk with the student about the origins of his/her trauma, or that the student is obliged to talk with you. You can acknowledge and work to lessen the stresses a student is experiencing without probing the past (unless the student clearly wants to talk with you about what has occurred in the past).
- Don't negate or downplay the trauma the student has experienced. Help the student understand that he or she is experiencing normal reactions to a negative situation.
- Study the student to identify triggers that cause a stress response.
- Help students who have experienced trauma understand what is going on in their bodies as a result of the trauma.
- Use emotional check-ins (by using a mood meter, quick conversations, or reflection opportunities).
- Help the learner identify the emotions he or she is feeling at a given time. Naming feelings can make them less frightening.
- Teach self-regulation strategies and strengthen them through regular use of mindfulness, positive self-talk, journaling, or physical exercise. Teach "channel switching" (like changing channels on a TV) so the student learns to move from negative feelings and impulses to ones that are more comfortable and productive—like changing channels on the TV. Helping a student focus on things to be grateful for can also be an empowering practice. (The point here is not to negate or deny the negative experience, but rather to help the young person look for positives that also exist.)
- Help students understand what they *can* control. Feeling that their world is out of control is common and understandable for children who experience trauma. As they can begin to feel in control of more elements in their environment, they will feel more empowered.
- Work with the student to develop some exit strategies so that when a collaborative or social context feels uncomfortable and stressful, he or she has options for leaving the setting calmly and smoothly.

- Encourage the young person to help others (for example, reading to younger children, sending notes or emails to a senior adult who is confined, taking part in a class or school community project).

To Provide Support When a Student Is Anxious, Angry, or Misbehaving

- Consider creating an area in the classroom that is away from the action and is furnished in a comfortable, inviting way where a student can take a break when emotions are building.
- Stay calm. Often, it is not *what* we say, but *how* we say it that a young person hears most clearly. If we seem anxious or angry, that may magnify their fears and intensify a negative response.
- Do not take the student's negative behavior personally. Instead, reflect on the emotional distress that is causing the behavior and understand that the student is trying to communicate through the behavior. The behavior, while it may be problematic, is not the root problem. The trauma experienced by the young person and the scars it has created are the *real* problem.
- Validate the child's feelings. Before you make any suggestions, reflect back or mirror the young person's emotions, for example, "It sounds like you're scared" or "I'm sorry you are so worried." Tell the student it is normal to feel anxious (when routines have changed, or when something unexpected happens, when you feel stressed, etc.).
- Restore equilibrium after an event triggers fear or alarm in a student. Wait until the student is more settled before talking with that student about the event.

To Respond to Major Negative Behavior

- Remember that when a student repeatedly acts out in class in ways that are disruptive, disturbing, or alarming, the behaviors are almost inevitably the symptoms of a problem and not the problem itself. It is wise to deal with those instances with the primary goal of guiding, teaching, and repairing rather than punishing.
- When punishment is clearly necessary, do what you can to ensure that the punishment is unlikely to impede the student's trust and learning.
- Instead of telling a child what you are going to do because of a behavior, talk with the student (when things are calm again), having the student describe with you what happened. Explore together ways in which you or the student might have eliminated or lessened the behavior. Make a plan together to avoid a similar problem in the near term (for example, the student being aware of stress building in his body, your signaling him when you become aware that he is tense or appears distressed, using mindfulness practices, or going to a quiet area in the room to calm down.
- Understand that students are "a whole lot more receptive when you're solving problems *with* them rather than doing something *to* them" (Greene, 2016, p. 21).
- Do what you can to ensure that when punishment that is clearly necessary, the punishment imposed is unlikely to impede the student's trust and learning. It is always important that the "remedy" we apply does not make the problem we are trying to address become more severe.
- Realize that a child who is impacted by trauma is not likely to become a model of classroom deportment as the result of a single problem-solving session. Healing is a long-term, stepwise process. Know, too, however, that collaborative problem solving can reinforce a student's trust in you as a caring ally and also reinforce the student's agency in developing and drawing on skills through which he or she can regain some control in life.

Teaching for Engagement and Success

- Be aware that trauma does not diminish a young person's capacity to learn but rather diminishes his or her access to that capacity for periods of time over time.

- Teach up to the student and provide emotional, social, and academic scaffolding that enables the learner to succeed with work that stretches his/her capacity.
- Connect curriculum with students' lives so they can see their stories in the lives of other people and realize that people can overcome difficulties and make significant contributions to others.
- Make sure the curriculum includes mirrors (opportunities for a student to see him/herself reflected in the content they are studying), windows (opportunities to learn about people whose lives and experiences are different in many ways from their own), and doors (opportunities to learn in the broader community and/or make contributions to that community).
- Provide structure, predictable routines, a consistent schedule, and clear directions and expectations for assignments to provide a sense of safety. Proactively providing for the needs of students who have experienced trauma greatly diminishes the likelihood that you will have to respond reactively to a problem.
- Prioritize safety and support over academic pressure. Academics are important, of course, but there are times when it is more important to support a student's mental health. Don't give up on learning. Support it, be a catalyst for it, but also let it ebb for a bit when academic pressure is becoming another stressor for a student during a time when that student's stress level is high.
- Encourage student voice and choice in how the classroom operates, topics for study, how to accomplish assignments, how to express learning, and other areas to help the student develop a sense of control, self-confidence, and agency.
- Teach the skills of working independently.
- Help students who have experienced trauma connect or reconnect with peers as they are ready to do that. Support their success in that process (for example, by modeling listening, or asking them to work with a peer whom you know is empathetic and sensitive to the needs of others).

- Teach the skills of working collaboratively.
- Differentiate instruction so the student can work with materials that are appropriately challenging; experience flexible time that enables him/her to complete work effectively; set personally meaningful and challenging goals that he/she can accomplish, earning a sense of satisfaction; choose topics that are personally interesting or personally relevant; choose ways of expressing learning; and so on.

To Partner With Parents or Caregivers

- Avoid blaming parents or caregivers for a child's pain. Much trauma is intergenerational, meaning that parents have suffered similar trauma over an extended period. In any case, parents need support, too, to provide continued support for their child. They also need to understand their role as partners with a teacher in a child's growth and success. That partnership is jeopardized if parents feel resentment or anger from the teacher.
- Let parents or caregivers know you care for their child and for them—that you want to be an ally in helping the student get better and continue to grow.
- Ask for insights about what triggers the young person's stresses and fears at home as well as for strategies the parents or caregivers find are helpful in helping him/her identify triggers, reduce stress, regroup after outbursts, and so on.
- Stay in touch with parents/caregivers throughout the year to help build a team of support for the learner. Be sure to share examples of student successes and growth.
- If you have reason to believe that parents, caregivers, or other relatives are abusing a child or are aware of and unresponsive to abuse by anyone, you are obliged by law and professional ethics to report your concerns to appropriate authorities.

Remember that you will likely have students in your classroom whose behaviors are a match for the manifestations of trauma but for whom there has been no identification of trauma by mental health professionals. It is quite possible also that you teach children who have experienced trauma and who, for a variety of reasons, have not told their parents or caregivers. Teachers certainly do not have the credentials necessary to make a diagnosis, but may at some point play a role in helping to connect a student with a mental health professional who can determine whether trauma is playing a role in a student's behavior and learning and be able to help the young person reclaim a life less dominated by fear, shame, anxiety, and stress.

As you build connections with learners who have experienced trauma, create a consistently positive and supportive classroom environment, listen, teach key coping strategies, help students realize and act on their strengths, help students feel in control of their lives, respond redemptively to students' behavior challenges so your students can develop agency and self-efficacy, see and appreciate their resilience, and look ahead with growing confidence. The student may not remember all the content you taught, but they will remember that you made them feel safe, cared for, and valued—and that you opened the way to learning.

NOTE

The following sources were consulted for this chapter. Full citations appear in the References section. Chaltain, 2016; Conn, Nelms, & Marsh, 2020; Gobir, 2021; Gorski, 2018; Greene, 2016; Haap, 2020; Hosier, n.d.; Institute for Child and Family Well-Being (n.d.); Keels, 2020; Merrill, 2020; Minahan, 2020; National Child Traumatic Stress Network, n.d; Rebora, 2020; Sorrels, 2015; Thiers, 2020; Institute for Child and Family Well-being, n.d.; Zacarian et al., 2020.

CHAPTER 9

Teaching Students Who Identify as LBGTQ

Our LGBTQ students are no different from our other students. They love some classes and hate others. They probably procrastinate too much. They laugh and love. They have struggles we know nothing about. They want what we all want: to feel like they matter in the world. Support them the same way you do all your students, by getting to know them. Be there for them during their struggles and celebrate their victories.

—Larry Ferlazzo

INTRODUCTION

Core to growing up are self-discovery, self-understanding, and self-acceptance. Core to *that* process is discovering and seeking to understand one's sexual orientation and gender identity—and feeling secure in that identity. For students whose gender identity does not conform to the binary, male or female standards on which society has long been predicated, the journey to self-understanding and self-acceptance can be frightening, lonely, isolating, and danger-filled.

Estimates are that somewhere around 10% of young people between the ages of 13 and 18 identify as LGBTQ (The Trevor Project, n.d.). Some young people begin to question their sexual orientation or gender identity at even earlier ages. Some who question their identity do so silently, afraid of the consequences of veering from the norm. Many of them feel unsafe, alone, invalidated, stigmatized, and even traumatized as they enter our classrooms. One national study found that over 85% of these students have experienced verbal harassment and 66% have been discriminated against based on their sexual orientation or gender identity. Students who experience more victimization are more likely to have lower grade-point averages and to report feeling depressed. It is not difficult to understand why they feel like "the other," unacceptable, voiceless (Gonzalez, 2017, Nov 5). Low self-esteem often

stunts their sense of possibility as learners and as participants in society.

Perhaps it is not surprising, then, to learn that over 45% of young people between 13- and 18-years-old who identify as lesbian, gay, bisexual, transgender, queer, or "questioning" seriously considered committing suicide during a recent year when a Trevor Project survey gathered data on the status of this group of students—young people who are in our classrooms every day (The Trevor Project, n.d.). That figure makes a chilling case that schools and classrooms need to create and maintain environments that feel safe and affirming to LGBTQ young people. We have no reason to expect that students who feel devalued or alienated will engage vigorously with learning.

If we as educators want to contribute to a world in which diversity is valued, in which respect and empathy are cornerstone values, then we need to see to the safety, well-being, comfort, and full participation of each learner in our classroom community. For students who identify as LGBTQ, we need to stand for their full worth, too; to affirm their experiences, dreams, and strengths; and to open doors of opportunity to nurture those strengths and give root to those dreams. As one teacher reflects, "It's scary, I know. For so many of us, this is uncharted territory. But to ignore this opportunity would be to operate in opposition to justice. To quiet students' voices would mean crushing autonomy, courage, and vulnerability. And as educators, we cannot and must not do that" (France, 2019).

Students who identify with gender identity and/or sexual orientation that differs from mainstream conceptions are, as is the case with all "exceptionalities," categories, and labels, *not* a heterogeneous group. Some of these young learners will be confident in their identity—others will be still unable to speak about it, even with friends. Some LGBTQ students will be English learners, or have a learning disorder or be academically advanced, or some combination of exceptionalities. There is no one-size-fits-all approach to working successfully with any group.

The following guidelines address common needs experienced by many LGBTQ young people. Your application of the guidelines will necessarily vary with the age of the students you teach. The list may appear less academic than affective or social in its focus. It is wise to remember the admonition "Maslow before Bloom." It is most often the case that until a student's more fundamental physiological needs and needs for safety and belonging are met, self-esteem—which is typically connected with learning success—is in jeopardy. Said differently, when we contribute to a student's affective health, we contribute also to that student's academic health.

SOME PRINCIPLES AND PRACTICES FOR TEACHING STUDENTS WHO IDENTIFY AS LGBTQ

To Create a Safe, Inviting Learning Environment for Learners Who Identify as LGBTQ

- Be aware of your biases—how you were taught to think/feel about people whose sexual orientation or gender identity differs from what society considers to be the norm—and ways in which those ideas shape your feelings and interactions.
- Look at each student with unconditional positive regard—that is, with full appreciation and valuing of each learner for who he or she now is—so that there is no need for a student to prove or do anything to earn your approval or positive attention (Gobir, 2021).

- Get to know each student as a three-dimensional person with distinct strengths, goals, personalities, learning preferences, cultures, and so on.
- Carefully and continually build a culture of inclusion in the classroom in which every learner finds acceptance, respect and empathy—a classroom in which it is safe to be oneself, one that encourages individuality and appreciates different points of view. Experiencing an inclusive environment from the earliest school years helps children learn empathy and respect for a full spectrum of peers as they connect, explore ideas, and work together in a variety of group contexts. Use welcoming language. Demonstrate consistently your belief that every student is important, that the perspectives of each student matter, that each student has roles to play in making the class the best it can be, and that we are stronger as a team when we work with individuals who bring to us a wide range of perspectives, experiences, and cultures.
- Be visible in your support (for example, by hanging a "safe space" sign on the classroom door and using a student's preferred pronouns). Let students know you are always happy to talk with them when they need or want an adult to talk with.
- Build trust with each LGBTQ student (as with every student in your class). Understand that when a student has reason to see the world as untrustworthy, building trust will take time. Students who have reason to distrust others will listen carefully to what you say and be quite attuned to what you do to determine whether you merit their trust. Be patient. Be sure to do all you can not to violate the trust you are building.
- Ensure that all students in your class have voice and choice and that all of them work as partners with you to create a classroom that is attentive to and effective in addressing the needs of all members of the class.

- Take care to keep private what a student tells you unless that student gives you permission to share with others.
- Work with administrators to be sure school privacy practices and policies adequately protect the rights and privacy of LGBTQ students.
- Work collaboratively with LGBTQ students to make sure they feel safe and supported at school and at home.
- Strive to use whatever terminology is currently embraced by the LGBTQ community to refer to their identities to show acceptance and respect (tricky because the language evolves over time).
- Respond clearly and firmly to anti-LGBTQ language or behavior. Not to act is to act.
- Support any student who is the target of negative language or behavior.
- Hold students whose words and actions are inappropriate accountable for negative behavior.
- Use situations that involve anti-LGBTQ language or behavior as teachable moments for the students involved and peers.
- Be supportive of LGBTQ students who come out. Listen. Ask them what they need— what you can do to support them.
- Be sure the school's anti-bullying policy includes LGBTQ students.
- Partner with parents whenever possible to understand strengths, interests, and needs a learner brings to school, to get suggestions of topics or approaches to learning that would be engaging, and to understand stresses the student has faced or is facing as a student whose gender-identity experience differs from many of his or her peers. Offer your partnership and insights to support parents as they support their child. Understand, too, however, that parental rejection is a reality for a significant number of LGBTQ learners. In those cases, much of the hurt a child experiences arises from the people who typically, and should, represent safety and acceptance in a child's life.
- Work with colleagues to learn more about how to work effectively and productively with LGBTQ students—for example, the GLSEN website (https://www.glsen.org) and materials as well as the Learning for Justice website and materials (https://www.learningforjustice.org/topics/gender-sexual-identity). Read blogs, read books, listen to podcasts, and talk with LGBTQ colleagues and friends.

To Teach for Engagement and Success

- Ensure that curriculum includes the perspectives, voices, and histories of LGBTQ individuals from many cultures, time periods, and societal contributions (for example: Ma Rainey, "Mother of the Blues"; Tim Cook, CEO of Apple; Alice Walker, Pulitzer Prize winning novelist; Edward Albee; Stephen Sondheim; Alexander the Great; Lorraine Hansberry, playwright of *A Raisin in the Sun*; Howard Ashman, song writer whose work is included in *The Little Mermaid*, *Aladdin*, and *Beauty and the Beast*; Jane Addams, founder of Hull House; Glen Burke, major league baseball player; Emily Dickinson; Ellen DeGeneres; Barbara Jordan, the first African American woman elected to the U.S. Senate from a Southern state; Sally Ride, astronaut; Frida Kahlo, artist; Langston Hughes, poet; and Katharine Lee Bates, poet and writer who penned "America the Beautiful").
- Create curriculum that includes mirrors, windows, and doors. Mirrors allow students to see themselves in what they study and to understand themselves more fully. Windows allow them to learn about people, places, and times that are different from their own in some ways, allowing students to expand their sense of the world. Doors allow them to connect with and contribute to the community. This kind of curriculum benefits all students by exposing them to more inclusive and accurate accounts of history, helping them understand LGBTQ people, encouraging them to question stereotypes, and promoting acceptance of LGBTQ people as full members of society. The curriculum benefits LGBTQ students by validating

their existence and experiences, reinforcing their value and self-worth, providing space for their voices, and connecting them with school and learning.

- Ensure that curriculum is inclusive and affirming for all students—teach students about the multiple identities all of us have and help them develop respect and support for a wide spectrum of identities, and to learn to collaborate with peers whose identities, experiences, and perspectives are both like and different from their own.
- Include in curriculum universal concepts that are relevant to a wide range of learners (for example: justice, tolerance, self-expression, diversity, perspective, equity, discrimination, freedom and responsibility, and persecution). These points of focus help students explore their own experiences and concerns, as those same concerns have existed and do exist in many times, places, and circumstances, causing students to feel less alone and more connected to the world in which they live—past, present, and future.
- Teach up to LGBTQ learners. Expect them to work with big ideas and complex content. Support them in becoming good problem-solvers and in developing agency as thinkers and learners. Help them develop voice so that they become increasingly comfortable in sharing their experiences and speaking up for all people who face any sort of discrimination, hatred, or rejection.
- Ensure that classroom and school library books and materials include varied kinds of families and people whose careers and other life roles do not conform to gender stereotypes. Likewise, be sure images you use on walls, handouts, websites, and so on are inclusive of gender, race, language, and sexual orientation.
- Help students learn about the evolution of civil rights as that topic relates to the LGBTQ community (as well as African Americans, immigrants, women, and other groups). Talk about both steps forward in civil rights and regressions.
- Avoid addressing the class as "boys and girls" or "ladies and gentlemen."
- Group students gender-neutrally rather than by boys and girls (e.g., as 1s and 2s or by birthday month or by interests, etc.)
- Evaluate your speech and materials for gender-normative assumptions (e.g., assuming boys will marry girls, asking boys to move the boxes, suggesting that girls like shopping and boys like sports, or that boys don't dance, girls don't play football, etc.).
- Take care not to have different expectations for behavior for males and females.
- Differentiate instruction so that learning is consistently a bit beyond a learner's current reach, and peer and teacher support are available as catalysts for growth—where student strengths and interests are emphasized as pathways to success, and choices of ways to learn and demonstrate learning are often available. Help students see learning as a way forward in an uncertain world.
- Use flexible grouping so that all students regularly work with a variety of peers, based on similar and different readiness needs, similar and different interests, similar and different approaches to learning, teacher choice, student choice, and random groupings.
- Teach student the skills necessary to collaborate successfully.
- Teach them the skills and attitudes necessary to be successful with independent work—to have increasing agency over their own learning.

LGBTQ students frequently come to school with a sense that neither teachers nor peers will understand or accept them. Those trepidations are born of experience. It is a daily act of courage for many LGBTQ learners to walk through the classroom door. Often their greatest need is to have an opportunity to rebuild trust in a world that has broken their trust at a young age. For students who have learned not to trust, the process of finding it again is long and risky. Remember that one teacher can make a profound positive difference in the direction a student's life will take. Work with the intent to be that teacher through your relationship with LGBTQ learners by creating an environment in which those students—and all students—can find safety, connection, and voice without sacrificing their identity.

NOTE

The following sources were consulted for this chapter. Full citations appear in the References section. Barile, 2017; DiPietro, 2012; Ferlazzo, 2021b; France, 2019; GLSEN, n.d.; Gobir, 2021; Gonzalez, 2017; Green, E., 2021; Kiebel, 2017; Learning for Justice Staff, 2017; Smith et al., 2020.

CHAPTER 10

Teaching Students Who Experience Poverty

It is a common condition of being poor . . . you are always afraid that the good things in your life are temporary, that someone can take them away, because you have no power beyond your own brute strength to stop them.

—Rick Bragg, Pulitzer Prize-Winning Journalist

INTRODUCTION

Poverty is defined as a lack of monetary resources necessary to meet basic needs such as food, clothing, housing, health care, child care, and education (Gorski, 2018). The standard federal measure of poverty is an annual family income of about $26,000 for a family with two adults and two children and about $20,500 for a family with one adult and two children. Figures vary from year to year. Currently, over half of students in the United States qualify for free or reduced-price lunches—another indicator of the degree of poverty among K–12 learners in the United States.

In 2019, the federal government reported that 14.4% of U.S. children lived in poverty (compared with 9.4% of adults from ages 18-64 and 8.9% of adults over 65). Distressing as it is, this figure is an underestimate of child poverty in the United States for at least two reasons. First, it does not include individuals experiencing homelessness because census surveys are sent to households and therefore exclude those without permanent housing. In addition, the census historically undercounts children of color as well as low-income and immigrant families. Not only does this skew our view of the scope of child poverty in this country, but it also results in a reduction in funding for vital services that rely on accurate counts for adequate funding—services that children living in poverty desperately need. Poverty impacts individuals and families from all cultures, ethnicities, regions, and settings. Some groups, however, disproportionally experience poverty. The

United States has one of the highest rates of child poverty among high income nations.

Eric Jensen (in Cooper, 2016) explores five different kinds of poverty:

- **Situational Poverty**—occurs when there is a family crisis or emergency such as a parent losing a job, a house fire, or a natural disaster that suddenly causes a family to lose everything.
- **Generational Poverty**—happens when several generations of a family have lived in poverty and continue to do so.
- **Relative Poverty**—occurs when a student lacks basic needs and has a standard of living significantly lower than most peers in the same area or school.
- **Urban Poverty**—found in large cities. In these concentrated areas of poverty, students suffer from chronic stress that impacts their daily lives. In addition, they typically attend underfunded/high-poverty schools that offer fewer advanced classes, tend to have a larger number of inexperienced teachers, and offer fewer resources that students in those schools need to moderate the effects of poverty.
- **Rural Poverty**—occurs in non-metropolitan areas. There is a predominance of single-parent homes in these locations, and rural schools generally lack basic services that would be available in cities and suburbs such as programs for students

with disabilities. Persistent underfunding of rural public schools contributes to low teacher salaries, benefits, and lack of access to professional development. In addition, having to prepare multiple subjects for various grade levels means that teachers cannot provide students with as much individual attention as they need. Rates of rural poverty are on the rise, with over half of the rural student population living in a low-income family.

In addition to lacking money, which can compromise a student's ability to develop a sense of personal agency, students who live with poverty often lack opportunity to develop three other kinds of capital that can benefit their development and sense of agency (Parrett & Budge, 2020):

Human capital—the skills, abilities, and knowledge that support learning in school (for example, the ability to deal with language, and comfort with the rules and language for reasoning). Schools and communities in which poverty is a central factor offer fewer opportunities than do wealthier communities (for example, libraries and medical facilities that promote healthy development).

Social capital—the ability to form formal and informal networks of people who are helpful as parents try to negotiate the bureaucracy of schools to negotiate for their children. People who live in poverty are often isolated from these networks and one another.

Cultural capital—Students from wealthier backgrounds enter school with a good bit of cultural capital because they have already been introduced to libraries, books, theater, travel, and knowledge about the world around them. This knowledge is typically rewarded in school (Parrett & Budge, 2020), and students who lack this sort of knowledge are at a disadvantage. The lack of these three kinds of capital magnifies the impact on learning that stems from the financial deficits that characterize poverty.

A report from Child Trends (cited in Public Schools First NC, 2018) found that while child poverty rates remained the same or decreased slightly from 2017 to 2018 for all racial and ethnic groups, the poverty gap between young Black and Hispanic children and their White peers under the age of 6 increased. Nearly 1 in 3 Black children (32.4%) and 1 in 4 Hispanic children (24.3%) were living in poverty in 2018, compared to less than 1 in 10 White children (9.1%). In 2018, young Black and Hispanic children lived in poverty at rates of 3.6 and 2.7 times higher than their non-Hispanic White peers.

Students living in poverty often have fewer resources at home to complete homework, study, or engage in activities that help equip them for success during the school day. Many families living in poverty lack access to computers, high-speed internet, and other materials that can aid a student outside of school. Parents of these families often work longer hours or multiple jobs, which means they may not be available to assist their children with their schoolwork.

Among other negative outcomes of living in poverty are the following:

- Children less prepared to enter school, including language and literacy development
- Greater likelihood of having developmental delays or learning disabilities than students who do not live in poverty (1.3 times more likely)
- Higher levels of persistent stress that make it difficult for students to succeed in school
- Health issues, often stemming from a non-nutritional diet
- Food insecurity
- Lack of access to medical treatment for illnesses
- Family stress and trauma
- Neighborhood risk factors
- Poorer mental health
- Housing instability
- Homelessness
- Higher rates of absenteeism
- Lower achievement scores
- Higher rates of repeating grades
- Higher dropout rates (7 times higher than those of students living in families with higher incomes), in part because students

living in poverty are more likely to have to work or care for family members

- Less likelihood after completing high school of enrolling in a 4-year college (fewer than 30% of students who experience poverty enroll in 4-year programs, and 50% of those who do enroll do not graduate from the programs)
- Lower prospects as an adult for a life of well-being and economic productivity

Young people whose families lack financial resources necessary to live economically stable and comfortable lives *do* bring challenges to school with them. However, those challenges cannot serve as an excuse to teach them in ways that contribute to weak outcomes. While their challenges may make their learning more difficult, they do not sentence students to a life of failure and future poverty if schools and teachers provide them with opportunities to succeed—including opportunities to develop human capital, social capital, and cultural capital. As Wiliam (2011a) notes, research findings indicate that in the classrooms of teachers whose students make the greatest progress in reading, students who are disadvantaged because of low socioeconomic status make as much progress as students from advantaged backgrounds—and students with behavioral disorders make as much progress as students without those disorders.

There are also countless stories of teachers who refused to "teach down" to students from homes that lack resources—innumerable teachers who helped those students build bridges to hopeful lives, including the skills and habits of mind that enable the students to realize their hopes. Following are some principles and practices that are important in helping students who experience poverty realize their full capacity and become contributors to their own welfare and that of others as well. Poverty is not a human trait. It is a consequence of societal and structural inequities. Teachers have the opportunity to help prepare those young people to find a way out of poverty and to be a voice in diminishing the inequities, policies, and structures that result in a significant segment of the population living in conditions that diminish their opportunity to live stable and preferable lives.

SOME PRINCIPLES AND PRACTICES FOR TEACHING STUDENTS WHO EXPERIENCE POVERTY

To Create a Safe, Inviting Learning Environment for Students Who Experience Poverty

- Monitor your thinking to eliminate deficit thinking and shed labels. Poverty is not located *in* students. It is a result of persistent societal inequities or human emergencies. Students who experience poverty have talents, strengths, interests, and capacity to accomplish great things. How we feel about poverty shapes how we teach students who experience poverty.
- Monitor your mindset. Students who live in poverty, like all students, have malleable brains and can learn as all students do when their teachers believe in them, communicate that belief to them, partner with them to learn important things and to learn how to learn, and teach them the skills and habits of mind necessary for success.
- Look for positives in all students every day and in all situations.
- Ensure that students who experience poverty see that you welcome them every day with unconditional positive regard (Gobir, 2021)—in other words, that they do not have to do anything or be anything other than who they are for you to accept and respect them.
- Work from the first day of school to establish a bond with each student, both personally and academically, so each student sees that you care about them as individuals and are invested in supporting their growth and success as learners. Your relationship with a student is probably the most important factor in that student's willingness to work against the odds of societal inequity.
- Create an environment that is physically and emotionally safe, welcoming, and comfortable and in which every student can feel capable and important.
- Learn students' names before the first day of school if possible. Consider using desk

nametags for the first week or two of school to help you with names and to help students learn one another's names.

- Use strategies like student-to-student interviews, "Me Bags" (students place in a small bag four or five objects or pictures of objects that are significant to them, and over time, each student has a chance to share with the class what is in his/her bag and to explain why it is important to them), or other strategies that create opportunity for students to learn about their classmates early in the school year.

- Make the classroom a place where students talk with one another often, laugh together, solve problems together, and help one another. Human beings are hard-wired to connect, and those connections are especially important for students who face significant challenges in their lives. Being part of a vibrant learning community makes a significant positive difference in a student's sense of belonging and possibility, and in their engagement in learning.

- Ask students to be your partners in creating a classroom that works for everyone. Ask for their suggestions about classroom norms. It is helpful to have just a few powerful and encompassing rules. For example: Work hard. No excuses. Be nice. Make good choices. Take care of this place. Take care of one another. Take care of yourself. Ask students to work together to describe how those norms would look in action—or make suggestions for modifying the basic set of norms.

- Regularly seek student input on what is working or not working for students and apply what you learn.

- Use flexible grouping so that students have regular opportunities to work with a wide range of peers. Consider also assigning each student to a long-term learning team on which they will work for an extended time (for example, a month or a marking period). Provide time for the long-term groups to work together daily, or at least several times a week, so that students can bond with one another, become skilled in drawing on the various strengths students bring to the group, and learn how to support one another's growth.

- Invest heavily in creating a classroom environment of respect, empathy, energy, optimism, and achievement. Surround students with conversations about and demonstrations of their progress—about the importance of taking their next steps. Talk with them about important things they will do in the future and steps they will take to get there. A classroom with these characteristics can make a major difference in how a young person sees the world and him/herself in the world.

- Do not plan classroom events that assume parents can contribute (for example, cupcakes for birthdays, pizza parties, valentine exchanges, holiday gifts, field trips).

- Use classroom circles for students to share ideas with one another. (Students sit in a circle. The teacher shares a prompt. Students take turns responding. The student who is speaking holds an object that indicates he/she is the only one who speaks at that moment. The teacher calls time when it seems appropriate and thanks students for sharing their ideas.) This approach can benefit student listening skills, empathy, and sense of connectedness with peers.

- Teach students breathing techniques they can use when they are stressed.

- Connect with students' families or caregivers in locations, times, and modes that are accessible to them. Let them see that you care about their child's learning and development. Be a positive constant for families that may lack those touchstones. Find out about ways in which they support and encourage their child's learning and development. Work with them to develop ways both you and they can extend that support.

- If you have had personal experience with poverty (or if your parents did), share those stories with your students. If you have not had personal experience with poverty, talk with colleagues or community members who have had those experiences. Read about the nature and impact of poverty to help you more deeply understand some of what your students experience. (But do not let that knowledge lead you to excuse work or behaviors that fall below the high standards for quality you and your students establish in your class.)

- Encourage students to share their stories and to listen respectfully to one another's.
- Make certain students have what they need in terms of materials and equipment needed to complete any assignment you give. If any student does not and there is no way for you to ensure the student can get what the assignment calls for, change the assignment so it does not require out-of-reach resources.
- If students may come to class hungry, be sure to have snacks in the room they can get easily (preferably without asking you). If students are coming to class in need of sleep, give them a place (or permission) to take a nap. If those problems are chronic, team with caring colleagues (principal, counselor, other teachers) to work toward solutions. Schools must be attentive to these basic human needs—because students cannot learn when those needs are unmet, but also because we cannot claim to care about the people we teach if we are unaware of or inattentive to their most fundamental requirements for sustaining life and growing.
- Be sure the classroom environment, teaching, and learning are all designed to be culturally responsive. (See Chapters 15 and 16 for information on culturally responsive teaching).

To Help Students Who Experience Poverty Develop Hope, Optimism, and Agency

- Make learning interesting, relevant, and lively. Students need to see learning as something of worth—an endeavor that taps into their curiosity, connects with their lives, calls on them to participate, and makes it

feel worthwhile to come to school. (Drill, practice, worksheets, and memorizing information add to a sense of pointlessness for many learners.) Your enthusiasm should be a catalyst for theirs.

- Have high expectations for each student's work and communicate those expectations clearly and consistently. Make sure students see your classroom as a place where achievement happens, where students support one another, and where they can count on your partnership in their learning.
- Set high expectations for yourself. Share those with your students and let them see over time how you are working toward those goals. When something does not work, share that with the class and let them see your determination as you analyze your next steps and continue working toward your goals. Model resilience and persistence.
- Use models of quality student work at or near a student's current level of readiness to help them see examples of what good work looks like.
- Help each student develop his/her voice, drive, effort, and intention. These are all teachable skills and are important in achieving self-efficacy, agency, and ownership of learning.
- Help students set their own goals for success based on class learning targets and monitor those goals as they work to understand their own progress and development. Use checklists weekly to have students reflect on their progress toward their goals (Where are you? Where do you need to be? How will you get there?). When a student is not progressing as he or she should, use small short-term goals the student can master in a relatively brief time frame that will lead them to the larger, long-term goal.
- Provide feedback to guide student work. Feedback should be clear, focused on what matters most, and actionable. Let a student know two or three things he or she has done effectively and two or three things that need additional attention. Provide suggestions of what the student might do to improve those areas.

- Scaffold student work as needed to help them accomplish goals that may seem out of reach to them. (But do not do the work for them. Help them figure out steps that will take them forward.)
- Hold students accountable for meeting expectations (not through punishment, but through requirements to complete unfinished work and revise work that misses the mark).
- Help your students experience the world outside their classroom and communities. Take them on field trips (real or virtual) to libraries, museums, parks, interesting buildings, recreation areas, or work sites where people are addressing problems or needs using math or science.
- When students become discouraged, give them a reason to keep on. Jensen (2019) suggests saying something like, "I care about you. I am good at what I do. I will work hard, persist, and learn from my mistakes. You do your part and I guarantee I'll do my part. I won't let any of you fail. Now, let's get to work."
- Help students learn about a range of careers that they are not likely to encounter on their own by inviting people in those careers to visit your class and through reading and student investigations. It is particularly powerful if invited guest presenters have experienced poverty in their lives. Be sure students come to understand the pathways to those careers and how they can begin accessing those pathways now.
- Invite students who went to your school and who grew up in poverty before going to college to come talk with your learners about the challenges they faced (and still face) and what they do to move around those barriers.
- Ensure that from the earliest grades, students who experience poverty read about and see communities like their own in ways that emphasize the positives in those communities rather than contributing to persistent stereotypes about people who experience poverty.

- Regularly share stories, books, articles, videos, and so on about people who grew up in poverty and became significant contributors to the arts, athletics, music, science, law, business, non-profit work, and so on.
- Help students learn how to take action on behalf of their hopes and dreams—to understand ways in which they can have agency over their current and future lives.
- Provide opportunities for your students to help other people (through classroom jobs helping younger students with their work, contributing to agencies in the community that serve community members, supporting one another). Encourage them to engage in acts of kindness every day. Both of these avenues are empowering to most people and particularly those who feel powerless much of the time.
- Work with leaders in your school (principal, assistant principal, counselors, social workers, parent volunteers) who will get to know your students personally, congratulate them when they achieve goals and personal successes, and engage in periodic conversations with them.
- Post affirmations and thought-provoking quotations in the classroom. Talk with your students about them. Change them from time to time. Seeing them and thinking about them can be useful to students who may not have those sorts of encouragements in their lives.
- Teach the social and emotional skills students need in their lives to make positive connections with others, express their feelings, and see beyond current problems.

To Teach Responsively to Students Who Experience Poverty

- Create curriculum that has mirrors, windows, and doors. Mirrors enable students to see themselves and their experiences in what they learn. Windows give them opportunity to understand other people, places, and experiences that are both like and unlike their own. Doors invite them to connect with and contribute to the larger community.

- Teach up. Create curriculum that emphasizes big ideas or concepts and principles, meaning, understanding, and complex thinking. Then scaffold learning opportunities in ways that support student success.
- Use concepts and principles across content areas that address equity and inequity, justice and injustice, bias, stereotyping, economics, change, voice, and other themes that enable students to understand how inequitable circumstances are created and how individuals and groups take action to diminish inequities. This approach enables students to relate to and understand content more readily, relate it to their own experiences, and transfer it to thinking about their future. The concepts can be catalysts for discussions, reading, writing, group investigations, and performance assessments.
- Teach students to recognize bias and to think analytically about it, and ways to respond when they encounter it.
- Make sure learning targets/goals (KUDs) are clear and that students understand them.
- Align instructional plans with the KUDs so that student learning is consistently focused on what is most important for them to master in a segment of content.
- Find out each student's interests, dreams, and aspirations. Use those as a basis for conversations with a student and for reading, writing, group investigations, expert groups, and performance assessments.
- Provide voice and choice as often as possible in what students learn, how they learn it, and how they express what they have learned.
- Make literacy the cornerstone of the curriculum across content areas, ensuring that students have opportunity and support necessary to learn to decode, comprehend/ make meaning of text, and reflect on their reading. Literacy also includes developing skills to understand, analyze, and recognize both the contributions and deficiencies of media.
- Create a classroom in all content areas where reading for pleasure is a high priority

and where students and teachers share their enthusiasm for reading. For many people who have lived in discouraging or demeaning conditions over time, reading has been a route to a better life.
- Whatever the grade level of your students, take time to read to them as well. *Hearing* the beauty of wonderful stories or exciting nonfiction read by an adult whom you trust or even emulate is powerful commendation of reading.
- Differentiate instruction based on students' evolving strengths, interests, and learning needs. Use highways and exit ramps (structure time and space) to allow you to address needs of the whole class as well as individual and small-group needs. Differentiation is necessary to enable students to do work that is a little too hard for them, find support to get it done, and experience frequent successes in order to learn and to believe in themselves as learners.
- Call on students to use what they learn in meaningful ways, connecting their work with the larger world whenever possible.
- Teach students the skills and attitudes they need to be able to work effectively (both independently and collaboratively).
- Create student profiles (in notebooks, index cards, online) that provide a place for you to make notes about students' interests, successes, dislikes, talents, and so on, so you continually grow in your knowledge about each student. Use what you learn to form student groups, talk with students one on one, generate examples or metaphors to help students relate to content, suggest reading materials, create problem scenarios for students to solve, and so on.
- Establish high standards for quality work and hold students to those standards. Remember, however, that excellence requires time, guidance, and patience. Reaching high ceilings requires building high ladders, and teachers are the primary ladder-builders.
- Post visual reminders in the room of the most important academic vocabulary, steps in key processes, and criteria for success.

- Be a warm demander—a teacher who clearly cares for and champions the success of each student but who will not accept behaviors or work habits that fall short of the high standards set for the class.
- Build students' learning skills by teaching them how to take notes, draw mind maps, and use mnemonic devices. Teach them to ask questions when they are uncertain about the work they are doing, summarize, track their own learning progress, think about their thinking, learn from errors, and use feedback as stepping stones to success.
- Use a range of instructional approaches and strategies to keep learning lively, fresh, and engaging. It will likely be helpful to change approaches during a class or subject period and/or inject physical activity about every 15 minutes. The constant stress felt by many students who experience poverty can make it difficult for them to focus, pay attention, and sit still. Classrooms in which instruction is dynamic, varied, and engaging facilitate learning for these learners.
- Review content in unexpected and engaging ways such as games, sketches, role-plays, and singing.
- Look for what *is* working for a student— and keep doing it. Look for what is *not* working—and change the approach.
- End class with a preview of what students will do in the next class in ways that help them look forward to the new learning.

To Ensure That Assessment Is a Positive and Productive Process for Students Who Experience Poverty

- Ensure that formative and summative assessments align tightly with learning targets (KUDs) for a unit or lesson.
- Use formative assessment to determine the degree to which each student is showing mastery of KUDs. When a student is lagging, adjust instruction accordingly (generally during exit ramp time unless there is a broad pattern of misunderstanding, misconception, or confusion around a topic or skill).

- Consider giving students re-do opportunities after summative assessments as a catalyst for them to persist in achieving mastery of areas in which they were initially weak.
- Whenever possible, use performance tasks for summative assessment so that students can use varied strengths, talents, and interests to demonstrate their mastery of key ideas and skills and can plan for sharing their products with significant audiences. With appropriate support for one another and the teacher, performance assessments provide an excellent means of helping students see themselves do things they've not thought possible—opportunities, quite literally, to see themselves grow and succeed. Opportunities to excel lead to empowerment, which then translates into academic competence, personal confidence, courage, and the will to act (Berger et al., 2014; Gay, in Jensen, 2019).
- Use both formal and informal formative assessment to become aware of each student's strengths and interests.

Cynthia Johnson (2013), a longtime classroom teacher, principal, and district project leader working often with students who live with poverty, poses the core question all educators should seek to answer when we serve those learners: "What bridges the gap between a culture of despair and a future of hope for children who live in poverty?" The answer, she says, is simple (although, of course, it is not). It is educators who refuse to settle for mediocrity, who will not accept excuses for why students who experience poverty can't learn, who are willing to do whatever it takes to help each child succeed, who establish supportive environments where children learn to bounce back from life's negative circumstances and thrive.

She reminds us that children who come from generations of poverty or those who find themselves there because of life's current circumstances still dream, have hopes, and want to achieve. They need teachers who see working with them not as a burden but as an opportunity to help young people in our care achieve in ways that turn dreams into realities.

NOTE

The following sources were consulted for this chapter. Full citations appear in the References section. "11 facts about education," n.d.; Berger et al., 2014; Collins, 1992; Cooper, 2016; ED100, n.d.; Gobir, 2021; Gorski, 2018; Harmon, 2018; Jensen, 2019; Johnson, 2013; Kearney, 2021; National Association of Secondary School Principals, 2019; National Center for Education Statistics, 2021; Public Schools First NC, 2020; Parrett & Budge, 2020; Riddell, 2020; Smith et al., 2020; Tucker, 2019; Wiliam, 2011a.

CHAPTER 11

Teaching Students With Autism

She didn't know how to be semi-interested in something. She was either indifferent . . . or obsessed.

—Helen Hoang, *The Kiss Quotient*

INTRODUCTION

Autism, or autism spectrum disorder (ASD), is a lifelong developmental disorder caused by a neurological dysfunction. Autism is not a disease to be cured but rather a way of being in the world. It affects the way a person experiences and interacts with their surroundings. Every individual on the autism spectrum is uniquely different from every other individual on the autism spectrum—just as any two typically developing students are different from one another in a myriad of ways. Students with autism are generally diagnosed at one of three levels of severity. Individuals who function at Level 1 require support and need assistance primarily in communication and connecting with people in social situations. They also often have inflexible behavior that can interfere with functioning in a variety of contexts, with switching contexts, and with organization and planning. Individuals who function at Levels 2 and 3 need increasingly more support in more areas. It is likely that most classroom teachers will work only with students who function at Level 1.

According to the Centers for Disease Control and Prevention (2020a), about 1 in 54 children has been identified with autism spectrum disorder (ASD). Autism occurs in all racial, ethnic, and socioeconomic groups and is four times more common among boys than girls, perhaps because females tend to manifest characteristics in less visible and potentially disruptive ways than boys.

Students with autism bring to the classroom a wide array of strengths and talents—and an array of challenges that are often broader, deeper, and more idiosyncratic than the challenges experienced by their typically developing peers. While people with autism have the same range of intellectual skills as the general population, they may have a number of other characteristics that can make education less accessible to them.

CHARACTERISTICS THAT STUDENTS WITH AUTISM MAY EXHIBIT IN THE CLASSROOM

Autism impacts the way individuals communicate, socialize, and behave with others. While most students with autism exhibit some behaviors that are generally associated with autism, the number, frequency, and degree of such behaviors will vary greatly among students with autism. It is important that a teacher get to know all students in order to teach them well. That quest is certainly important for teaching a student with autism. Among the challenging behaviors students with autism may demonstrate are the following:

- difficulty with comprehension, abstract thinking, problem-solving, inference, and judgment
- weak organizational skills, difficulty following simple directions
- difficulty with flexibility in thinking
- difficulty adapting to change
- obsessive routines such as hand-flapping, rocking, twirling a pen, wanting to wear the same clothes over and over, or eating the same kind of sandwich for lunch every day

- engaging in repetitive behaviors
- preoccupation with a particular topic of interest
- unusual attachment to particular objects
- tendency to take language literally—inability to understand abstract language like figures of speech and idioms, irony, or sarcasm
- problems with social relationships—behavior that seems odd to peers, difficulty making and keeping friends, may seem arrogant or impolite, difficulty reading social cues
- difficulty in understanding or communicating feelings, inability to empathize with others
- inability to pick up on nonverbal cues, poor eye contact, tendency to miss instructional cues
- hyper sensitivity to sounds, tastes, smells, textures, and so on that others may not perceive—resistance to touching
- poor coordination, clumsiness, poor gross motor skills

ANXIETY AT THE HEART OF CHALLENGING BEHAVIORS

Life for students with autism can be perpetually confusing. They may not understand what people around them are doing. They receive regular signals that they are not in sync with that world. A steady stream of negative feedback from a variety of sources can erode self-confidence and cause a young person to feel worthless or hopeless. In fact, individuals on the autism spectrum are at least four times more likely to experience clinical depression than are members of the general population.

Students with autism learn through repeated experience to expect feeling overwhelmed, overstimulated, and shunned. Their sense of self is fragile. Anxiety is always in the mix—and the twists and turns in a school day are, at the very least, persistently confusing.

On any typical day in an inclusion classroom, new lessons, topics, and projects—each with its own set of rules and expectations—come at them every few minutes. Bodies move in unpredictable directions; conversations veer off on inscrutable tangents; teachers and students come and go; peace and chaos ebb and flow. On some days there are assemblies, field trips, absent teachers and service providers, fire drills, lockout and lockdown drills. The cafeteria runs out of pizza. A classmate vomits. Even activities thoughtfully designed to engage and excite students—those one-minute dance parties, quick-writes, turn-and-talks, group projects, or trips to the makerspace—can be incapacitating for students on the spectrum unless carefully presented in advance, and, if necessary, carefully adapted. (Boroson, 2020, p. 30)

Many things can trigger anxiety for students with autism, and when the trigger occurs, the student may experience sensory overload. Flexibility and rationality may abandon them. Self-regulation may be out of reach. Communications skills may shut down so the student can't access language to ask for help. In those instances, the only mode of expressing the anxiety may be behavior.

Needless to say, the better able a teacher is to understand, anticipate, and avoid triggers, the better the day will be for the anxious student, for classmates, and for the teacher. Boroson (2020) suggests several broad categories of triggers:

- Something New—A new school year with new names, new faces, new routines and rules, and new expectations—all at once—maybe even all on the same day.
- Unfamiliar Activities—Anything unfamiliar, even basic classroom processes and activities can feel unsafe to a student with autism—far outside the comfort zone they work diligently to protect.
- Something Unexpected—Changes in a schedule, alterations in the way the classroom is arranged, a clock that says the wrong time, the teacher is absent, a familiar object is broken. Once again, the anxiety index rises.
- Something Different—Transitions between parts of the school day that may be insignificant or even pleasant for many students feel disorganized, noisy, and frightful. Separation from parents or other caregivers each day can be wrenching and can make other difficult elements (such as riding the school bus) even more

disorienting. Leaving a trusted teacher or a comfortable spot in the classroom can be a mighty challenge for a student who values predictability and even rigidity.

A key factor in shaping a day that eliminates or at least reduces anxiety for a learner with autism is the presence of a teacher who is alert to anxiety triggers and proactive in attempting to address them. While most students with autism who are in general education classrooms have fewer of these characteristics and/or milder manifestations of them, it is useful for a teacher to be acquainted with all of the characteristics because of the variability among individuals with autism spectrum disorder.

Children and teens with autism are, first and foremost, young human beings. They are funny, likeable, and interesting and need their teachers to love and support them just as those teachers love and support any other student they teach. Following are some guides for teachers that can be helpful in working with students who have autism. The goal is not to use all the strategies with any one student who has autism. Understand suggestions as a repertoire from which you can consider options that seem likely to benefit a given learner at a particular time, in a specific context.

SOME PRINCIPLES AND PRACTICES FOR TEACHING STUDENTS WITH AUTISM

To Learn About a Student With Autism

- Talk with the student to begin to get acquainted if he or she is able to communicate through dialogue.
- Talk with parents or other caregivers to share with you ways they have learned to effectively support their child.
- See if parents/caregivers are willing to share with you brief videos of the learner taking part in community activities or engaging in a variety of activities at home or can share stories about how their child approaches varied settings and activities.
- Ask the student to create for you a list of tips to help teachers work well with students who have learning differences.

To Create a Safe, Inviting Learning Environment for Students With Autism

- Work consistently to create an ethic of inclusion, empathy, respect, and kindness in the classroom. Help students be reflective about their own feelings and how they respond to actions that make them feel inferior or excluded. Support students not only in treating others as they want to be treated, but also in treating others as *those* individuals want to be treated. Model those behaviors, talk about them, teach them, and acknowledge examples of those approaches at work in the classroom.
- View and interact with the student with unconditional positive regard—meaning that the student does not need to do or change anything to earn your acceptance or respect (Gobir, 2021).
- Help students understand autism as a difference and not a disorder, and let them know that while an individual with autism may sometimes speak or act in ways that are unusual, they are not intended to offend anyone.
- Point out strengths and contributions that many individuals with autism have made to the world—past and present. Michelangelo and Mozart were likely autistic. More recent figures who have contributed significantly to the world include actor Sir Anthony Hopkins, scientist Albert Einstein, author and autism activist Temple Grandin, filmmaker Stanley Kubrick, and Pokémon creator Satoshi Tajeri. Throughout the year, help students develop awareness of one another's strengths and talents—including those of students with autism.
- Be a consistent student of each student with autism. Look for strengths and interests (including obsessions). Be an astute observer of what makes the student feel comfortable and what triggers anxiety and subsequent behaviors that can derail learning for that student and for others. Take note of what helps the student regain equanimity after a disruption. Study how the student interacts with others (including you), speech patterns,

eye contact, and other clues that will help you work with the student in productive ways.

- Watch for signs of high anxiety (for example, a student putting his hands over his eyes or ears or engaging in repetitive behaviors) and work with the student to know how and when to use calming objects or strategies (for example, going to a quiet place in the room, putting on headphones to listen to quiet music, using a stress ball).
- Create a variety of inviting seating options—for example, a rocking chair, wiggle seats, wobble cushions, a beanbag, or a carpeted area—that are available to all students.
- Reduce direct light or provide a visor for students who are sensitive to light. Florescent lights can be especially problematic for some students with autism.
- Provide earplugs or headsets when noise in the classroom is distracting or troubling to students.
- Keep spaces in some part of the classroom free of clutter and image overload. Use portable carrels for times when a student needs to work in an area that is visually "busy."
- Support students who need help with organization. For example, a teacher might ask all students to copy down assignments, pack their book bags, and straighten up their seating areas as the class or school day ends. Picture-based communication cards or lists can be useful to depict the steps in a process for students who are concrete in their thinking. Some students with autism will readily follow schedules or procedures presented in words—on paper or digitally.
- Provide classroom routines that are structured and predictable. These include how to turn in homework, how to come to class prepared, how to line up to go to the library, and so on. Visual charts or storyboards showing and describing each step in a routine can be quite helpful for some students with autism.
- Consider using visual daily schedules for students with autism as well as posted daily schedules for the class.

- Consider providing visual charts of appropriate behaviors in varied situations.
- Teach skills like creating to-do lists, deciding which tasks to do first, making timelines for work, setting goals, checking progress toward goals, and so on.
- Teach social and emotional skills as regular aspects of content instruction and integrated into students' learning experiences—for example, how to listen carefully to one another, how to collaborate effectively, how to monitor and regulate one's feelings, how to work through difficulties that arise between peers, how to give feedback that is useful to the progress of others, and so on.
- Make sure the classroom is a place where students know they can make mistakes safely and, like all people do, learn though making mistakes and understanding them.
- Help all students understand the negative impact of bullying. Speak up against it. Enlist the help of students in minimizing it. Help all students develop strategies for dealing productively with it. Teach students with autism to stay away from kids who bully, to stay in view of adults so adults can intervene when bullying occurs, and to find peers to whom they can turn for help. Peer support networks can be powerful tools for safety and inclusion.

To Effectively Teach a Student With Autism

- Most students with autism who are in general education classrooms have the same learning expectations as other students of their grade and age. Therefore, they should work from curriculum that is engaging, understanding-focused, relevant to their lives, and that requires them to think in complex ways. The nature of that curriculum is described at several places in this book (see, for example, Figure 5.3). When a student with autism has challenges (for example, difficulty with organization or communicating with peers), provide scaffolding and support in those areas so that they are not barriers to the student's success.

- Teach to the learner's strengths, interests, and passions. Linking class content to something a student with autism cares deeply about opens the way for the student to relate to and invest in content and skills which might not otherwise capture the learner's attention. It can be especially helpful in the case of some students with autism to lead with the student's interest and build learning from there.

- Differentiate content, process, and/or products based on a student's readiness/ entry points into a lesson, interests, and approaches to learning based on formative assessment insights, as you do with all learners. Using accessible materials and technologies, designing learning experiences, and ensuring means through which a student can demonstrate what he or she has learned is key to a student's sense of safety, security, achievement, and growth.

- Use strategies that give the student a voice in learning activities. For example, Think-Pair-Share or Turn-and-Talk can provide a sheltered or safe opportunity for a variety of students who have communication challenges to express ideas. Instead of asking students who can provide an answer to a math problem or who can point to the error in a sentence, the teacher might say, "Stand up if you think you know the answer."

- Give students choices as often as possible— for example, whether to work alone or with a group, whether to read in the quiet corner or with a classmate at a table, which 4 of 8 math problems he or she will complete, whether to write with a pencil or on the computer, whether to take notes in words or pictures, and so on.

- Use demonstrations, visuals, illustrations, and videos whenever possible to support learning. Many students with autism learn more effectively through visual rather than auditory channels. Visuals are also often effective because they make ideas and directions more concrete than words alone.

- Share your expectations with clear, direct words. Don't count on students with autism reading your facial expressions or body language. The "teacher look" will often fail you with students on the spectrum.

- Make directions as simple and clear as possible. With multistep directions, consider presenting the steps one at a time to students who are confused by multiple parts of a task.

- Explain clearly and explicitly why you are asking students to do a particular assignment or engage in an activity. Help students grasp why something is important and how new information and ideas connect with previous learning and with students' lives. These connections can help students construct a big picture of what they are being asked to learn—to place it in a meaningful context. Timelines, concept maps, graphic organizers, comparison and contrast charts, and similar tools can be quite useful in building understanding.

- Encourage a student to handwrite just a few words or a sentence on paper rather than a longer response, or allow the student to use a computer or even a typewriter rather than pencil/pen and paper. If a student has motor difficulties, being able to write in the least restricting way possible allows the student to focus on content rather than motor skills that feel restrictive.

- Support transitions between settings and assignments. For example, use a visual timer so students can see when time slots are coming to an end; give heads-up reminders just before a transition is about to occur; use consistent transition activities like writing down homework or (for younger students) singing a particular song; ask peers to help out (walking from place to place in the classroom with a partner in the lower grades or asking the student to choose a peer to accompany him or her during class-to-class transitions in the upper grades); or provide a transition aid such as a toy, a stress ball, or a picture.

- Make it possible for the student to take breaks, for example, walking around the classroom, walking up and down the hall, or sitting in a rocking chair or on a sofa in the classroom while other students work at their desks. It's even useful sometimes to ask everyone in the class to walk around the room as they think about an idea, problem solution, or next step in their work.

- When a student on the spectrum breaks a rule or engages in disruptive behavior, avoid the urge to apply "discipline" as a consequence. Impulsive, often dramatic reactions to surprise or change are not choices for students with autism. The triggering event and its resulting impact on a student's emotions wipe out the student's ability to think, remain calm, or otherwise cope with what happened.
- Threat of punishment is likely to heighten the student's anxiety, break trust with you, and eliminate any possibility that you can work with the student to help him or her identify and draw on coping skills. Empathy is a far better tool than harshness of any kind under most circumstances. Reinforcement of desirable or appropriate behaviors is likely to be far more productive than punishment of undesirable or inappropriate ones.
- When someone has been wronged or injured as a result of behavior from a student with autism, consider a restorative justice approach instead of punishment. Restorative justice helps a student learn what went wrong, why it was wrong, who was harmed by it and in what way(s), develop strategies for handling a situation in the future, and collaborate to find ways to rebuild damaged relationships. "Restorative justice not only addresses situations in individualized, differentiated ways, but also places an emphasis on skill building and facilitating a positive, mutuality-based school culture—all indispensable factors when addressing behaviors of students on the spectrum in an inclusive setting" (Boroson, 2020, p. 124).
- When a behavior from a student on the autism spectrum is unusual or questionable but not dangerous, disruptive, or destructive, consider letting it pass. The behavior may just be different, and different is okay. Students with autism have a lot to work on

without adding unnecessary targets. You have a lot to work on, too, without taking on less significant challenges.

- Ensure that the classroom is truly inclusive so that a student with autism has opportunity to be with a variety of classmates in a variety of learning and social configurations. It is often important for students with autism to observe peers in order to learn how they communicate with one another, handle emotions, and go about their work. It is also important for all students in the class to understand and value peers whose lives and experiences are both like and different from their own.

A Few Additional Ideas

- Think about substitute teachers in advance. If a substitute who is already on board in your school has experience in working with students on the autism spectrum, that is ideal. Otherwise, it is important to include one or more substitutes in professional development on supporting the needs of students with autism. When possible, having the same substitute work with your class whenever you are absent is quite helpful.
- Bring colleagues on board. Talk with any teachers or support personnel in the school who will also work with your student who has autism. Proactively discussing a student's strengths and needs, triggers, preferences for learning, routines, and so on can make both teaching and learning smoother for everyone.
- Plan for unexpected disruptions in the classroom. Despite your best intentions, it is impossible to completely avoid the unexpected. Plan for how you will handle "emergencies" in the classroom to minimize fear and resulting outbursts from a child who reacts intensely to what feels like a crisis to that learner. You might carry a card in your pocket every day that reassures the student and explains that you will be back to talk with him or her as soon as possible. You may send another student to get a teacher next door or a custodian, counselor, nurse,

or office assistant who can help. Planning ahead can minimize the likelihood of escalating disruptions that inevitably occur in all classrooms.

- Think about and plan for events such as fire drills, lockdown drills, school evacuations, early dismissals, and so on. It is wise to proactively plan with the student for these occurrences to reduce the element of surprise or shock as much as possible—including use of visual, step-by-step "schedules" for these events. It may also be necessary to plan for additional support to work with you, or with the student in an alternative location, during events such as these. Remember that students who have milder degrees of autism are unlikely to exhibit extreme reactions to potentially stressful events.

- Once calm is restored after a disruption or upsetting event, talk with the student about what went well and what both you and the student might do differently if a similar, unexpected event happens again. Taking the opportunity to teach strategies that may help a student feel more control is helpful for the student and others who may be part of such events in the future as well. The teaching will need to be clear, specific to the situation, and not emotionally charged—and will often require multiple revisitations for the student to understand what you're saying and how to translate that into action.

- Understand that parents of some students with autism (as parents of any student with exceptional needs) may (or may not) feel a sense of grief and loss, marginalization and difference, unworthiness, guilt, self-doubt, frustration, resentment, hopelessness—and exhaustion! Meet them as they are, where they are, and work collaboratively with them to enhance their child's growth and development.

- Learn as much as you can about autism. Talk with parents, read, use resources of organizations that support people with autism, and, when you realize YOU need support to be successful in teaching a student with autism, call on the experts in your school, including special education teachers, counselors, teachers who have experience in working with students on the spectrum, and colleagues who have a child with autism.

We live in a world that is learning to be more inclusive of all its citizens—a world that has more learning yet to do. Teachers in inclusive classrooms have proven themselves willing to learn and would no doubt volunteer that they still have much learning to do. There is something both natural and important, however, in classrooms where teachers help young learners experience and understand that diversity is the way the world is. We have differences in culture, religion, hair color, styles of dressing, language, and physical and emotional challenges. The list is long. Still, we share the same core needs as human beings—to be understood, to be accepted, to learn, to have friends, to contribute, to make our way in life. Understanding our shared humanity makes us less afraid and suspicious of differences, more accepting of one another. That makes us wiser and the world a better place. We are all part of that fabric of reality, including students with autism. There is much to learn from one another.

NOTE

The following sources were consulted for this chapter. Full citations appear in the References section. Applied Behavior Analysis, n.d.; Boroson, 2020; Bryant et al., 2020; Callahan, 2020; Centers for Disease Control and Prevention, 2020a, 2020b; Chaltain, 2016; Gobir, 2021; Karten, 2017; Kluth, n.d.; National Autistic Society UK, n.d.; National Education Association, 2006; Scholastic, n.d.; Smith et al., 2020; Star Autism Support, n.d.; Waterford Foundation, 2019b.

CHAPTER 12

Teaching Students With ADHD

Sometimes I've got too many thoughts at once. It's like there's a four-way intersection in my brain where everyone's trying to go at the same time.

—A. J. Finn, *The Woman in the Window*

INTRODUCTION

If you're a teacher, you know these kids: The one who stares out the window, substituting the arc of a bird in flight for her math lesson. The one who wouldn't be able to keep his rear end in the chair if you used Krazy Glue. The one who answers the question, "What body of water played a major role in the development of the Ancient Egyptian civilization?" with "Mrs. M, do you dye your hair?" (Segal & Smith, 2020)

Attention-deficit/hyperactivity disorder, or ADHD, is a neurodevelopmental disorder and is a chronic condition that usually becomes apparent in childhood and affects a person throughout life. While symptoms vary in degree and kind among individuals affected by ADHD, characteristics of ADHD usually involve difficulties staying focused, keeping organized, planning, managing time, and controlling impulses. These traits can make it difficult for a student to fit in in the classroom, achieve, and make friends. They can also make teaching frustrating.

The teacher can see the students have the capacity to learn what they need to learn, but their disorganization, lack of focus, and restlessness often disrupt students who are trying to learn. At that point, it is helpful to recall Ross Greene's (2014b) reminder that when adults, teachers included, get frustrated with a child whose behaviors are challenging, they often say, "He *could* do the work if he just *would*." In reality, Greene says, "The student *would* do the work if he or she just *could*." Doing better is largely out of the young person's control. Students with ADHD do not want to be out of step with expectations and with peers. They want to succeed and have friends, as all young people do. Without targeted support, they simply find it almost impossible to do what school asks of them and to experience the kinds of satisfaction from learning and establishing friendships that many students take for granted.

Without effective intervention during their school years, students with ADHD are more likely to make lower grades, turn in fewer assignments on time, have higher rates of absence, and develop lower self-esteem. As they grow older, they may be at risk for lower educational outcomes, higher rates of unemployment, higher rates of accidents (including traffic accidents), higher levels of drug abuse, lower levels of social functioning, and higher rates of family problems than the general population. Effective treatment improves long-term outcomes.

ADHD is one of the most common learning disorders. Approximately 10.8% of all K–12 students in the United States will be diagnosed with it at some point in their lives (Centers for Disease Control and Prevention, 2020b). The incidence of ADHD is roughly the same in boys and girls, but teachers, on the whole, are far more likely to refer boys than girls for identification. As a result, while about 14% of boys in K–12 are identified as having ADHD, only about 6.9% of girls are identified. Part of that disparity may be a result of gender bias that causes teachers to react more strongly or negatively to "acting out" behaviors in boys than in girls.

On the other hand, the acting-out behaviors of girls with ADHD are often more subtle than those of boys. More girls have only the inattentive symptoms of ADHD and can be viewed as just dreamy or ditzy. If they have the hyperactive symptoms, girls are more likely to be seen as pushy, too talkative, or overemotional. Impulsive girls may have trouble being socially appropriate and struggle to make and keep friends. Another reason that girls are diagnosed and labeled as having ADHD is that girls often knock themselves out to compensate for their weaknesses and to hide their embarrassment about falling behind in work, losing things, feeling different, or being socially awkward.

Because students with ADHD can achieve at the same levels as students without ADHD, some experts suggest thinking of it as a condition rather than a disability. Among many noted individuals who have or had ADHD are Simone Biles, U.S. gymnastics champion; Stevie Wonder, musician; Howie Mandel, actor; Emma Watson, *Harry Potter* star; Whoopi Goldberg, comedienne and actress; David Neelman, founder of Jet Blue Airways; Robin Williams, actor; Michael Phelps, U.S. Olympic swimming gold medalist; Adam Levine, front man for Maroon 5; Jeffrey Siegel, classical pianist; and will.i.am, rapper, singer, and songwriter.

Characteristics often associated with ADHD can be classified in two categories: inattentive behaviors and hyperactive/impulsive behaviors.

Inattentive behaviors include (but are not limited to) the following:

- Short attention span
- Daydreaming
- Making careless mistakes in schoolwork, overlooking details
- Being easily distracted or sidetracked
- Having difficulty following written or spoken directions
- Concentration issues (for example, listening to the teacher while taking notes)
- Seeming inattentive when spoken to directly
- Forgetfulness
- Having trouble with organizing time, tasks, or belongings
- Poor study skills for age group
- Failing to finish schoolwork or chores at home or in the classroom

- Avoiding tasks that require sustained mental effort, including doing homework and class assignments
- Losing things
- Losing homework assignments, completed homework, books, jackets, backpacks, sports equipment

Hyperactive behaviors include (but are not limited to) the following:

- Fidgeting or squirming
- Having difficulty staying in his/her seat
- Running and climbing when and where it is inappropriate
- Having difficulty playing or working quietly
- Inability to stay on task, shifting from one task to another without bringing any to completion
- Being extremely impatient, not being able to wait for his/her turn
- Seeming to always be "on the go"
- Talking excessively

Impulsive behaviors include (but are not limited to) the following:

- Interrupting or intruding on others' conversations, activities, or possessions
- Having difficulty waiting for his/her turn in school or in games
- Blurting out answers instead of waiting to be called on
- Taking frequent risks without thinking before acting

Some students have combined-type ADHD in which both impulsive and inattentive behaviors are evident. In fact, combined-type ADHD is the most common type of ADHD.

When you consider that school is all about sitting, listening, following directions, remembering what you hear, being quiet for long stretches, and getting along with others, the challenge for students with ADHD is evident. Their teachers can feel it as well. Below are some guides for teachers that are helpful in working with students who have ADHD. The goal is not to use all these strategies, of course, but to understand them as a repertoire from which you can consider options that seem likely to benefit a given learner at a particular time, in a specific context.

SOME PRINCIPLES AND PRACTICES FOR TEACHING STUDENTS WITH ADHD

To Create a Safe, Inviting Learning Environment for Students with ADHD

- Create a classroom culture of inclusion with respect, empathy, and appreciation of human differences at the core of how everyone in the classroom functions.
- See the student with unconditional positive regard—that is, the student does not have to do or change anything to have your approval or respect (Gobir, 2021).
- Avoid seeing the student with ADHD as "a problem" or as deficient. Instead, look for the student's strengths, interests, and positive traits. Keep those in mind as you plan for the student and build on them consistently.
- Help all your students understand the challenges of ADHD but also its positives.
- Keep books in your classroom library in which main characters have ADHD and biographies or articles about people with ADHD who persisted in learning and developing their strengths and talents, and who ultimately made a positive difference in their communities or the world at large. This helps normalize ADHD.
- Establish and maintain trust with the student so he or she knows you are on their side, that you want to help them grow, and that you enjoy their company.
- Emphasize the positive in your communications with all students. For example, talk with them about what you want them to do rather than what you do not want them to do in terms of behaviors, establishing classroom rules or norms, and working together.
- Offer positive feedback regularly to students with ADHD so they trust you and know that you have their best interests in mind.

Acknowledge their positive behavior and academic progress far more often than you correct or point out problems.

- Be sensitive to the impact of ADHD on emotions, such as self-esteem issues or difficulty regulating feelings.
- Observe the student carefully to try to understand what helps and what supports or detracts from learning. Ask the student what is helpful in paying attention, reducing movement, organizing work, and so on.
- Establish clear routines and stick to them as fully as possible.
- Create an auditory signal that indicates the start of a lesson (e.g., a clicker, chime, specific piece of music). Use additional cues to show how much time remains in a lesson.
- Seat the student with ADHD away from windows, doors, pencil sharpeners, bookshelves, and talkative peers to reduce distractions.
- Consider whether the student would work more effectively if seated near your desk.
- Seat the student with ADHD in a row of seats that support focusing on the teacher, rather than having students seated around tables or facing one another in other arrangements.
- Create a quiet area that is free of distractions where a student can sit quietly, take a test, study quietly, or complete a class assignment. Make cardboard carrels available for any student who wants or needs a quiet, visually spare space to work.
- Minimize clutter.
- Avoid sensory overload, information overload, and work overload.
- Make eye contact when you are talking with a student who has ADHD.
- Provide alerts before transitions and changes in routines and for return to routines after a break (for example, flicking the lights or using a hand signal that the students mirror as they see you use it).
- Stay in touch with parents or caregivers and encourage them to work with you to make the year successful for their learner. Learn strategies and tools they use at home to successfully to support their child. Ask

also about approaches they have learned to avoid. Establish periodic check-in times to update one another and to plan together for their child's continued growth. If the child is on medication for ADHD, ask parents to share with you how the medicine generally affects the learner and learning in both positive and potentially problematic ways. Remember that parents or caregivers who have children with ADHD may themselves be tired or frustrated. Hear their concerns, learn from them, and be a trustworthy touchstone for them when you can.

To Help the Student Develop Organizational Skills

- Consider giving a student with ADHD a checklist of steps to take in completing an activity or product.
- Have the student keep a notebook with a separate, color-coded section for each subject. Help the student check to be sure everything that goes into the notebook is put in the correct section. Color-code materials for each subject.
- Provide a three-pocket notebook insert for homework assignments, completed homework, and mail to parents (permission slips, information about school events, etc.).
- Make sure the student has a system, such as a daily planner, for writing down assignments and important dates and uses it.
- Allow time for the student to organize materials and assignments for home.
- Provide the student with a list or chart that shows steps in preparing to leave school with whatever the student needs to complete work at home.
- Talk with the student periodically about strategies for self-regulation and self-management. Work with the student to set goals, monitor progress, and develop new skills and strategies to support achieving the goals.
- Work with the student to understand and apply the habits of mind and work that

lead to successful learning—and to success beyond the classroom as well.

To Provide a Curriculum That Supports and Inspires Success

- Most students with ADHD who are in general education classrooms have the same learning expectations as other students of their grade and age. Therefore, they should work from curriculum that is engaging, understanding-focused, relevant to their lives, and that requires them to think in complex ways. The nature of that curriculum is described at several places in this book, including in Figure 5.3 on pages 53–54. When a student with ADHD has challenges (for example, difficulty with organization, focus, sitting still), provide scaffolding and support in those areas so they are not barriers to the student's success.
- Teach up to the student. Maintain the goal of having the student do meaningful work, engage in complex thinking, and make connections between the content and his or her life and experiences. Because ADHD does not typically suggest cognitive impairment, you should expect the student to master core content and competencies with support to work through or around the symptoms of ADHD.
- Be clear about the knowledge, understanding, and skills that are most important for a student with ADHD to focus on at a given time. Helping a student maintain that focus is critical to his or her making meaning of the content, navigating an assignment without getting lost in details, and developing intellectually.
- Students with ADHD may be very good at memorizing information and at providing right answers in the short term. At the same time, they may lack understanding of what they are studying and within a few days "lose" what they "knew" a few days earlier. While a lack of understanding content limits the learning of all students, lacking understanding is certainly a common inhibitor of durable and useful

learning for students with ADHD. It is important to focus students with ADHD on understanding, to check for understanding often, and to ask the students to apply what they are regularly learning both to develop and reinforce understanding.

- Teach to the learner's strength and interests. Linking class content to something a student with ADHD cares about opens the way for the student to relate to and invest in content and skills that might not otherwise capture the learner's attention.

To Teach Responsively to a Student With ADHD

- Differentiate content, process, and/or products based on a student's readiness/ entry points into a lesson, interests, and approaches to learning as often as possible. Using accessible materials and technologies, designing learning experiences, and ensuring that means through which a student can demonstrate what he or she has learned is key to a student's sense of safety, security, achievement, and growth.
- Differentiate directions, materials, timelines, steps in a process, and so on to be a fit for a student's readiness levels, interests, approaches to learning, and to be responsive to specific issues related to ADHD in order to maximize the student's learning.
- Communicate expectations clearly through both oral and written reminders, including rubrics for long-term work.
- As you begin a lesson, tell students what they are going to learn, what your expectations are, and exactly what materials they will need.
- List the activities or steps in the lesson on a wall, board, or screen.
- Have students work with the most difficult material early in the class period or early in the day.
- Walk by the student often as he or she is working and as you are talking with the class. Use the opportunity to notice and comment on things the student is doing

well and to supportively redirect the student when that seems important to do.

- Use paired learning or peer tutoring, linking the student with ADHD to a willing and mature classmate to provide extra support for learning. These pairings can also aid students with ADHD in developing or refining social skills.
- Use charts, pictures, color coding, drawings, and so on to support visual learning.
- Use colored highlighters to mark the most important sections of texts, directions, rubrics.
- Create outlines or graphic organizers for note-taking that help the student arrange information to support understanding as you deliver it.
- Use worksheets and tests with fewer items or highlight the parts of the work that are most important for a student to complete.
- Provide wait time for the student to process questions or ideas and to tap into his/her working memory.
- Vary the pace of instruction and include different kinds of activities. Many students with ADHD do well with competitive games or other activities that are rapid and intense.
- Provide extra time for a student to complete an assignment that is taxing.
- Experience-based learning, in which students develop their own products or performance assessments, design and perform experiments, and go on field trips, works well for most students with ADHD.
- Incorporate movement into learning that involves the whole class, for example, gallery walks, forming opinion lines where students arrange themselves on a line to demonstrate an opinion or preference, turn-and-talk and think-pair-share while standing, "stand if you . . ." (know the answer to this question, have ever helped a neighbor or relative or friend who needed help, can say the names of the planets in our solar system . . .) or "stand up/sit down" (stand up if you have ever traveled by bus, train, or car; sit down if you have ever traveled by train; stand up if you have ever

lost something important; sit down if you found it . . .).

- Plan for differentiated, active engagement in all subjects for students with ADHD and others who benefit from "doing" (for example, in social studies, the student has sticky notes with the names of continents and moves around the room to place the continents in locations that simulate a world map; in science, a teacher places his students in human electron configuration to teach the Pauli exclusion principle; in language arts, the student uses the NCTE comic creator or similar tool to create a dialogue from a scene in a book the class is reading; using manipulatives or models in math (Karten, 2017).
- Allow the student frequent breaks.
- Allow the student to stand and/or to sit on a bouncy ball or wiggle chair while working.
- Allow a student to walk in designated areas of the room during work time, to stand at his/ her desk to work, and to stand and stretch.
- Use hands-on materials to teach concepts, information, and skills.
- Allow the student to use a stress ball, squeeze a rubber ball, or tap something that does not make noise as an outlet for stress.
- Invite a student with ADHD to take on jobs in the classroom that need to be done and that require movement (for example, passing out materials, collecting materials, erasing boards, running errands to the office).
- Use a timer to signal a student when it is time for a break. (For example, a student must listen to a lecture for 5 minutes and write down three important facts or ideas from the lecture, then the student can take a 2-minute break.) The timer can also indicate when a break is over. Visual timers that show the passage of time without using numbers are available for classroom use and via app for individual devices. As a student improves with paying attention, increase the time necessary to attend before a break.
- Have an unobtrusive, pre-established cue set up with the student who has ADHD, such

as a touch on the shoulder, a hand signal, or placing a sticky note on the student's desk, as a reminder to stay on task.

- Connect content with a student's interests and use the connection to activate and sustain learning. Use stories, games, questions, YouTube videos, music, and so forth to pique student interest.
- Provide choices as often as possible (for example, a book to read, which assignment to work with first, how to practice a skill, how to express learning).
- When students have free-choice reading time, give them the option to read comic books, graphic novels, and books that are of high interest to them.
- As with any student, avoid asking a student with ADHD to perform a task or answer a question publicly that is likely to be too difficult. It is helpful for some students with ADHD for you to give the student a private heads-up that you will be asking him or her a question in about 10 minutes. Share the questions with the student. The heads-up enables the student to organize his or her thinking rather than being startled by cold-calling.
- Teach study skills regularly and explicitly to align with work students are doing (not out of context or as a separate subject).
- Teach social skills such as how to collaborate with peers, how to disagree with someone politely/empathetically, and how to express appreciation.
- When you give a class assignment, ask a student to repeat the directions or post the directions on the board or online, or ask the class to read the directions in unison.
- Be specific about what students will need to take home to complete an assignment.
- Make sure the length of time required for a homework assignment does not exceed the student's ability to attend to a task.
- As you end a lesson or class period, summarize key points.
- Check in with the student often during long-term assignments to monitor progress and student understanding of goals for the

work and quality of work. Partner with the student to set goals for next steps in his/her work.

- Use appropriate apps to address a student's need for practice with various skills.
- Encourage students to use technology to learn and express learning, including apps (such as Explain Everything, Nearpod, Soundtrap, Flipgrid, and Seesaw) that support students in using varied modes of expressing learning and collaborating with peers.
- Accept late work, within limits, and allow re-dos of assignments that are not completed adequately as an encouragement for a student to persist in achieving difficult goals.

To Use Assessment to Improve Teaching and Learning

- Continue to monitor the student for awareness and understanding of unit KUDs (learning targets).
- Be sure all assessments are tightly aligned with unit and/or lesson KUDs.
- Use frequent formative assessment (both pre-assessment and ongoing assessment) to understand where the learner is in a learning trajectory—to understand his/her status with unit and lesson KUDs.
- Avoid long tests and reduce the number of timed tests.
- Emphasize clear, targeted, actionable feedback rather than grades. (It is likely to be unhelpful for most students to grade formative assessments, homework, and other practice.)
- Know that for any student, it is acceptable to differentiate any aspect of an assessment (time, using a computer rather than a pencil or pen, providing an answer orally rather than in writing, drawing, labeling a diagram instead of writing a paragraph, etc.) except the learning targets (the knowledge, understanding, and skills the students should all demonstrate on the assessment). If a student has an Individualized Education Plan (IEP), that document can specify different learning targets as well.

- Assess students with ADHD in ways they do best (for example, orally, fill-in the-blank, creating a video or animation). A good assessment maximizes the opportunity for a student to show as much as possible of what he/she has learned.
- Be sure the student understands the learning targets he or she must address regardless of the format of the work.
- Allow the student to dictate responses to a peer, parent/caregiver, aide, volunteer, and so on rather than writing them.
- Divide long-term projects into segments with completion goals, check-in dates, and due dates for each segment.
- Help the student reflect on his work and feedback on that work to help him/her develop agency as a learner.
- Use grading protocols that report achievement/performance, working processes/habits of mind and work, and progress/growth separately (not averaged). It is important for students with ADHD and their parents or caregivers to understand the student's status in all three areas and to understand how the second and third areas contribute to growth in the first area.

To Work Positively with Disruptive or Potentially Disruptive Behavior

- Maintain a positive attitude toward the student and understand the challenges he/she faces. A combination of warmth, humor, and firmness is often effective in working with students who have ADHD.
- Let the student know you are looking for positive behavior—and be sure to follow through in noticing it.
- To be proactive in reducing or eliminating behavior that might disrupt the work of other students, establish a couple of warning signals with the student who has ADHD (for example, a hand signal, an unobtrusive tap on the shoulder, or a note on the student's desk).
- Favor positive reinforcement rather than punishment. Especially do not take away things like recess, breaks, free time, and choice.

- Ignore mildly inappropriate behavior if it is unintentional, is not distracting other students, or is not disrupting the lesson. Pick your battles.
- When a behavior absolutely requires some sort of punitive action, ensure that you use the interaction you have with the student as a teaching/learning opportunity. If punitive action is necessary, make sure the consequence for the student with ADHD is relevant to the behavior infraction (for example, repairing or replacing an object that broke when the student shoved a classmate and repairing the relationship that was damaged).
- If it is necessary to discuss a student's behavior with that student, do so privately—away from view of other students or teachers.

Students with ADHD seem always to be out of sync with the rhythms of the classroom, the easy conversation of peers, and the behavioral norms that win approval. Their challenges in learning can be quite significant. These same students, however, develop resilience, coping skills, and the ability to think outside the box to solve problems. Their unusual way of experiencing the world often feeds their creativity. Their sense of humor is generally quite healthy. Their cognitive capacity is not diminished by their symptoms although the symptoms can sometimes make it challenging to harness that potential. In the company of teachers who understand them, who create a classroom environment that is respectful and appreciative of human differences, and who can help a student with ADHD circumvent or at least lessen their challenges, they will grow and succeed. In turn, they help teachers who invest in their growth to develop attitudes and instructional approaches that benefit all learners. It is a worthy partnership.

NOTE

The following sources were consulted for this chapter. Full citations appear in the References section. Bryant et al., 2020; Centers for Disease Control and Prevention, 2019; Education & Behavior, n.d.; Gobir, 2021; Johns Hopkins Medicine, n.d.; Karten, 2017; Low, 2020; Miller, n.d.; Parrish, 2018; Scholastic, n.d.; Segal & Smith, 2020; Shaw et al., 2012; Smith et al., 2020; Thorne et al., n.d.; Waterford Foundation, 2019a.

CHAPTER 13

Teaching Students With Specific Learning Disorder

Dyslexia is not a pigeonhole to say you can't do anything. It is an opportunity and a possibility to learn differently. You have magical brains, they just process differently. Don't feel like you should be held back by it.

—Her Royal Highness Princess Beatrice Elizabeth Mary of York

INTRODUCTION

If we lived before the advent of books, formal schooling, or technology, the issue of a reading disability would not exist. Now, however, a young person who does not learn to read readily and confidently is in jeopardy. Reading is at the core of nearly all school-based learning. A reading deficit can impact learning in subjects such as math, social studies, science, and others. A reading deficit that prevails into adulthood can narrow an individual's career opportunities and economic welfare.

There are many reasons a student may struggle to learn to read, including speaking a primary language that is different from the language of the classroom, brain injury, trauma, emotional disorder, attention deficit disorder, and so on. This chapter focuses on students who have diagnosed reading difficulties involving phonological awareness, word recognition, spelling, and comprehension.

Over time, the indicator used to specify that set of reading challenges has shifted in some quarters from "dyslexia" to "specific learning disability." While the two terms overlap and the change in language is somewhat controversial, the two are not synonyms. One way of framing the difference between the two terms is to think of a reading disability as part of the larger and newer category known as "specific learning disability," whereas dyslexia is a more specialized term for a particular type of specific learning disability in reading. More to the point, while the medical field continues to use the term "dyslexia," public

schools generally do not. The term "dyslexia" is no longer a term used in federal education law.

The Individuals with Disabilities Education Act (IDEA) defines specific learning disability as a disorder in one or more of the basic processes involved in understanding or in using language, spoken or written. Thus, in public education, the term "learning disability" or "specific learning disability" is most often used to identify and serve students with particular *reading* difficulties.

In other contexts, "Specified Learning Disability" is a broader category that may manifest itself in a student's imperfect ability to listen, think, speak, read, write, spell, or do mathematical calculations. In those contexts, "dyslexia" is one category of Specific Learning Disability (SLD) and is the most common SLD category.

Students with SLD may

- struggle with reading,
- have trouble sounding out words,
- find it difficult to recognize common words in text,
- find it difficult to memorize sight words,
- avoid reading aloud,
- have poor spelling and grammar,
- have memory deficits,
- have difficulty understanding what he/she has just read,
- confuse the order of letters in a word,
- find it difficult to listen,
- have difficulty rhyming,

- find it difficult to follow a set of directions, and
- struggle to organize thoughts while speaking.

Some, but not all, students who have SLD also have difficulty with writing, including

- illegible handwriting,
- slow and labored writing,
- mixing print and cursive letters,
- spacing letters and words oddly,
- poor spelling and grammar,
- difficulty gripping a pencil,
- incorrect punctuation,
- run-on sentences and lack of paragraph breaks, and
- trouble organizing information and ideas when writing.

In other words, students with SLD experience reading as a slow, labored, and error-prone activity while many of their peers without SLD seem to read and write almost automatically. The primary goal of reading instruction for children with SLD is to help them acquire the knowledge and skills they need to understand printed material and/or write at a level consistent with their verbal ability or aural comprehension skills.

SLD is common, with estimates as high as 20% of children having the reading difficulty. That means it is likely that most general education teachers will have at least one student with SLD in their classroom at a given time. SLD is chronic. The severity of symptoms varies along a continuum for students with SLD and students will master important skills on varied timelines. People do not "outgrow" SLD. Having SLD can erode a learner's sense of self-confidence and agency. Those feelings and their consequences can endure for a very long time.

SLD is not caused by laziness, lack of motivation, poor vision, or lack of ability. In fact, SLD is often associated with students who have average or above average intelligence. Because students with SLD are fully capable of achieving on a par with their peers, the "D" in SLD is often used to represent the word "disorder" rather than "disability." Some schools continue to use disability, while a growing number use disorder. In general, this book uses disorder.

Among noted individuals who have or had SLD are: Charles Schwab, Steven Spielberg, Whoopi Goldberg, Richard Branson, Michael Phelps, Cher, Jay Leno, John Lennon, Jamie Oliver, Nicola Tesla, Salma Hayek, Anthony Hopkins, Steve Jobs, Bill Gates, Tommy Hilfiger, Anderson Cooper, Muhammad Ali, Greg Louganis, and Ingrvar Kamprad (the founder of Ikea). Based on biographies and historical accounts, it appears likely that George Washington, Woodrow Wilson, Leonardo da Vinci, Louis Pasteur, Albert Einstein, and Alexander Graham Bell are among a long list of other major contributors to society who also had SLD. It is not uncommon for students with SLD to have ADHD as well. However, while the two exceptionalities appear with some frequency in the same individual, they call for very different treatments and supports.

Students with SLD do not pick up the skills of reading and writing casually or with little instruction. They need learning opportunities that are personalized, organized, focused, consistent, and persistent in an environment of encouragement, patience, and with an emphasis on growth so that each student can systematically build new skills on existing skills.

A classroom teacher is not a specialist in working with students who have SLD and will probably need to partner with a special educator or reading specialist for guidance in the sorts of reading instruction and support a student needs in order to learn most effectively. Nonetheless, a classroom teacher does have the opportunity to positively change the life of a student by taking the time to understand what SLD is and to provide classroom supports that enable the learner to access information that he or she is capable of learning through alternate formats. Following are some guides for successfully teaching students with specific learning disorder. This group of students is not homogeneous, of course, so the goal is not to try to use all the strategies or the same strategies with all students who have SLD. Rather, use the ideas as a repertoire from which you select approaches based on the needs of a particular student, in a particular context, at a particular time.

SOME PRINCIPLES AND PRACTICES FOR TEACHING STUDENTS WITH SPECIFIC LEARNING DISORDER

To Create a Safe, Inviting Learning Environment for Students With SLD

- View each of your students with unconditional positive regard—that means you are fully accepting of each student and that the student does not need to do or change anything to earn your respect and partnership (Gobir, 2021).
- See the whole child. Get to know each student, looking particularly for strengths and interests around which you can build instruction. Many students with SLD have strong problem-solving skills, including creative ways of learning, coping, and expressing ideas. Be sure they are conscious of those strengths and continue to develop them.
- Monitor your thinking about the student to be sure you are not engaging in deficit thinking.
- Communicate to the student your belief in his/her capacity to succeed and your partnership in that success.
- Understand that SLD does not go away. Students can't "fix it," and neither can you. Be careful not to spend so much time trying to "fix" what's "broken" that you end up "breaking" what's "fixed." Ensure that the student spends most of their time working with ideas, skills, and talents that are energizing and promising rather than frustrating and discouraging.
- Create a classroom environment of inclusion and respect for individuals and the differences that inevitably exist among them. Help students understand that every student differs in significant ways from other students and that those differences are enriching in a classroom because they help us think about people and the work we do more broadly.
- Tell students about role models like Richard Branson, Steven Spielberg, Nobel Prize–winning scientist Carol Greider, and others listed in the introduction to this chapter who have or had dyslexia or SLD. Let them know that there is real benefit in being a different thinker and that our society benefits in countless ways from contributions from people with SLD.
- Develop and maintain reliable schedules—and give students a heads-up when those schedules or routines must change so they are prepared for the differences.
- Acknowledge a student's achievements, including small ones in relation to reading and writing, but also achievements in their talents and areas of interest. Help the student recognize their progress and let the student know you are watching and recognizing his/her growth in a full range of pursuits.
- Help the student understand that mistakes are the way we learn. Make the classroom safe for making mistakes. Share your own mistakes with students and show them how you learned from a mistake or how you created a new opportunity from a mistake.
- Partner with parents or caregivers to learn from them and to help them understand how you are supporting their child's growth not only in reading but also academically, socially, and emotionally. Discuss their aspirations for their child and ask them to share with you strategies that work at home and that have been successful in other classes to help their child develop as a reader and as a person. Check in with them often to coordinate home and school. Be sure to let parents or caregivers know about successes in multiple aspects of their child's life at school.

To Teach Responsively to Students With SLD

- Students with SLD who are included in general education classrooms have the intellectual capacity to use the same curriculum as their classmates. Therefore, they should work from curriculum that is engaging, understanding-focused, relevant to their lives, and that requires them to think in complex ways. The nature of that curriculum is described at several places in this book. See, for example, Figure 5.3. When a student with SLD has processing difficulties related to his or her reading disorder, provide scaffolding and support in those areas so that they are not barriers to the student's success.

- Teach up to the student. Establish, share, and maintain expectations that the student with SLD will learn important content, explore significant ideas, think in complex ways, solve problems or address issues that are meaningful in a content area and in the world, and create products or performances that demonstrate academic and intellectual growth even if they need to access information in ways other than reading text.

- In all aspects of learning, emphasize ideas and the power of those ideas over mechanics. Clearly, a student with SLD needs ample support and instruction in areas impacted by the disorder, but a steady diet of practice, worksheets, and skills out of context does little to commend learning. Tap into student curiosity, interests, talents, aspirations, and friendships to create learning opportunities that engage the learner's mind. Integrate into those assignments important skills of reading and writing. Then support the students in focusing first during those assignments on the ideas involved, *then* on editing the work that is meaningful to the learner.

- Talk with a special educator or reading specialist who can help you understand the student's strengths as well as aspects of reading such as phonemic awareness, reading fluency, and comprehension that will need your careful attention and how best to teach the student in those areas.

- Talk with the student often to learn about tools, materials, learning options, and teaching alternatives that make learning more accessible for him or her. Give the student a voice in setting goals, designing work, and monitoring progress. This helps the learner build agency and self-determination, which are important in student confidence and motivation to learn. Ultimately, help the student become a self-

advocate for effective support in addressing his or her learning needs.

- Build highways and exit ramps into all your teaching plans to ensure there is time for individual and small-group work as well as whole class work.

- Reduce stress in the classroom whenever possible, including shorter or fewer assignments, more time to work on assignments, more time to process ideas, and additional practice options for students with SLD.

- Use a systematic process to organize lessons to make assignments predictable and accessible to students with SLD (and many other students as well)—for example, set up the lesson with an advance organizer or some other approach that previews the lesson, demonstrate a skill that the lesson is designed to develop, provide guided practice, offer corrective feedback, ensure time for independent practice and/or small group practice, monitor practice, review student progress, and then plan next steps accordingly.

- Work consistently with the learner to strengthen memory and metacognition. Both are required for effective reading.

- Use mnemonic devices to assist students with SLD learn, retain, and generalize concepts.

- Offer help without doing the work for the student.

- Use multi sensory modes of presentation so students can see, hear, move, and so on to support learning. Pictures, picture books, videos, demonstrations, audio recordings, role-plays, and hands-on learning are a few options that can promote learning for students with SLD and many others as well.

- Model and demonstrate processes and skills.

- Provide clear, concise directions.

- Provide graphic organizers that help a student grasp the flow of ideas in a lesson or topic, understand points at which note-taking is important, and review key points over time.

- Provide step-by-step directions and chunk the work to enable students to complete multi-step directions one part at a time when a multi-part assignment feels overwhelming.

- Help students learn to chunk assignments themselves.
- Balance your oral presentations with visual information and participatory activities. Also, use large-group and small-group, and individual activities as well as assigning groups based on student readiness, interest, and approaches to learning.
- Simplify written directions for students with SLD—for example, using more accessible vocabulary, making sentences shorter, using bullets to indicate separate steps in a process or parts of a direction set, using more white space on the page or larger fonts.
- Highlight the most important elements in a set of directions for a student to read first and to return to throughout the assignment.
- Make directions available on video or audio recordings so students can hear them more than once—and online so they can review directions at home.
- Give students self-monitoring checklists and guiding questions for reading comprehension.
- Record lectures, key explanations, and demonstrations (audio and/or video) so students can listen to them again and use them for review.
- Use the "Contemporary Lecture" format if you lecture, clarifying goals for the lecture (KUDs), ensuring that the lecture aligns with those KUDs, providing organizers or lecture outlines that help a student grasp the flow of ideas in a lesson or topic and understand points at which note-taking is important, stopping about every 7–10 minutes to engage students in brief, paired conversations about the lecture content (summaries, projections about what will come next, taking on a pro or con stance with evidence, and so on), and making time for whole-class conversation around key points in the lecture.
- Provide a copy of the teacher's lecture notes for students who have difficulty following a lecture or taking notes on it.

- Write key vocabulary, dates, and so forth on a SMART board or chalkboard as a lesson or lecture progresses.
- Use mnemonic devices to help students remember key vocabulary, important names, or steps in a process.
- Review previous learning or lessons at the start of a new day or new lesson to help students connect new information with prior knowledge.
- Use flexible time options so that students with SLD (and other students) can have extra time, when needed, to complete assignments thoroughly and thoughtfully before turning them in. Also provide extra time for students to process ideas and information during class.
- Explore assistive technologies that can support skills like reading and writing that are challenging for students with SLD. Speech-to-text technology allows students to "talk" their ideas onto a page rather than writing them. There are many examples of such technologies for reading from a desktop or laptop computer (for example, Natural Reader, TalkButton, Browsealoud, and ReadSpeaker) or from a tablet or phone (for example, Voice Dream Reader, KNFB Reader, Captura Talk, and Read & Write). The Livescribe smart pen allows students with SLD to write notes on paper while it also records the speaker. In addition, it can also transfer written notes to the computer. Read-aloud technology enables students to hear text read aloud rather than reading it themselves. This technology enables students to read books on or beyond grade level, hear correct pronunciation of vocabulary, pause a reading to take notes, and improve comprehension. Read-aloud technology enables students to read an assignment more than one time, which is important for reading development. Both speech-to-text and read-aloud technologies also give students a sense of agency as learners. Closed captioning can also be an important support for students with SLD and is now available in a growing number of books and videos. Making these technologies

available to all students can both benefit the learning of a wide range of students and normalize the use of varied pathways to learning. Books on Tape are generally available to students with SLD and can also be a great boon to learning. Learning Ally and Bookshare also provide recorded books. Goodreads' Young Adult fiction list and ALA/YALSA's Amazing Audiobooks lists provide a wide range of books designed for middle and high school readers that are available on audio.

- Use apps and tools that support students in reading and writing—for example, spellcheck, which is commonly available on varied devices. No Red Ink helps with grammar, punctuation, and spelling, and Flocabulary helps students learn vocabulary in an entertaining and memorable way. Phonics Genius supports young learners in phonemic awareness and in speaking, reading, and recognizing words through their sounds. Newsela and Smithsonian's Teen Tribune, Tween Tribune, TT Jr., and TT Español provide a wide range of nonfiction readings at different levels of complexity so that everyone in a class can read the same text at degrees of difficulty that are appropriately challenging for their current development; Storyworld and CommonLit provide a range of fiction readings at varied levels of complexity, again allowing everyone to read the same selection as appropriate for their current reading development. Podcasts are increasingly available on a broad range of topics, providing an accessible tool for learning about content in many disciplines. Podcasts often include scripts of the text, giving students a way to extend both their auditory and visual skills. Take time to explore the *many* other tools that are also useful to students with SLD and/or to their teachers.
- Use Hyperdocs and similar instructional strategies that invite use of video, audio, photographs, and other art forms that students can walk through at an individual pace and use as modes of learning on the topic around which the Hyperdoc is based. Hyperdocs also enable teachers to provide varied links to reading material on the same topic at different levels of complexity. They make learning experiential and provide varied ways to help students explore and come to understand a topic.
- Use apps that make it possible for students to learn and to present what they are learning in varied ways. These apps also support student collaboration and development of creativity. Among the many and growing number of such apps are Flipgrid, Explain Everything, Nearpod, SeeSaw, and Soundtrap.
- Use real-life applications of reading and writing that exist beyond worksheets and texts (for example, creating to-do lists, making labels and signs for the classroom or school, reading community newsletters, looking at recipes on cooking websites such as children's cooking site spattulata.com, making grocery lists, texting, tweeting) (Karten, 2017).
- Make sure students have a study buddy they can call or text when they are working on assignments at home.
- Provide samples of work that is complete and accurate to serve as models for the student.
- Emphasize ideas in student products, not just mechanics.
- Use an intranet site where class assignments are posted for students who may need a backup to what they have written in their planner. Also on the intranet site, highlight key words/steps required to successfully complete an assignment.
- Avoid calling on students with SLD to read aloud in class unless the student volunteers or has time in advance to practice the passage. Other students who struggle with reading, who are shy, and who grapple with anxiety and other emotional challenges would echo this recommendation.
- Highlight the most important sections in a chapter or article.
- Offer line markers to help a student follow the text.

- Use "windows" cut into cardboard that will allow a student to focus on a section of text and be less distracted by surrounding text and other elements that might be distracting.
- Provide spaces in the room where a student can work with minimal distractions—or use noise-reducing headsets or cardboard carrells for the same purpose.
- Front-load or pre teach vocabulary before a unit begins to students who may struggle with words, including, but not limited to, students with SLD.
- Front-load an upcoming unit with students who have difficulty following large amounts of information (again, including, but not limited to, students with SLD). Sharing and discussing the "story" or flow of key segments in a unit, much like a trailer for a movie or video, can help a student develop a frame of reference for what they will learn.
- Build in additional practice opportunities focused on essential vocabulary and essential skills (for example; instructional games, peer teaching, self-correcting materials, computer software programs, and additional worksheets).
- Be sure that homework assignments are within reach for a student with SLD so that the student learns from the work rather than becoming discouraged or frustrated by trying to complete it.
- Provide a glossary of important terms to support reading in a topic or content area.
- Encourage students to use calendars or assignment notebooks to record assignments and plan their completion.
- Meet regularly with students who have SLD, individually and in a variety of small groups, to introduce ideas, teach, reteach, clarify, and respond to questions.
- Read aloud to your students so they hear voices with effective inflections and see what it looks like when someone reads with feeling. Consider recording key or favorite readings so students can listen to them again and perhaps even follow along in the book or other text from which you read.

To Ensure That Assessment Is a Positive and Productive Process for Students with SLD

- Work with a specialist to assess the student's proficiency with phonics, comprehension, spelling, and writing to have an understanding of areas in which you will likely need to modify assessments.
- Pre-assess students with SLD (and other students) for important prerequisite skills and reteach those that appear weak.
- Use ongoing formative assessment to monitor a student's development with essential knowledge, understanding, and skill. Use what you learn to plan next steps in instruction.
- Emphasize growth over competition and comparison. Help each student learn to accept responsibility for taking his or her own next steps in class every day and to feel a sense of accomplishment and satisfaction when they do that.
- Allow extended time for taking tests that call for considerable reading and/or writing.
- Provide choices of ways for students to show what they know—and encourage them to suggest other options as well.
- Emphasize performance assessments rather than primary reliance on right-answer tests to measure student growth and understanding.
- Allow students with SLD to use an electronic dictionary, speller, or thesaurus; computers; and talking calculators during tests.
- Allow a student to audio-record answers or to use speech-to-text technology to provide responses. It is also helpful to many students with SLD to be able to use a word processor to write rather than being required to write with a pen or pencil.
- Provide sentence-starters that support students in seeing how a response might be framed.
- Avoid counting off for spelling errors on a test. A better alternative is marking important words that are misspelled for student review and/or for the student to consult while doing writing assignments.

Graded assignments should be assessed on student ideas, not mechanics, for students with SLD.

- Allow the student to work in a quiet area if necessary.

Most teachers work hard to establish a classroom environment that is conducive to helping each student learn effectively, including those with specific learning disorder. That is easier said than done, of course. To reach that goal, teachers must plan and teach intentionally to ensure that students with learning differences feel comfortable in the classroom. Drawing on the student's strengths and interests and incorporating instructional strategies that make reading more accessible go a long way in helping a student with SLD grow and achieve

success. Working in partnership with special educators and/or reading specialists as well as with the student(s) for whom reading is an ongoing challenge makes the process both more fruitful and more enjoyable as well.

NOTE

The following sources were consulted for this chapter. Full citations appear in the References section. Bailey, 2019; Bryant et al., 2020; Centers for Disease Control and Prevention, 2020a; Dyslexia Help, 2021; Dyslexia Resource, 2020; Eide, n.d.; Gillis & Kessler, n.d.; Gobir, 2021; International Dyslexia Association, n.d.; Karten, 2017; Kelly, n.d.; Mizerny, 2018; Sandman-Hurley, 2014; Smith, 2021; Smith et al., 2020; Understood.org, 2018; Waterford Foundation, 2014; Worthington, 2021.

CHAPTER 14

Teaching Students With Emotional and Behavioral Disorders

Students with emotional and behavioral disorder do not choose to exhibit challenging behavior any more than a child would choose to have a reading disability. They'd prefer to be doing well just like the rest of us. Just like the rest of us, they do poorly when life demands skills they're lacking.

—Ross Greene, *The Explosive Child* (5th Edition)

INTRODUCTION

Emotional and behavioral disorder (EBD) is an umbrella term under which several distinct diagnoses (such as anxiety disorder, manic-depressive disorder, oppositional defiant disorder, and more) fall. These disorders are also termed "emotional disturbance" and "emotionally challenged." The Individuals with Disabilities Education Act (IDEA) defines emotional disturbance as a condition that exhibits one or more of the following characteristics over an extended period of time and to a degree that negatively impacts a child's educational performance:

- An inability to learn that cannot be explained by intellectual, sensory, or health factors.
- An inability to build or maintain satisfactory interpersonal relationships with peers and teachers.
- Inappropriate types of behavior or feelings under normal circumstances.
- A general pervasive mood of unhappiness or depression.
- A tendency to develop physical symptoms or fears associated with personal or school problems.

Students who suffer from emotional and behavioral disorders, or EBD, often find it very difficult to control their behavior and to focus on their work in the classroom. They also often lack the impulse control and the emotional balance that is necessary to handle social interactions with other students effectively. Thus, the emotional difficulties experienced by students with EBD spill over into their cognitive and social skills as well, translating into behaviors such as:

- hyperactivity, which shows up as short attention spans and impulsiveness;
- aggression or self-injurious behavior, like acting out or fighting;
- Withdrawal from social gatherings due to excessive fear or anxiety;
- Emotional dysregulation like inappropriate crying, temper tantrums, and poor coping skills; and
- not paying attention in class and performing below grade level.

Under the umbrella of emotional and behavioral disorders are two categories: psychiatric disorders (such as bipolar disorder, eating disorder, anxiety disorder, obsessive-compulsive disorder, and psychotic disorder) and behavioral disabilities (such as oppositional-defiant disorder and conduct disorder). Students with psychotic disorder generally need intense and specialized medical support. Teachers who have students with these conditions in their classrooms will need to work closely with special education professionals to provide appropriate support. Students with conduct disorder are likely to need placement in special education classrooms until their behavior improves enough to be successful in a general education setting.

Attention deficit/hyperactivity disorder (ADHD) is generally classified in the literature of psychology and psychiatry as an emotional-behavioral disorder. This book addresses ADHD in a separate chapter (Chapter 12) because schools most often address ADHD as a category separate from emotional and behavioral disorders.

Behavioral disorders are one of the most common forms of disability among children and young adults and are the most frequently cited reason for referral to mental health services. Following are approximate percentages of children who have a diagnosis of behavior disorder:

- 3.6% of children ages 3–5
- 8.7% of children ages 6–11
- 6.85% of children ages 12–17

The appearance of behavioral disorders in classrooms is increasing significantly. Further, behavior disorders, anxiety, and depression often exist together.

- Almost three-fourths of children 3–17 with depression also have anxiety.
- Almost half of children 3–17 with depression also have behavior problems.
- About 20% of children 3–17 with depression also have anxiety and behavior problems.

While many young people exhibit some of the behaviors associated with EBD at some point as they grow up, it is the persistence and severity of the behaviors that suggest the possibility of a behavioral or emotional disorder.

If left untreated, EBD can result in serious short- and long-term problems, including suspension or expulsion from school, difficulty maintaining employment, strain on or dissolution of marriage, and threatening violence and committing violent acts. The earlier a behavioral disorder is diagnosed and properly treated, the more likely it is that a child or adult suffering from it will be able to control their

behavior. Helping young people learn to manage their behavior is the key goal of both clinical and classroom support. Following are some guides for teachers that are helpful in working with students who have emotional and behavioral disorders. The aim is not to use all of these strategies, of course, but to understand them as a repertoire from which you can consider options that seem likely to benefit a given learner at a particular time, in a specific context.

SOME PRINCIPLES AND PRACTICES FOR TEACHING STUDENTS WITH EBD

To Create a Safe, Inviting Learning Environment for Students With EBD

- See students with EBD with unconditional positive regard—that is, with the belief that they do not need to change anything or do anything to earn your acceptance (Gobir, 2021).
- Work consistently to create an ethic of inclusion, empathy, respect, and kindness in the classroom. Mentor students in understanding that human differences are normal, natural, and positive.
- Get to know your students—and let them get to know you (post family pictures, share funny stories, let students know what you enjoy doing when you are not working, share with them when you have failed at something and regrouped, tell them about what you are reading or listening to—and give them opportunities to do the same).
- Throughout the year, study students to understand any elements in their lives that will help you teach them more effectively. Understanding a student's interests, recognizing triggers for negative behavior, determining how the student responds to various ways in which you might communicate with him or her, and becoming adept at reading moods are examples of areas in which teacher knowledge about a student can be especially helpful in working with students with EBD.

- Help all students be reflective about their own feelings and how they respond to actions that make them feel inferior or excluded. Support students not only in treating others as they want to be treated, but also in treating others as *those* individuals want to be treated. Model those behaviors, talk about them, teach them, and acknowledge examples of those approaches at work in the classroom. These attributes contribute to a student's sense of safety, belonging, and worth. It is the teacher's attitudes, words, and actions that are most likely to help students in a general education classroom respond positively to students with learning differences.

- Serve as a model for students with emotional and behavioral disorders (as for other students). Your actions need to be consistent, mature, controlled, and caring. Theirs sometimes cannot be.

- Be sensitive, a good listener, a careful observer, and patient. Throughout the year, help students develop awareness of one another's strengths and talents and the benefits of drawing on the strengths and talents of many students to extend one's own reach and development.

- Look for and work from the student's strengths. Teachers who focus on developing a student's strengths rather than on fixing problems are more successful in helping the student feel hopeful and grow in a positive direction. When a student with EBD behaves in ways that are challenging and even harmful, it is wise to recall that the behavior is often a means of communicating pain and/or fear. Instead of thinking of the student as disruptive, think of him or her as a young person who is hurting. That change may not solve the behavior problem but will put the teacher in a better frame of mind to work with the student toward a solution.

- Work consistently to ensure that classroom relationships, processes, and rules support growth, and foster self-esteem and self-efficacy.

- Recognize and acknowledge positive behaviors.

- Show confidence in the student's ability to succeed, and present challenges that are achievable with effort and support.

- Make time throughout the year to talk with the student about his or her strengths, needs, and goals for the year.

- Take time often to spend just a couple of minutes talking with the student who has EBD about things that have nothing to do with school—what the student watches on TV, sports and teams the student follows, an event the student is looking forward to. Spending as little as 2 minutes a day over a 10-day period focused on this kind of conversation between a teacher and a student with emotional or behavioral challenges can result in improved student behavior and a stronger student–teacher bond (Wlodkowski in Woolf, n.d.).

- When a student with EBD wants to push you away (often to prove that no one is trustworthy), don't let that happen. The student needs you to maintain the relationship.

- Be a consistent source of support and encouragement for the student.

- Acknowledge the contributions of a student with an emotional or behavioral disorder in any aspect of a class—as you would with all students. Success is very important to most students with EBD.

- Establish well-defined rules, limits, and expectations. Work with your students to develop or modify those elements and understand them. Class rules, limits, and expectations work best if they are simple and clear and should be developed to help students focus on learning and to make the class work for everyone. Phrase them as positive statements, indicating what the student *should* do rather than should *not* do.

- Develop, teach, and implement clear and predictable classroom routines. Students with emotional and behavioral disorders tend to struggle with unexpected events and with transitions. Routines help them feel grounded and being able to see the routine is reassuring.

- Clearly distinguish unstructured or less structured from structured activities in terms of time, place, and expectations.
- Post daily and weekly schedules visually so students can refer to them readily.
- Ask teachers who have previously taught the student with EBD to share strategies that were effective in supporting that student's growth and success.
- Remember that when a student with EBD is withdrawn, unresponsive, angry, or disruptive, those behaviors are not about you. Do not take it personally.
- Be patient for student success. Students with EBD generally carry heavy weights on their shoulders. Understand backsliding. Recognize incremental steps forward. Look for overall growth.

To Teach Responsively to Students With EBD

- Most students with emotional and behavioral disorders who are in general education classrooms have the same learning expectations as other students of their grade and age. Therefore, they should work from curriculum that is engaging, understanding-focused, relevant to their lives, and requires them to think in complex ways. The nature of that curriculum is described at several places in this book (see, for example, Figure 5.3). When a student with EBD has challenges (for example, difficulty with organization, communicating with peers, or speaking in anger), provide scaffolding and support in those areas so that they are not barriers to the student's success.
- Teach up to the student. Establish, share, and maintain expectations that the student with EBD will learn important content, explore significant ideas, think in complex ways, solve problems or address issues that are meaningful in a content area and in the world, and create products or performances that demonstrate academic and intellectual growth.
- Teach to the learner's strengths and interests. Linking class content to something a student

with EBD cares deeply about opens the way for the student to relate to and invest in content and skills that might not otherwise capture the learner's attention.
- Make sure the curriculum has mirrors, windows, and doors. Mirrors enable students to understand themselves and their experiences more fully. Windows provide opportunities for students to learn about people whose lives and experiences are different from their own in significant ways. Doors provide opportunities for students to connect with the broader community and to contribute to it.
- Differentiate content, process, and/or products based on the student's readiness/ entry points into a lesson, interests, and approaches to learning, as you do with all students. Using accessible materials and technologies and designing learning experiences that are in a student's Zone of Proximal Development are key to a student's sense of safety, security, achievement, and growth. The fact that the work is achievable reduces fear and tension for the student. Support growth in areas where a student needs help to master skills or knowledge from past years so the student can progress. This will likely bolster the student's confidence as a learner (and trust in you!).
- Give the student choices whenever possible (for example, deciding which of two assignments to do, selecting a mode of expression, deciding whether to work alone or with a partner, choosing a book to read or a topic for an inquiry). Choosing not to complete the assignment is not an option, but enabling a student with EBD to feel a sense of control over aspects of the assignment can be empowering for that student (and other students as well).
- Establish clear learning targets that are expressed in terms of the knowledge, understandings, and skills students need to master (KUDs). Make sure students know and understand what the KUDs are at any point in a learning sequence.
- Plan for student engagement from the outset. Using analogies, activities that

require movement, videos, images, questions, quotations, discussions, debates, opinion lines, and other engaging strategies can capture student attention and imagination and help them connect what they are learning to their own lives and to issues and problems they care about in the world outside the classroom.

- Ensure that much/most of the student's learning focuses on understanding the big ideas or concepts and principles around which a discipline is organized. Concepts such as equity, alienation, exploration, justice, fairness, conflict, and peace provide an opportunity for students with EBD (and other students) to see their lives in the content they study. Concept-based teaching also helps the brain organize information so the learner can remember it, retrieve it, and apply it more readily.
- Align instruction with KUDs carefully and consistently.
- Include learning activities that make it possible for students with EBD (and other students with learning challenges) to participate with the class as a whole (for example, response cards that indicate a student's current comfort with the ideas and skills they are learning, unison responses, reader's theater, guided notes).
- Provide opportunities for the student to make choices. It is helpful to begin with two or three choices from which the learner selects one option. Let the student know how long they have to make the choice. Review the selection with the student so both of you are clear on what the choice is and what the criteria for success are for that choice.
- Review key knowledge, understanding, and/ or skills from the previous lesson by asking reflective questions.
- Provide clear goals for an upcoming lesson.
- Differentiate instruction in ways that focus on individual needs, support success, and reduce frustration (for example, student-specific goals, breaking longer assignments into small chunks, allowing the student to work at his/her own pace on longer

assignments, and adjusting task difficulty to be at a doable degree of difficulty).

- Use apps that provide the same reading materials at multiple levels of complexity (for example, Newsela, Smithsonian's Teen Tribune, Tween Tribune, TT Jr., TT Español, Storyworld, and CommonLit). Khan Academy can provide useful support in math.
- Use visual depictions to show steps in a process, sequence of events in a story, or an event in history. Concept maps, flow charts, diagrams, and storyboards are a few tools that can be helpful for this purpose.
- Stop regularly to give students an opportunity to catch up. It is also helpful to allow students time extensions and independent work times to complete unfinished work.
- Use small-group instruction to teach skills in which students are lagging and that they are not likely to master without direct teaching. Individual and small-group instruction most often happens during "exit ramp" time and allows students to work on aspects of learning that are most important for their continuing growth. (See, for example, Figure 4.4 on page 39.)
- Plan small-group participation when feasible so the student with EBD is part of a group that includes mature and thoughtful members to support the student's sense of community and shared contribution to the work of the class.
- If a student has difficulty adapting to a group, begin by having the student observe the group, then move to paired work. When the student becomes comfortable with working in a pair, move into work that will span a short period of time in groups of three or four.
- Consider using mnemonics with the student to help with knowledge retrieval.
- Write the student brief notes during the day (perhaps using restaurant order pads, prescription pads, or notepads with the school's name and mascot printed on them). The notes can be a greeting, an acknowledgment of positive behavior or

completed work, or to make a request. It is just a way to indicate your presence, attention, and support.

- Determine whether the student is on medication, what the schedule is, and what the medication effects may be on his or her in-class demeanor with and without medication. Then adjust accordingly.
- Consult with specialists like the special education teacher, school psychologist, or counselor to discuss strategies that may be useful in helping the student become more skilled in managing emotions and behavior.
- Connect with parents or caregivers at times and in ways that match the demands on their lives. Share positive information with them. They may be struggling along with their students and worried about their child's present and future prospects. Listen to their concerns and respond thoughtfully. Ask for approaches they find beneficial to their student at home, and approaches that do not work well. Talk together about ways in which you can partner with them to coordinate efforts to benefit their child. Check in regularly to learn from one another and plan together.

To Ensure That Assessment Is a Positive and Productive Process for Students With EBD

- Align assessments tightly with the learning targets you have specified (KUDs).
- Be sensitive to the student's reactions to the various aspects of assessment.
- Have students create portfolios of examples of their work (quizzes, class assignments, projects, performance assessments) that demonstrate what the student has learned during a unit of study. Portfolios often show a student's development far more effectively than test results. (If a student cannot develop a portfolio alone, work with the student to accumulate and organize the work.)
- Understand any special needs a student may have that would compromise a testing situation and adjust the context as needed. (For example, a student might work in a smaller room, with a proctor present if necessary or use a carrel or noise-cancelling headphones to block distractions.)
- Formatively assess students often so you can discover problems in their learning early in a unit or learning sequence and can address the problem before it is too late.
- Provide clear, specific, actionable feedback to the student as soon as possible after he or she completes an assignment or test. Be sure to note what is correct as well as a couple of areas that need additional attention.
- Help the student reflect on feedback, decide on next steps in the current work that will help him/her move forward, and establish a timeline for taking those steps and checking in with you to talk about outcomes.
- Consider adding as a final item on formative and summative assessments a statement such as, "Please share with me anything else you know about this topic that was not included on this test." This is likely to be helpful to many students, not just those with learning challenges.

To Teach Skills That Lead to Success for Students With EBD

- Provide ongoing opportunities for students with EBD to work with students whose behavior is positive.
- Provide opportunities for students with EBD to be responsible in the classroom. When teachers give students an opportunity to act responsibly, they often do.
- Make plans with the student to work on specified behavior challenges. Make sure the student has the plan in writing with a way to document levels of success in meeting the goals.
- Teach and explain how specific target behaviors (both academic and social) should look, why they are important, and steps a student can take to develop the skills that lead to a target behavior.
- Make specific plans with the student for him or her to replace inappropriate behaviors with positive ones during a specific component of the class. Follow up with a

conversation emphasizing what the student accomplished and looking at next steps. Keep the planning, teaching, and reviewing process going.

- Consider using a "Kudos to You" box to help all students recognize and reinforce positive behaviors in one another. Students look for peers helping one another, following classroom rules, making extra effort, helping to solve a problem, and so on. They write what they saw on a slip of paper and put the paper in the Kudos Box on the teacher's desk. The teacher can then acknowledge the recognitions to individuals and/or to the class. This process helps students look for peers who are "getting it right" while also providing motivation to get it right yourself.

- Teach the skills of collaboration to all students (for example, making sure everyone understands the task and success criteria, careful listening, disagreeing respectfully, drawing on the strengths of group members, summarizing at intervals to make sure everyone has a shared understanding, and supporting one another when a group member feels unsure).

To Work Productively With Student Behavior

- Build mini-breaks into the day. Students with EBD often lack emotional balance, stamina, or maturity to remain focused for extended periods of time.

- Designate spaces in the classroom where a student can go to step away from a tense or escalating situation before it becomes volatile. Help students learn to recognize those moments and use the safe space to regroup.

- Establish cues with the student that you will use to signal a need for him/her to change or stop a behavior (for example, making eye contact, standing close to the student's desk, putting a note on the student's desk, a hand gesture, or picking up a particular object from your desk and holding it for a minute or two).

- Remember that students with EBD often lack the judgment and restraint that a teacher may expect from peers of the same age or grade. Their misbehavior is not planned. It is not manipulative. Productive behavior is simply beyond their reach much of the time. That is the genesis of an EBD diagnosis. A primary goal for a teacher who works with a student who has EBD should be helping the student understand his/her emotions and to work with them in ways that are less hurtful/more productive both to that student and people in his/her life.

- When a student commits a minor infraction, use "planned ignoring." If the misbehavior does not disrupt the class or cause harm, it is often wise to overlook it. Continually correcting or scolding a student with EBD can escalate the student's sense of rejection and anxiety. Further, teacher intervention during minor infractions can itself disrupt the class.

- Remember that rewarding positive behavior is ultimately far more effective in the long run than punishing negative behavior. Often, students with EBD see punishment as a personal attack. Punishment, then, often compounds problems that already exist.

- Celebrate the successes of students with EBD. When they receive positive feedback and rewards, they begin to see that there is a positive benefit to good behavior and will also be more likely to see you as an ally rather than an adversary. Because students with EBD often have a store of negative experiences with school, emphasizing the positive can be an effective motivator to invest in their work.

- When a student breaks a rule, remain calm. The student often cannot!

- When consequences need to follow a negative behavior, be sure the student understands the connection between his or her action and those consequences.

- Think very carefully before you buy into a zero tolerance policy in regard to rules. While the idea of zero tolerance is appealing because that approach makes discipline seem clean and fair, the approach requires teachers to overlook the deep-seated and intractable problems some students fight against but are not equipped to conquer for a time in their lives. No teachers want a zero tolerance friend. No one wants a zero tolerance boss or neighbor. In our legal system, zero tolerance policies have often created suffering that is disproportional to an offense. Mendler and Curwin (2007) recommend that teachers be as tough as they need to, but not be bound to delivering a pre-prescribed punishment without regard to the student who will be the object of the rule. We dehumanize our students and ourselves when we fail to look at the circumstances that brought a student to behave in a destructive way. Differentiation and inclusion call on educators to look at students as distinct individuals and to respond appropriately in light of the child's needs. It is important that we not relinquish that goal.

As students with emotional and behavioral disorders learn to manage their own behaviors productively, they are more fully able to succeed academically and socially. Along the way, they need teachers who see their promise, believe in their capacity to grow, and are diligent in being architects of classroom experiences that support that predominant goal. Academic learning still matters, of course, but until the student can function with growing agency and confidence, behavioral and emotional growth should be in the foreground. For these students, the aim is to help the student understand they are contributors to their life circumstances and not just products of those circumstances (Solar, 2011).

NOTE

The following sources were consulted for this chapter. Full citations appear in the References section. Bryant et al., 2020; Centers for Disease Control and Prevention, 2021; Council for Exceptional Children & Council for Children with Behavior Disorders, 2020; Desautels, 2017; Gobir, 2021; Greene, 2014b; Karten, 2017; Loveless, 2021; Lukowiak, 2010; McKibben, 2014; Mendler & Curwin, 2007; National Science Teaching Association (n.d.); Positive Action, 2021; PsychGuides, n.d.; Resilient Educator, 2018; Smith et al., 2020; Solar, 2011; Woolf, n.d.

CHAPTER 15

Teaching Students From Diverse Cultures

Education must be not only a transmission of culture but also a provider of alternative views of the world and a strengthener of the will to explore them.

—Jerome Bruner

INTRODUCTION

"Culture" refers to the shared assumptions, values, and beliefs of a group of people that result in characteristic behaviors of people in that group (Storti, 1999, p. 5). It is a way of perceiving the world and interacting with it. Culture can be seen as the growth of a group identity fostered through social patterns unique to that group. Those patterns encompass religion, what we wear, how we wear it, music, beliefs about right and wrong, how we sit at the table, when we do or don't make eye contact, how far away from a person we stand during a conversation, how we see the world around us, how we define family roles—*and how we learn in a classroom,* to name just a few ways our culture shapes us.

Culture has both an invisible dimension (for example, assumptions, values, beliefs) and an observable dimension (behavior). The things we say and do stem from what we assume, value, and believe in, and those assumptions, values, and beliefs are learned through group membership. In other words, there is a cause-and-effect relationship between the invisible dimensions of a culture and the visible or behavioral dimensions of that culture.

A child's assimilation into a culture begins at birth, if not before, and can be so subtle, so automatic, that the child may not even realize that he or she is a product of enculturation. That young person is simply doing what the others in the environment do—acting as those others act—and learning "how we do things around here."

As we encounter people from cultures whose values, beliefs, and actions differ significantly from our own, we begin to notice the cultural differences, and we often respond to those observations by thinking (or saying), "Why does she do *that*? It makes no sense!" In truth, however, the action or behavior makes perfect sense in light of the beliefs and values that individual has come to represent as part of the culture in which he or she has grown up.

The more opportunity we have to encounter people from other cultures, the more likely we are to realize that cultural differences are not only inevitable but interesting rather than foolish or wrong. Those who interact with people from a range of cultures will develop a greater awareness of the "givens" of their own culture than they would otherwise have and will be enriched, as they have the opportunity to see life through different lenses.

Many Americans, however, grow up in places where nearly everyone they encounter more or less shares their beliefs, embraces their values, and behaves as they do. That is particularly true for individuals who are part of the dominant culture. It is easy for those individuals to conclude that all classrooms function, and should function, as their classrooms do—to conclude that when they study history, they are studying the history and perspectives of all Americans, and that the stories and novels they read in English class offer a reasonable representation of the important ideas and experiences that exist in our country and the world. While that is not the case, it is difficult for most of us to imagine ways of being that are significantly different from the way we have always been.

Cultural diversity is not just about traveling to a country different than our own or getting to know someone in the United States who came here from another country. There are numerous cultures within any country beyond those introduced into that country by immigrants. For example, Native Americans, Alaskan Natives, African Americans, Southerners, New Englanders, people who live in rural areas, those whose roots are in the Appalachian Mountains, and individuals with disabilities are just a few examples of cultures whose beliefs and practices are, in many ways, distinct from those of "mainstream" Americans or "the dominant culture" (though defining "mainstream" or "dominant culture" would be difficult to do without including the many cultures that have shaped and continue to shape our sense of who we are as a people).

Culture is at the core of everything we do in school. The question that looms large at this point in our history as a nation is whether we as teachers can open up the classroom to be welcoming of, and sensitive and responsive to, the cultures of the diverse students who are in our care—or whether we will continue to "do school" as we have always known it to be done.

When a young person's culture is in sync with his or her classroom, that place feels quite user-friendly to that learner. On the other hand, if the culture of the classroom represents different beliefs, values, and practices than those represented in a student's home culture, it feels confusing, off-putting, and even hostile. For example, the role of the teacher varies considerably across cultures, as does the role of the student. Expectations for parental roles relative to schools differ considerably as well. Further, the way a culture presents child/adult relationships, homage to authority, the meaning of time, the relative importance of feelings versus information, and the primacy of individual versus group will markedly shape how classrooms function.

Look, as an example, at the set of continuums in Figure 15.1. Children who grow up in some cultures are likely to be enculturated to learn, work, and communicate in ways that represent the approaches in the left-hand column, while children who grow up in some other cultures are equally likely to be enculturated in ways that reflect the right-hand column of approaches. Still, of course, there will be differences among individuals in a culture so that some individuals for whom the left column is the cultural norm will move toward the center of the continuum in some traits, or perhaps even all the way to the right of the continuum. Conversely, some people for whom the right column is their cultural norm will function more to the center of one or more of the continuums—or even all the way to the left (adapted from Dack & Tomlinson, 2015).

If you grew up in mainstream schools in the United States, consider which of the two columns you think those schools generally reflected. The likelihood is that the values, beliefs, and behaviors in the left-hand column were dominant in your schools. At the same time, many students whose first cultures were outside the United States, the United

Figure 15.1. Cultural Continuums of Behavior or Action

Continuum of Behaviors That Are Predominant Across Cultures	
Focus on the individual	Focus on the group
Motivated most often by external reward	Motivated most often by internal satisfaction
Needs to observe how things work	Needs to test how things work
Needs external structures	Creates own structures
Competitive	Collaborative
On-demand response	Reflective response
Challenging of authority	Respectful of authority
Conformity	Creativity
Reserved	Expressive
Fixed sense of time	Flexible sense of time
Information-driven	Feeling-driven

Kingdom, and a few European countries, as well as a number of cultures in the United States whose cultural norms differ from some mainstream norms, identify much more strongly with the values, beliefs, and behaviors in the right-hand column.

Schools in the United States still tend to function well to the left on the continuum because that column represents the dominant culture in the United States. Many students whose cultures tend to represent the right-hand column, and who increasingly attend those left-hand-column-schools, find classrooms in the United States to be disorienting. They may think, "Why does this school put so much emphasis on the individual when group welfare and group contributions seem much more 'normal'? "Why do so many students talk so much of the time when it clearly seems that listening is more polite and fruitful?" "What is the reason for so much emphasis on competition in schools and classrooms when collaboration builds community?" "Why does everyone have to finish work at the same moment when the work of some students would be better if there was opportunity for those learners to work a bit longer?"

When *any* learner becomes part of a classroom in which the values and behaviors seem in conflict with the values and behaviors of that learner, the student can feel almost like he or she is working in a house of mirrors where everything is distorted and disorienting. Not surprisingly, learning is likely to be diminished for that learner.

When you combine the likelihood of a cultural mismatch in the classroom for many students from diverse cultures, both inside and outside the United States, with the parallel realities that that student will likely be a member of a cultural minority in the United States, may speak a primary language or dialect other than the language of the classroom, may live in a low-income home, and may also have additional learning challenges, the road between that student and academic success can feel eternally long and lonely to the young learner.

At a time when it seems that everyone in the world lives everywhere and when the nations of the world are more and more closely intertwined than in the past, the need for classrooms that are culturally responsive is more pressing than ever. The personal and societal costs of failing to provide such classrooms would be difficult to overestimate.

Culturally responsive teachers are passionate about the students they teach and are determined to teach students from culturally diverse backgrounds with the goal of continually considering what students see, hear, feel, and experience as individuals in a learning environment that constantly affirms who they are and what they can become as a result of being in the company of that teacher and being in that teacher's classroom. In that environment, culturally diverse learners learn content and learn about themselves. They discover who they are, their own capacities, and their own potential. They are discovering their own worth and value and developing their voices (Kafele, 2021).

An education that introduces young people to a variety of cultural practices and perspectives and that embraces the contributions of students from a wide range of cultural backgrounds is good for all students. Enacted effectively, such classrooms provide all students with "mirrors" in which they can see and understand themselves more fully, "windows" through which they come to understand other people and other cultures, and "doors" that invite them to connect with and contribute to the community. Students learn to think more deeply and more critically as they gain perspectives much broader than their own. They learn the value of accepting people whose backgrounds differ markedly from their own and respecting the contributions of those individuals to their own growth and development. One of the great challenges and opportunities for educators in the years ahead is to understand cultural differences, translate those understandings into classroom practices that invite success for all comers, and model the attributes of cultural respect.

One caveat bears repeating in this introduction as well, however, just as it does in each of the chapters of this book. There is no such thing as a "typical American" or "typical Latinx" student, no single person who represents "Asian culture" or even "Japanese culture," no single image that comes close to representing "an immigrant" to the United States, "an individual with special needs," or "a female." Not only do cultures differ across times and places, but there is no truly homogeneous culture in any time and place. Personal temperament, personal circumstances, and personal experiences mediate culture so that no two people experience a culture in the precisely same way or translate its tenets into the same practices. The caution is, as always, do not generalize to groups. Instead, provide opportunity and support that enables all sorts of individuals from all sorts of cultures to learn and grow comfortably, consistently, and confidently in the classroom you lead.

While cultural differences may challenge us, cultural similarities give us a foundation of shared understandings and experiences in which we find common ground. An idea sometimes reflected in classrooms of teachers who seek to create a classroom climate of respect for and affirmation of each student is, "Our similarities make us human, our differences make us individuals." That idea holds when thinking about cultural similarities and differences. Our need as educators is to understand that idea deeply, believe in it fully, embody it faithfully, and demonstrate it daily to the young people in our care.

Following are some guides for teachers who seek to create culturally responsive classrooms that are invitational to and supportive of the success of learners from all cultures. The goal is not to use all these strategies and certainly not to assume that every strategy will work for every student from a particular culture or equally well across all cultures. Rather, the goal is to consider the principles and practices as a repertoire from which you can consider options that seem likely to benefit a given learner, at a particular time, in a specific context.

SOME PRINCIPLES AND PRACTICES FOR TEACHING STUDENTS FROM DIVERSE CULTURES

To Create a Safe, Inviting Learning Environment for Students From Diverse Cultures

- Develop an increasingly clear sense of your own ethnic and cultural identities. What are the beliefs, values, traditions, and behaviors that are core to you? How did you develop those beliefs and practices? What do they suggest about who you are and how you approach life? What biases may stem from your cultural experiences?
- Consider your degree of personal commitment to achieving equity for all

students and your belief that you are capable of making a positive difference in your students' lives.
- Examine your mindset. When we fully believe that each student is capable of learning what is required of them (and more), we will teach in ways that support their success. When we see students as able and teach them as we teach able learners, they nearly always demonstrate that ability. Always look at culturally diverse learners (as all learners) through an asset-based lens rather than a deficit-based perspective.
- View each of your learners with unconditional positive regard—that is, the assurance that you accept and value that person as he or she is, with no need for them to change anything or do anything for you to care about them (Gobir, 2021).
- Work consistently to develop a strong bond with each of your students. Build a learning environment in which everyone consistently feels respected by and connected to one another. Make a culture of inclusion, respect, and empathy "the way we do things in this classroom." Help students understand why that way of doing things matters. Model those attributes for them consistently.
- Pronounce students' names correctly from day one. This is a simple and meaningful way to show respect. Significant damage can occur when vulnerable students hear their names pronounced incorrectly.
- Ask students what they would like to be called. Avoid substituting an "American" nickname or a shortened version of the student's name unless the student clearly prefers a nickname or abbreviated name.
- Avoid thinking of culturally diverse students as "the other." When that view prevails, students whose cultures differ from your own or from the majority of students will be seen as deficient, inconvenient, or even "wrong" in the ways they approach school and learning.
- Help students understand and respect both their commonalities and their differences.
- Help them learn to be responsible for one another both in and out of the classroom.

- Teach students behaviors and actions that are common in their new culture, so they are prepared for success in different contexts such as the classroom, lunchroom, community, and home.
- Take care also to help your culturally diverse students maintain their sense of cultural pride and identity as they learn the culture of the school. Help them learn to be bi-cultural and to see biculturalism as a sign of their strength, providing them with new ways to understand the world around them, new avenues for solving complex problems, and new possibilities for making their way through the world successfully.
- Create a safe way for students to ask background questions about how/why things are done in a certain way at school (or in the community) or about vocabulary that may be unfamiliar to them. One possibility is a "That's a Good Question" box on or near the teacher's desk in which students can place their questions for a response from the teacher, who can answer the question privately to an individual or for the whole class.
- Identify and work to dispel cultural stereotypes in your students, your colleagues—and yourself.
- Structure collaborative environments in which students (including those with special needs and English learners) regularly work with a broad range of peers and teach the skills necessary for students to collaborate productively (for example, inquiries, collaborative controversy, jigsaw, think-pair-share, round-robins, and Paideia seminars). This enables students to share experiences, support one another, and contribute to the success of the group.
- Give students voice and choice in as many aspects of their learning as possible. Ask them regularly for feedback on what is working well for them in class and what is not. Seek their suggestions for making the class better, even if it appears to be working well. Act on student suggestions and consult them on whether changes are working effectively for them.

- Welcome parents or caregivers of culturally diverse learners to your classroom, always showing respect for them and the beliefs and traditions they bring with them. Set meetings at times when parents can most likely attend. When necessary, secure translators to assist in conversations.
- Learn as much as possible about the expectations parents or caregivers may have for a teacher's role in the classroom and for a parent's role in helping their students learn.
- Learn from parents or caregivers what their aspirations are for their children and invite them to share information with you about their child's learning, talents, and interests that will help you teach that learner more effectively.
- Help parents or caregivers learn additional ways they can partner with you to support their children's learning. Support them in being a key part of decision-making regarding their children's education.
- Get to know students' communities. Attend events in those communities that allow you to see your students in the places and with the people they most value.

To Teach Responsively to Students From Diverse Cultures

- Teach every child from an asset-based rather than a deficit-based perspective.
- Teach to ensure that culturally diverse students not only *maintain* their cultural pride and practices in the classroom but that they also *grow* in their understanding of and pride in their cultural heritage through their classroom learning opportunities and experiences.
- Teach up! Communicate, through words and actions, high expectations of success for every student and the belief that every student can succeed, and persistently support the learner in achieving that success. Be their partner in developing the knowledge, understandings, and skills necessary to do high-quality work. Ensure that students engage in reciprocal teaching as well, working together as a team to support the success of all members of the team.

- Differentiate instruction to meet students where they are in their entry points into the curriculum, their interests, and their varied approaches to learning. This is a pivotal element in a student's growth, motivation, and trust in the teacher.
- Provide all students with academically challenging curriculum that calls on them to understand and apply what they are learning and to develop higher-level cognitive skills.
- Teach around "big ideas," or concepts and principles that are relevant in many cultures and contexts (for example, power, conflict, friendship, community, voice, change, inclusion/exclusion, poverty/plenty, human rights, fairness, justice). Help students understand both the commonalities and differences in how varied cultures experience and make sense of those ideas/ concepts across time and place.
- Ensure that learning goals (KUDs) are clear and that students know and understand them.
- Use a variety of approaches and methods when you teach and when you plan instruction to reach the full range of students you teach. As you extend your range of effective and inclusive instructional approaches, you are likely to see more and more of your students engage and succeed.
- Give students a voice in what they learn and how they learn it. Be sure students have choices of what and how to learn that enable them to learn about and grapple with ideas that are significant in their lives.
- Teach the skills of agency or independence so students can progressively take charge of their own learning success.
- Use highways and exit ramps to ensure that all students work with rich, meaningful ideas and that they have time and support to practice skills necessary to support complex, meaning-rich work.
- Emphasize the human purpose of what students are learning, how it can improve the prospects of people and communities, and how it relates to student experiences.
- Provide encouragement when a student needs it. Let the student know you are convinced they can succeed with the task. Ask the student how you can help him or her "get unstuck." Coach the student in taking those steps rather than doing the work for the student.
- Use instructional approaches that help students make meaning of what they are learning (for example, critical questioning, guided reciprocal peer questioning, problem-finding, decision-making, investigation of definitions, historical investigations, experimental inquiry, experiential learning, invention, art, simulations, and qualitative research methods) (Wlodkowski & Ginsberg, 1995).
- Use games as learning tools to gain student attention, support active processing of content, make connections, and collaborate. Games are motivating to many learners and are particularly effective in supporting learning for students from cultures that have strong oral and active traditions.
- Draw on the cultural resources your students bring to school to help them connect to and find success with the challenging curriculum. For example, many culturally diverse students come from backgrounds with strong oral traditions and therefore readily use spoken, rhythmic, and interactive methods of learning. Therefore, when teachers use (and call on students to use) rhyming, call and response, choral reading, readers' theater, music, poems, or riddles as ways to remember and process information, students who are comfortable and practiced with those approaches learn more readily and comfortably.
- Draw on the funds of knowledge students from various cultures bring into the classroom with them. Students from rural areas may have knowledge of nature that is richer and more detailed than their urban counterparts. Students from many countries will be able to share examples from their home countries of topics often taught in the United States (for example, pollution, disease, natural resources,

the arts, the divide between wealth and poverty, pollution, and human rights). Including experiences and perspectives on those topics as they exist in a variety of cultures expands the importance of the topics for all learners and makes learning about the topics more relevant for students from cultures in which the topics are examined. Students from a range of cultures can become experts by learning more about how a topic plays out in their home cultures (including the United States) and by sharing what they learn with classmates.

- Integrate the arts from a wide variety of cultures into teaching and learning in your classroom.
- Provide lesson previews to help students develop an orientation for what is coming next and use summaries at the end of lessons to support students in focusing on what is most important about the work they have done.
- Share content and ideas in story form. Oral cultures have passed along learning through stories for centuries. All content tells a story, whether it is math, art, history, science, music, and, of course, literature. Even grammar has a story to tell. Share the content in story form (who are the characters/protagonist/antagonist, what is the problem, what is the context or setting, where is the rising and falling action, what is the resolution, what is a takeaway theme). Alternatively, integrate the content into stories about your students or you. Ask students to create and share stories into which they weave big ideas, vocabulary, important information, and so on.
- Plan instruction that focuses on students creating meaning about content in an interactive and collaborative environment in which students come to see the varied contributions of group members as a highly positive resource. This draws on and continues to develop the communal nature of many cultures and helps all students grow in their appreciation of the richness that comes from looking at varied perspectives on ideas and issues.

- Use a wide variety of small groups working together on assignments (for example, peer teaching, one-on-one time with the teacher, skills-based groups, interest-focused groups). Whole-class instruction is often not the best way to teach for many learners. Students in a culture-friendly classroom will benefit from different kinds of small groups at different times in a learning cycle based on cultural practices and students' development as learners. Many cultures place considerably more emphasis on the group's success rather than the individual's success. For students from these cultures, group collaboration has the double benefit of supporting academic growth and helping them feel at home as a learner.
- Incorporate students' home cultures into the curriculum so they can see themselves in what they learn, and build on the experiences they bring to the classroom with them.
- Bring culturally diverse guest speakers into the classroom.
- Invite students to use their home languages in class—including the opportunity to write responses first in their primary language and then translate the response into English.
- Make available reading materials and other resources in students' primary languages whenever possible so students can read in a language that "makes more sense" to them as they also use English sources.
- Read books (to the class, as a class, and individually) that reflect the experiences of culturally diverse learners.
- Ensure that the curriculum consistently includes the contributions and perspectives of the different cultural groups that are represented in your class(es) and others that are representative of the cultural groups in society.
- Encourage students to learn in their first languages to enable them to work at a level of intellectual challenge. Being required to work only in English almost inevitably lowers the intellectual challenge level of student work for English learners and diminishes a student's opportunity

to maintain and develop strength in the language of their home culture.

- Encourage students to use home dialects for conversation in small groups and with the class as well as teaching them when to code-switch for some more formal uses of language.
- Provide authentic reading and writing experiences through which students immediately apply what they are learning in whole-class instruction to their own reading and writing. This reinforces the new learning while showing students that what they are learning is relevant to their own lives.
- Consider using peer feedback, peer tutoring, study squads, "experts of the day," parent or community volunteers, and other avenues of providing ongoing support for culturally diverse students, including students with special needs (and other students) who need extra support. Remember to prepare the helpers and the students who will work with them to work together productively.

To Ensure That Assessment Is a Positive and Productive Process for Students From Diverse Cultures

- Use a range of formative assessment strategies that help you learn more about each student, including how they approach learning, their entry points into various units or skills, the nature of their interactions with other students, and their strengths. The more fully you understand students, the more effective you are likely to be in planning for their growth.
- Make sure all assessments align tightly with the learning goals/KUDs for a unit and that students understand the success criteria for their work.
- Develop tasks and assessments that are authentic—in other words, work that mirrors the work of professionals in a discipline, focuses on real problems and dilemmas, and connects to students' lives and experiences.

- Use formative and summative assessments to support instructional decision-making for the class and for individual students.
- Consider using procedures and structures that draw on and reinforce intrinsic motivation to learn, such as formative feedback, authentic assessment tasks, portfolios and process folios, tests and testing formats critiqued for bias, self-assessment, narrative evaluations, credit/no-credit systems, and contracts for grades (Wlodkowski & Ginsberg, 1995).
- Teach students the skills of self-assessment and provide opportunity and support for students to self-assess their work both formatively and summatively throughout a learning cycle.
- Guide students in learning the skills and habits of mind that characterize successful learning (for example, establishing clarity about prescribed and personal goals and criteria for success, asking questions that move thinking ahead, checking for understanding while reading/using resources, learning from feedback, understanding that making mistakes is a pathway to learning, revising work to improve its quality, persistence, etc.).
- Provide feedback that is clear, focused, and actionable. Let students know what they have done correctly and point to two or three areas in which they can take next steps to continue their growth. Work with students to plan for taking those next steps so a student understands not only *what* to do next but also *how* to do it.
- Encourage students to make choices of assessment methods based on their experiences, values, needs, and strengths so they can represent knowledge, understanding, and skills in ways that maximize their opportunity to share what they have learned.
- Ensure fair and clear criteria for success. Include students in developing success criteria both for the class and individual goals.
- Connect the assessment process to the students' world, frames of reference, and values.

- Emphasize performance, process, and progress in all aspects of classroom life (3-P grading; Guskey, 1994, 2000). When reporting student outcomes, provide the three indicators separately on report cards—not averaged. Use addenda or direct communication to ensure that parents and students understand a learner's status on each element if the report card does not allow for recording the three.
- Look also at Chapter 7 on teaching students in our schools who are learning English as well as academic content.

As teachers learn more about and come to value the varied cultures around us and around the world, we extend our reach in being effective catalysts for growth in the full range of learners we serve. As we teach our students to appreciate both the similarities and differences in cultures, we extend their reach as well. They are better prepared to live in today's world—to live and work in partnership with neighbors, colleagues, and even adversaries in ways that can improve life conditions for all of us. Appreciation of cultural diversity, in fact, adds to our store of knowledge and wisdom, deepens our empathy, and enables us to collaborate more fruitfully, thus contributing to the mission of schools to support the intellectual, emotional, and social development of young people.

NOTE

The following sources were consulted for this chapter. Full citations appear in the References section. American University School of Education, 2020; Bryant et al., 2020; Cole, 1995; Collaborative Classroom, n.d.; Dack & Tomlinson, 2015; Ferlazzo, 2021a, Feb.; Ferlazzo, 2017; Gay, 2018; Hammond, 2015; Kafele, 2021; Ladson-Billings, 1994; Lindsey et al., 2018; McGraw Hill, 2019; Miller, 2019; Pesce, n.d.; Storti, 1999; Teacher Vision, n.d.; Tomlinson & Imbeau, 2010; Zimmerman, 2017.

CHAPTER 16

Teaching Students of Color

How does it feel to be a problem?

—W. E. B. Du Bois, *The Souls of Black Folk*

INTRODUCTION

African American students comprise about 15% of total enrollment in U.S. public schools, Hispanic students represent about 27%, and Asian/Pacific Islander students about 6%. American Indian and Alaskan Native students make up 1% of the public school population, and students of mixed race constitute about 4% of the U.S. student population (National Center for Education Statistics, 2020). Race should not be an inhibitor of learning for any of those young people who now constitute the majority of K–12 public school learners. Of course, the world is frequently not as it should be, and so it is the case that students in the United States whose race positions them as part of a "minority group" are often at significant risk of encountering persistent barriers to accessing equitable learning opportunities and the supports that can open the way to realizing their full potential.

Among the systemic barriers, policies, practices, and stereotypes that work against young people of color in public schools are continuing segregation by race in many schools, unequal school resources, unequal academic opportunities, fewer highly qualified teachers available for students of color, lack of access to social networks and out-of-school learning opportunities, lower-quality curricula for many learners of color, over representation in special education and low-track classes and under-representation in programs for students identified as gifted and in advanced classes such as Advanced Placement and International Baccalaureate classes, and harsher discipline and punishment. Those school-focused barriers exist in the company of societal barriers to quality housing, health care, higher education, employment opportunity, salary equity, and justice through the legal system, all of which can significantly diminish learning. The consequences of failing to ensure educational success for students of color are far-reaching, long-term, and will almost inevitably be reflected in future opportunities to participate in the world community.

It is always essential to recall that we should never assume any label represents a homogeneous group—despite the implicit assumption that a label should do so. There are African American, Hispanic, Asian, and Native students who are the sons and daughters of doctors, scientists, teachers, entrepreneurs, and so on. Their lives are predictably shaped by opportunity, resources, and ample adult support. There are also many young people of color who grow up greatly impacted by racial bias, inequity, and animosity but who nonetheless achieve against the odds, developing economically secure and contributing lives. Some students of color have lived only in the United States. Others have immigrated here only recently or are second- or third-generation immigrants. Some have ADHD, some have a specific learning disorder, some are identified as gifted, some experience trauma, some identify as LGBTQ; they live in cities, small towns, and rural areas; and, of course, they span the spectrum of possibilities in terms of talents, interests, and experiences. Some speak only English; others are fully bilingual. Some are brand new to the language of their new home. We fail our students and ourselves when we see any group as unitary—or any student as "representative" of a group or label. Impactful teaching is necessarily about seeing the individual, understanding the individual, and teaching in response to the individual. That caveat may apply to students of color more than to any other label-bearing group in our schools. Striving to adhere to that caveat is the cornerstone of quality inclusion, quality differentiation, and thus to achieving Everybody Classrooms.

Many students of color bring to school with them fears related to their own safety in society, an awareness of societal inequity and injustice that increases as they grow up and as they draw the experience-based conclusion that teachers, peers, and school leaders often see them in a negative light. Many of those students also experience ongoing bullying or taunting at school. When in the classroom, they may feel rejected, suspected, stereotyped, invisible, and absent from the academic content they are asked to learn.

For example, bullying of Muslim students is much higher than the national average across groups. Muslim girls are especially targeted for bullying when they wear a hijab, which makes their group identification visible. Twenty-three percent of African American students, 23% of Caucasian students, 16% of Hispanic students, and 7% of Asian students reported being bullied in school in 2019, but the incidence of bullying aimed at Asian students rose radically in 2020 as a result of public comments blaming Asians for the arrival of COVID-19 in the United States. While bullying is harmful to anyone who is bullied, race-related bullying is significantly associated with negative emotions and physical health effects (PACER's National Bullying Prevention Center, 2020; Russaw, 2019).

For African American learners, these deterrents to learning are wrapped in the long, painful history of race and slavery in the United States. Latino and Asian students, as well as students whose families come to the United States from other locations, see themselves as part of an enduring history of discrimination against immigrants. American Indians and Alaskan Natives continue to experience a centuries-long history of oppression, disregard, and cultural erasure. It is also unhelpful that while 51% of students in grades K–12 are children of color, 80% of their teachers are White. That imbalance means that many students of color seldom, if ever, have teachers who can genuinely understand their lived experiences. It means that many of these students will have few same-race role models as they make their way through school.

In the end, many (though certainly not all) learners from these groups feel discouraged, afraid, and angry even as the school day begins. And they also come to school with hopes, talents, and rich experiences that are ingredients for success. While appropriately and justifiably wary about school, in the company of teachers who see and act on their promise, many of these learners will flourish.

Students of color need teachers who are fully committed to the principles of equity and excellence for their students. They do not need teachers who propose that they are color-blind and do not see race when they teach. Students of color see race and live with race as a core part of their identity all day every day. They are simultaneously proud of their heritage and confined by it. They need teachers who understand that reality; who acknowledge, accentuate, and celebrate the races of their learners; and who help those young people feel completely secure, empowered, and comfortable in their skin (Kafele, 2021).

Following are some guidelines for effectively teaching students of color. The goal is not to use all these strategies, of course, but to understand them as a repertoire from which you can consider options that seem likely to benefit a given learner at a particular time, in a specific context.

SOME PRINCIPLES AND PRACTICES FOR TEACHING TO ELIMINATE RACE AS A BARRIER TO LEARNING

Building a Foundation for Successful Teaching

- Reflect on your growth mindset. Do you believe that children of color can learn to the same degree as Caucasian students—that every student has great hidden capacity that can be drawn out with the right support? Do you teach every day with the understanding that your mindset about the potential of each learner will shape that learner's mindset about his or her own potential? What is your degree of commitment to providing a range of support for students of color that enables them to regularly see themselves as capable and successful, thus developing a growth mindset orientation about themselves?

- Reflect on your equity mindset (Kafele, 2021). An equity mindset in the classroom involves a teacher recognizing that people do not all start from the same place and that it is necessary to adjust our teaching to address the imbalances in learners' starting places. A teacher with an equity mindset identifies and determinedly seeks to overcome intentional and unintentional barriers to learning for a student who needs different treatment and support to make their opportunities the same as another's opportunities.
- Think reflectively about your own culture and heritage. Until we understand how experiences, perspectives, and assumptions in our past have shaped *our* lives, we are not able to understand how the experiences, perspectives, and assumptions of others have shaped *their* lives.
- Study the cultures of the student you teach to understand more deeply the struggles, strengths, victories, and contributions that shape those cultures. It is not possible to understand your students in a meaningful way without knowing their cultures and without understanding the role of race and culture in the lives of those students.
- Look for practices and structures in your school that may reflect bias, stereotyping, and inequity. Advocate for students of color by working to replace those practices and structures with equitable ones.
- Understand the opportunity that is ours to teach students of color to succeed beyond what they had imagined to be possible. Understand, too, the cost to those young people, their communities, the broader communities we all share, and the world if we fail them.

Creating a Safe, Inviting Learning Environment for Students of Color

- See each student of color with unconditional positive regard so that each learner understands that he or she does not need to change anything or do anything to earn your respect and support (Gobir, 2021).
- Work consistently to create a culture of inclusion in which students learn respect, empathy, and appreciation for the contributions of each member of the class. A teacher who regularly models those traits and commends them to students is likely to see them enacted by the students as well.
- Help students learn a sense of responsibility for one another's well-being.
- Build bonds of trust with each learner and take care not to break the trust. If you feel you have damaged a student's trust (which can happen to any teacher), talk with the student about what occurred, apologize, and make clear your intent to do better.
- Make sure your students of color feel seen, valued, empowered, and have a sense of belonging that begins on day one and develops consistently through the year. This is an essential for all students, but even more so for students who feel (and often are) marginalized and even invisible in the world.
- Strive to create an "innocent classroom" (Pate, 2020)—one in which students of color feel free of the negative expectations, the weight of judgment, stereotype, and inequity—a place where they are free to thrive, not just survive (Love, 2019).
- Make your classroom a place where all students share stories, experiences, and laughter—where they make positive memories together.
- See each student as a unique individual, in cultural identity, social and emotional development, academic background, and life experiences, not just as a student of color or as an immigrant or as African American, Latino, Native American, Asian, and so on.

- Take care to see each student as multifaceted. While struggle *is* a factor in the lives of many students of color, their lives are also marked by joy, friendships, celebrations, talents, aspirations, and a host of other defining dimensions. Those dimensions should be in the foreground of teaching and learning.
- Learn each student's name and its correct pronunciation—before the first day of school, if possible.
- Understand that many children of color come to school knowing a great deal about failure. Work to ensure that when they come to school, they learn how to succeed (Collins, 1992) and that their successes are acknowledged and celebrated.
- Value students' primary languages and dialects or community languages and allow them to use those languages in the classroom. Teach them the conventions of language they will need to move forward in the larger society, but ensure that they understand those conventions are *in addition to* the conventions of communication that are important in their homes, neighborhoods, and circles of friends, not a replacement. Help them see themselves as multi lingual, not language-deficient. Most importantly, respect primary languages and community languages so students from diverse cultures can fully embrace them as well.
- Support students in developing positive racial and cultural identities. Students of color and students who experience poverty need to experience antidotes to the devaluing and disparagement they often experience in the world. The classroom needs to honor the cultures represented in it, taking care to point out achievements in areas beyond sports, music, and acting. Students of color need to grow in understanding of their own cultural backgrounds as part of coming to understand history, art, music, language, literature, and other content taught in school. Schools and teachers need also to provide opportunities and support for students to learn in depth about their own cultures.
- Work to be continually more aware of students' feelings, emotions, and needs. Get better at listening and watching beyond the surface. Responsive teaching is rooted in the knowledge we have about our students, and that knowledge is rooted in listening and watching.
- Demonstrate "authentic caring." That sort of caring is sustained, respectful, trusting, and reciprocal. Work consistently not only to care *about* your students (enjoy their company, think about them when you're away from school, attend events that are important to them) but to care *for* them as well (enact the "caring *for*" by doing your best to be sure they get whatever they need to grow and flourish) (Gay, 2018).
- Make sure there are always books available in the classroom in which students can see themselves. It is not uncommon for students of color to be in school for years without reading texts, stories, and novels and without seeing visuals in which the characters, actors, or authors sound and look like them and have experiences like those of your students. For example, a 2015 survey of children's literature found that 73.3% of the books had a main character who was white, 12.5% featured a talking truck or animal, 7.6% had an African American protagonist, and a scant 2.4% of the main characters featured were Latino (Minkel, 2018).
- Connect with families. Ask parents and caregivers of students of color to form partnerships with you to ensure their child's academic, social, and emotional growth. Ask them to share with you their aspirations for their child as well as insight into the student's interests and aspirations. Share with them your plans and aspirations for their child in the school year ahead. Check in regularly to share the student's progress at home and at school, to set goals, and to address concerns and invite them to check in with you.

- Emphasize community in the classroom by giving students many and varied opportunities to work together. Teach the skills of collaboration so they can build networks of appreciation and trust. Many students of color come from cultures that emphasize the importance of community over individuality. Schools in the United States most often emphasize individuality at the cost of community. Building community in the classroom benefits all learners and will make the learning environment considerably more hospitable to students of color and students who experience poverty as well.
- Help students see that it is safe in your classroom to make mistakes and that, in fact, mistakes are necessary for growth. Share your mistakes with them, explaining what you learned from a mistake and how it has helped you do better.
- Ask students who are in the minority in your classroom, and who may both feel and be seen as having little to contribute, to share experiences or interests with the class that make them the expert in a discussion or exploration. For example, a teacher may read or assign a book that takes place in a country that was the first home for a student in the class. That student may be able to explain a game the character is playing, why the character is so excited about an upcoming event, or who a national hero in the story is. One teacher I know occasionally provides groups with key materials needed to complete an assignment in a language spoken only by one or two students in the group. In those instances, a teacher "flipped the expert," ensuring that a student who might normally recede to the background became a source of information and success for his or her peers.
- Share with your students, and with their parents or caregivers, resources that are available in the community to support learning and positive development in the young person and to assist the adults in their homes in a variety of ways as well.

To Teach Students of Color Responsively

- Students of color who do not have disabilities or disorders that inhibit learning in some ways should be expected to use curriculum that is designated for use by students of their age/grade level in their school. The caveat here is that the "standard" curriculum should be engaging, focused on student understanding of critical concepts and ideas in the topic or discipline, and require critical thinking and problem solving as well as metacognition (awareness of one's own thinking). Unfortunately, curricula in many schools do not match that description, and that results in large segments of the K–12 population being less well educated than they need to be and less drawn to learning. Curriculum that is "flat," rote, test-oriented, and disconnected from students' lives will be even more detrimental to students of color and students who experience poverty than it is to others in the school population because it will mirror for students of color the low expectations they experience regularly in their school lives.
- Call on students of color to apply and problem-solve using what they learn. Scaffold students who need additional support to work successfully with those assignments providing graphic organizers, using resources at varied levels of complexity, encouraging students to use resources in their home languages, sharing models of student work that are near the performance levels of varied students in the class so they can see quality work a little above their current performance levels, encouraging and supporting peer collaboration, providing choice in how to express learning, providing clear and focused feedback, meeting with students in small groups to focus on shared needs, and so on.
- Write learning targets in clear, user-friendly language. Ensure that students are fully aware of their learning targets and criteria for success and that they consistently understand the relationship between those

elements and the work they are currently doing. Work to ensure that students feel they "own" their goals rather than the teacher owning the goals.

- Be enthusiastic about what you teach and about students' learning. That will be a catalyst for student enthusiasm.
- Teach as if each learner, regardless of background, ethnicity, or socioeconomic background, were the son or daughter of Harvard or Yale graduates (Collins, 1992), and support students of color in developing the habits of mind and work that undergird success as well as in mastering the complex content. Teaching up to students of color and students who experience poverty (Tomlinson & Javius, 2012) even more than to other groups of learners is necessary because much of their schooling too often has a remedial focus, which rarely helps students catch up or move ahead, and reinforces the student's sense of low expectations for students of color and students who experience poverty. Teaching down to students of color is corrosive. (See Chapter 17 on Teaching Advanced and Advancing Learners for more information on teaching up.)
- Create a culture of achievement in the classroom. That should not suggest a culture of competition, but rather a culture in which students support and celebrate one another's strengths and successes.
- Emphasize literacy development in all aspects of the learning of students of color by, for example, giving students control over what they read and write about as often as possible, providing assignments at levels of challenge appropriate for varied students, establishing clear goals for assignments, providing actionable feedback quickly on literacy-related work, making certain that reading and writing intersect with students' interests and life experiences, and actively supporting students in learning and applying the skills of literacy. It is particularly important for African American males that they regularly encounter characters and issues that honor their identity in fiction,

and that they have abundant opportunity to read nonfiction that teaches them something new and that legitimizes the male experience as they understand it (Tatum, 2005).

- Ensure that what students learn and how they learn it supports students in developing positive racial and cultural identities. Honor the cultures represented in the class, school, and broader community. Help students learn about achievements from their cultural backgrounds in a wide range of roles. Provide opportunities for students to learn more deeply about their own cultures and those of others as well.
- Talk with students often about going to college and other interesting and rewarding paths to a strong and contributing future. Help them learn about the process of preparing for college, applying to college, support that is available to help them through that process, and preparing for a range of contemporary jobs that they may not yet know exist. Understand that while many students seem to be born knowing that college comes after high school, many are not. It is critical for that latter group to come to see college and cutting-edge jobs as part of the narrative of their lives.
- Mentor students in understanding that developing character, empathy, and the skills of collaboration and leadership are equally as important in their lives as learning about history, music, math, or science.
- Help your students of color—and all students—develop the knowledge, skills, dispositions, and voice necessary to be active advocates for social justice for all people—including their own communities and themselves.
- Stress the richness that comes from understanding multiple perspectives on events and ideas, ensuring that your students develop their voices as they contribute their perspectives to meaningful discussions.
- Understand that success is a step-by-step process. Work to help each student move

ahead each day from where they were the day before and to help them realize the connection between working both hard and smart—and success. Differentiate instruction so students work consistently with work that is a little beyond their current point of competence and with teacher and peer support to succeed. Use these opportunities also to develop their talents, link to their interests, and offer a range of ways students can learn and express learning.

- Meet individually and regularly with your students of color (as with other students) to establish and nurture connections, to assess student strengths and needs, to determine what is or is not working in class for a student, and to understand more ways in which you can connect academic learning with student interests, experiences, and aspirations.

- Engage students regularly in planning for their own success, including establishing personal goals and articulating what success will look like in an assignment, assessment, or performance.

- Encourage students to draw on their prior knowledge to prepare for new content. New learning works best when students can connect it to something they already know or have experienced.

- Help students develop agency as learners. Apathy, disconnection, and lack of self-esteem that cause students to disengage with and give up on school is learned behavior. Put students back in the driver's seat by showing them how to be in charge of their own success. Help them channel negative emotions that stem from ongoing discrimination and inequity and/or poverty toward positive actions that can improve their own lives and the lives of others.

- Be sure the curriculum has mirrors, windows, and doors. Mirrors allow students to see themselves and other people from their culture, enabling them to establish deeper cultural roots. Windows provide opportunity for students to see, learn about, and understand cultures and perspectives beyond their own, helping them to value diverse cultures and viewpoints. Doors give them the opportunity to use what they are learning to benefit others and to develop an appreciation for the power of learning in people's lives to enable them to make the world safer, more just, and more humane.

- Make sure students of color study history that includes them and represents their past accurately; stories, music, and art that narrate the experiences of their culture; math that offers opportunity to improve the lives of people in their own communities and across the world; science that pertains to their everyday lives and communities and to a world they want to inherit; and stories that are their own. This enables students to nurture a positive identity as a member of their race or ethnicity *and* to choose excellence and success as a way forward.

- Tie concepts/big ideas from the curriculum to the students' lives and communities to make their work more contextual and relevant. Teach from "big ideas," or concepts that are explanatory across cultures and lives—for example, power, systems, justice and injustice, scarcity, culture, oppression, and equity and inequity. Discuss difficult topics like justice, equity, and power directly with students, helping them grapple with the past and look ahead to more positive change. Help students see how something they are learning in class matters now in their school, community, or country. Use the concepts you are exploring with your students to create projects or performances that enable students to draw parallels between their lives, cultures, and histories and the concept—and to apply and transfer what they are learning in authentic contexts.

- Embed required standards in meaning-rich, active, hands-on activities and authentic assessments that capture student interest and imagination. Make learning joyful—or at least satisfying. Reducing curriculum to mastery of a set of decontextualized standards extinguishes motivation to learn.

- Be conscious of representation of people of color in texts, supporting materials, and media you elect to use with your students. People of color are often underrepresented in both foreground roles and behind-the-scenes leadership roles in media. Texts and other teaching materials as well as the media continue to contribute to negative and/or stereotypical images of people of color, or to largely omit some racial and cultural groups from their education-related materials.

- Check often during lessons for student understanding.
- Use highways and exit ramps to allow you to address the need of the class as a whole and to provide opportunity to work with individuals and small groups on their particular next steps.
- Give students options of working on assignments independently, with one classmate, or in a small group as often as feasible.
- Use a broad range of instructional strategies that take into account the differing instructional, social, and emotional needs of all learners and that give students opportunity to develop voice and make choices both in what and how they learn.
- Use materials that point to the contributions of African American, Latino, Asian, and Native cultures to society, both past and present. Teach the histories, literature, music, and art of all the cultures of the young people you teach—throughout the year, not just in a designated week or month.
- Bring in speakers of color (including first generation college students, no matter the age of your students). All students need experiences that run counter to the stereotypical images of people of color that are so often portrayed in the media.
- Be a "warm-demander." These are teachers who deeply care about each student they teach—and the students know it. They also have little or no tolerance for excuses or "messing around" with either their behavior or their work. The combination of love and high expectations for both academics and

behavior has proven quite successful as a catalyst for growth in students of color. Warm demanders have empathy for their students, but never pity. They understand that to excuse a student from the rigors of real learning is to enable the difficulties that diminish the student's life to persist well into the future.

- Be enthusiastic about what you teach, and give your students reason to become enthusiastic as well.
- Teach students to be reflective about their work so they can identify the strengths and gaps in their work and can plan for increasingly strong outcomes.

To Ensure That Assessment Contributes to Student Growth

- Use ongoing formative assessment to help you be continually aware of students' varied learning paths. Plan instruction to meet students where they are and help them move them forward based on what you learn from formative assessment.
- Make certain that formative and summative assessments as well as instruction align tightly with learning targets (KUDs) specified in your curriculum.
- Provide choices for how students express learning on formative and summative assessments as often as possible, and invite them to propose other options as well.
- Use apps (such as Flipgrid, Nearpod, Explain Everything, Soundtrap, Seesaw, and many others) that support student collaboration and expressing learning in a wide variety of modes.
- Focus assessments on understanding and applying learning rather than largely on repeating information.
- Use performance assessments and authentic audiences for those assessments as often as possible. Sharing ideas, talents, and insights with authentic individuals and groups is far more "stretching" and motivating than turning in a paper to the teacher.
- Emphasize feedback over grades and growth over competition.

- Teach students how to provide effective feedback, help revise one another's work, encourage one another, and study together.
- Work with students to analyze their assessments in light of learning targets and success criteria and to teach them the skills of successful learners so they consistently develop agency in their work.
- Use 3-P grading (Guskey, 1994, 2000, 2019) to enable students, their parents or caregivers, and other key stakeholders to understand a student's current level of *performance* or proficiency with learning targets (KUDs, standards), their working *process* or habits of mind and work, and their *progress* since the previous grade report. All three Ps and the interrelationship among them are important in developing a growth mindset and therefore the motivation to persist in the face of difficulty. If report cards or other formats cannot accommodate the three grades (which should *not* be averaged), create an addendum; send an email or letter to parents/caregivers with the three grades and an explanation of their importance in understanding a student's development; and/or communicate with parents in conferences or phone conversations. Be certain, of course, to emphasize regularly in class and in conversations with individual students the significance of the three Ps and to involve students in tracking and analyzing their status in all three areas.

Addressing Behavior Challenges

- Understand the sources of anger in many students of color. Schools suspend students of color at more than double the rate of white students, and statistics show that a student who is suspended or expelled is three times as likely to be in contact with the juvenile justice system the following year. Realize that misbehavior is a symptom of a young person experiencing conditions that rightfully evoke anger. Misbehavior is communication and protest. Understand also that when students of any ethnic or racial group are disproportionally seen and dealt with as "problems," that reality becomes another form of injustice and a source of fuel for anger.
- Rather than immediately imposing a punishment when a student has broken a rule, committed a wrong against another student, or been disrespectful to the teacher, consider using a shared problem-solving strategy or restorative discipline. In both approaches, an adult works with the student to agree on what happened to determine what took place and to find a way forward that can be more instructive than punitive. In restorative justice, the goal is to answer the questions, "Who has been hurt?" "What are their needs?" "Who has the obligation to remedy those needs and address the harm that has been done?" In schools where these approaches are consistently and appropriately used, office referrals and suspensions are reduced considerably, and the classroom and or school environments are less tense and more amenable to learning.
- Avoid zero tolerance policies. While some infractions of rules or policies may necessitate that educators impose serious consequences, mandating that the same punishment be issued to any person under all circumstances makes it impossible for an educator to take into account extreme circumstances in a child's life that contribute to an infraction. Zero tolerance policies in the judicial system have often proven more harmful than helpful. They have often been applied disproportionally to individuals of color.
- Help students learn to channel anger in productive directions that can enable them to address inequities and make positive change in the classroom, at home, in the community, and in the world.

Keep Learning, Keep Doing Better

- Team up with colleagues who want to be a positive force in the lives of the students of color whom they teach. Work together to understand connections between race and schooling in the lives of your students—and teachers who regularly help students of color succeed. Become "critical friends" as you work together to adapt your teaching to better address the needs of each of the learners in your care.

- When you hear colleagues make comments that are unhelpful—or racist—say something. "It's OK if your face turns red, or you blurt out something that doesn't quite line up as a sentence, or it takes you 12 hours to come up with the line you wish you had said. The important thing is to make a little gash in that conversation, so the comment does not go unnoticed or unchallenged" (Minkel, 2018).

- Continue actively learning about race. Grow in your understanding of the origins of race-based disparities in your community, the country, and the world. Talk with colleagues whose experiences have led them to understand the complex and often devastating impact of race on the education, health, and future prospects of students of color. Listen to their stories. Read. Seek out quality professional learning opportunities. Get involved in groups that make a positive impact on the lives and communities of students you teach.

Long ago, the German poet Johann Wolfgang von Goethe observed that if we treat an individual as he is, he will remain as he is. If we treat that individual as if he were what he could be and ought to be, he will become what he ought to be and could be. In education, we have ample evidence that when students are treated as though they are smart, they are likely to demonstrate that capacity

We know that when we provide instructional scaffolding, students can move from what they know to what they need to know. We know that in order to do those things, the focus of our classroom for every student must be learning that is consistently challenging, dynamic, relevant, and complex. We know that effective teaching requires us to have in-depth knowledge of both the content and the individual students we teach. And we know how to make those things happen. The question of our will to enact those principles into classroom realities is less clear.

There is no greater opportunity (and obligation) for schools at this point in our history than to redraw the boundaries of opportunity for students of color, to reconfigure our thinking about the potential of those students, and to find the will and develop the skills necessary to contribute remarkably to a history of opportunity and promise for these young people. To continue to fail them is to fail society, the world, our profession—and ourselves as individuals.

NOTE

The following sources were consulted for this chapter. Full citations appear in the References section. American Psychological Association, 2017; Annie E. Casey Foundation, 2006; Anti-Defamation League, 2021; Berger et al., 2014; Burnham, 2020; Cole, 1995; Collins, 1992; El-Mekki, 2017; Gay, 2018; Gobir, 2021; Greene, 2014, 2016; Guskey, 1994, 2000, 2019; Horn et al., 2021; Kafele, 2021; Kam, 2020; Ladson-Billings, 1994; Love, 2020; Milner, 2006; Minkel, 2018; National Association of Colleges & Employers, 2021; PACER's National Bullying Prevention Center, 2020; Pate, 2020; Randolph, 2021; Russaw, 2019; Tatum, 2005; Tomlinson & Javius, 2012.

CHAPTER 17

Teaching Advanced and Advancing Learners

How do we create and support communities that help all students *believe* that they are smart?

—Karen Economopolous, Center for Curriculum and Professional Development

INTRODUCTION

In the first half of this book, I used the first-person pronoun often for two reasons. First, I was sharing ideas from the model of differentiation with which I have worked in various contexts for over 50 years. In other words, the ideas about differentiation, while supported by research, and applied and refined by many, are my professional focus. Second, using the first-person pronoun enables me to tell stories. Those stories, in turn, provide illustrations of the ideas in which they are embedded and often help us relate to, recall, and draw on ideas more readily than if they were only delineated.

In this second part of the book, I have, to this point, largely avoided using first-person references—again for two reasons. First, I have drawn on knowledge from experts in a range of specialties with experiences that have informed my thinking about learners who need particular attention in their classrooms in order to grow and flourish, so the ideas in this section are not generally my primary professional focus. In addition, this second section of the book is intended to present brief and accessible "how-tos" rather than to elaborate or illustrate ideas, and stories are not a match for the goal of brevity.

The exception to the use of the first person in this second component of the book is this chapter (Chapter 17) where I will use it often. Here, I am once again sharing ideas that are integral to my work over several decades, as well as reflective of the work of other researchers and practitioners, and I will again share examples or stories that come from my work as a teacher.

The logical title for this chapter would have been "Supporting Students Who Are Identified as Gifted," or "Supporting Students Who Are Advanced Academically or Intellectually." Neither of those titles, however, reflect the perspective that has evolved in my thinking over time. My hope is that sharing my perspective on the topic will prompt your continued thinking individually as well as for conversations among colleagues about this area of educational practice that is important, complex, and controversial. Following is a brief capsule of that thinking and therefore of the direction the principles and practices this chapter will take.

- I believe that our schools are not what they could or should be until every student can go to school confident that they will be supported in moving forward from their current points of development every day. Plus-one teaching, as John Hattie (2012) terms it, calls on the teacher to plan for each learner to move forward every day *at least* one step (one chunk, one skill, one idea, one insight . . .) beyond that student's entry point on that day. That is not a call for perfection, but rather a call to work from intention.
- I believe that many students in our schools do not have the opportunity to grow +1 each day. Our general tendency to teach one-size-fits-all lessons is reinforced by our sense that covering standards and trying to prepare everyone alike is a necessity for a test that is highly standardized. This sense of

necessity results in a great deal of teaching that is uniform, low-level, and rushed.

- I believe students whom we think of as advanced intellectually or academically are among the many students for whom school tends to be less than challenging, engaging, dynamic, or exciting. Like all students, these learners ought to be able to regularly encounter learning that is all those things—and +1 growth.

- However, I believe that the time-honored approach of trying to identify who is "truly gifted" and then teaching them separately in programs or classes as we have often done in public schools is problematic in several ways.

  » The measures we use to identify students as gifted typically represent a narrow conception of ability, omitting, for example, creativity, talent areas, insight, and leadership abilities.

  » Few schools have the time or staff required to support the kind of assessment process that would be necessary for stakeholders to have high confidence that the process is trustworthy.

  » Common identification processes *do* find students who *are* advanced (that is, perhaps not too many "false positives"). However, the system is replete with "false negatives" (that is, excluding from consideration students who have the capacity to achieve at high levels but whom the process overlooks or rejects as appropriate for identification). For example, schools or districts with cut off scores for identification as gifted commonly decide not to identify a student as gifted whose score on an aptitude test is 1 point or 2 or 5 below the cut-off indicator when there is no evidence that 2 or 5 or maybe even 10 or 15 points predicts that the individual who came up short has less capacity to learn advanced content or to benefit from advanced learning opportunities than the student who made the slightly higher score and was accepted for services.

» Of concern in many identification protocols is the small number of students of color, students from poverty, second language learners, and students with learning challenges (that do not suggest cognitive restrictions) who are identified as gifted. While there has been more attention to the disproportionally low identification of students from a variety of groups as "gifted" in the last few years, therefore denying them access to "advanced" learning opportunities, that problem is far from solved at this point.

» When we identify some students as the smart ones, the non identified students often draw the conclusion that they are *not* smart. Many members of that group see the exclusion as additional evidence that school is not their thing.

» Sadly, it is also easy for general education teachers to feel relieved of the obligation to do instructional planning for advanced students, since identified students are generally removed from their regular classrooms for varied (and often brief) periods of time so a specialist can teach them. A common outcome is that few general education teachers have the opportunity or motivation to develop the understandings and skills necessary to teach at high levels that are required to support complex learning. When that is the case, *all* students in their classrooms are poorer as a result.

» Once students are identified as eligible for services as gifted, the programs that serve them are often characterized by one or more of three problematic approaches:

  1. Students are asked to learn "more of the same stuff faster."
  2. Students are taught "higher-level thinking skills," but out of context from meaningful disciplinary-based content that shapes those skills and is necessary for

a student to be able to transfer those skills.

3. Students do "creative, enriching" activities that *may* be entertaining but that often have little to do with authentic creativity and discipline-based learning.

In a fourth approach to designing curriculum and instruction for students identified as gifted, students *do* consistently engage in work that *is* discipline-based, *is* anchored in the big ideas or concepts and principles that frame the disciplines, *does* call on students to solve problems and think in ways that are similar to those of experts in the discipline, *does* help students develop the skills and habits of mind that support further development of their abilities, and *does* require students to create authentic products or performances for meaningful audiences to demonstrate their learning.

This fourth approach *is* aligned with what experts in the field of gifted education advocate for students identified as gifted. However, this sort of program appears not to be dominant among services for students identified as gifted. Even if it were, there would still be at least two problems that would be difficult to surmount.

- First, many/most classes for students identified as gifted are taught as though all students in the class were fundamentally alike, overlooking the reality that ability comes in many forms and develops along many timelines. Services for any group of students—high ability included—fail many of its members unless they make room for their varied strengths, needs, backgrounds, and points of development (academically, socially, and emotionally). In addition, students whom teachers conclude "cannot do the work" readily in those classes are often seen as "not really gifted" and/or are removed from the services. This is particularly damaging to students who have not had the level of opportunity to learn and the support for learning that many more affluent students in those classes *have* had. These two factors, combined with

identification processes that are not robust in identifying ability in students of color, students who live in poverty, students from a wide range of cultures, and students with learning differences, have much to do with the reality that programs for gifted learners continue to struggle with the perception that they are elitist.

- Second, in those programs where students identified as gifted *are* regularly involved with work that is discipline-based, anchored in the big ideas or concepts and principles that frame the disciplines, and so on, as outlined above, there remains another problem that is difficult, if not impossible, to overcome. Those characteristics of curriculum and instruction are commended broadly by experts in education, psychology, and neuroscience as not only appropriate but as foundational for curriculum and instruction for the great majority of learners in our schools (for example, Borland, 2003, 2018; Erickson, Lanning, & French, 2017; Fullan, Quinn, & McEachen, 2018; National Research Council, 2000; Schlechty, 2011, Sousa & Tomlinson, 2018; Wiggins & McTighe, 2005).

So, *even if* prevailing practices in thinking about ability were expanded, *even if* identification mechanisms for those programs were more encompassing, and *even if* most programs for students identified as gifted functioned at what would now be considered best practices for teaching students identified as gifted, and *even if* those programs operated in ways that were responsive to the varied manifestations of ability in the widest possible range of young people, there would still remain the confounding problem that schools are often focused on finding a small group of learners who "deserve" or "need" the kind of curriculum and instruction that, in fact, schools would offer to most of its students *if* schools employed curriculum and instruction that research and experience suggest belongs/ought to belong to most of their learners.

Dylan Wiliam (2011b) reflects that schools tend to function as talent refineries. That is, when they see talent that is evident, they provide opportunities to further develop that talent—opportunities for those students to take advanced classes or participate in programs for gifted students. Schools then sort students into layers (which I sadly once heard a small group of educators refer to as "the definitlies," "the maybes," and "the no-hopes"). The maybes and the no-hopes are seldom pushed to excel. They can opt out of classes that don't seem to be "their thing." As Wiliam points out through an analogy, coaches don't have that luxury. They have to win games with whoever is on the team. They can't say, "The quarterback is weak this year, so we won't play." It is a coach's job to make the quarterback the best he can be—likely better than either of them thought he could be. Coaches cannot just refine evident talent; they must incubate it—not just nurture it, but even produce it.

My sense at this point in my journey in education is that schools and teachers need to take on the roles of the coaches that Wiliam describes. That is, schools should function as talent incubators. We live in a time when our villages, towns, cities, states, nation, and the world need the best that every young person can possibly bring into adulthood. We cannot afford to look for and try to extend evident ability in only a few young people. We ought not to begin by saying, "Let me see who appears obviously smart, talented, and creative so I can make sure *their* ability is extended." Rather, we need to begin with the assertion, "Each student who comes into my classroom has far more potential than is visible to them or to me. I will do the best I know to do and can learn to do to provide opportunity and support to elicit and extend that capacity—including in those learners who are working well in advance of their peers" (adapted from Tomlinson, 2021).

To be clear, I think it is not only unwise, but professionally unethical to allow students who have evident advanced abilities to spend much of their school days waiting for classmates to learn skills and amass knowledge that they have already mastered. It is unproductive and usually alienating to ask advanced learners to do more work than others as a way of "challenging them" or "meeting their needs." While, in my opinion, teachers should work diligently to create environments in which all students genuinely learn to respect and support one another, it is *not* an appropriate use of the school time of advanced learners to spend *significant* parts of a day serving as tutors for peers. Likewise, it

seems inappropriate either to place a few students in "special" classrooms that will serve only students identified as gifted but where the students' traits are not likely to be extended in meaningful ways, or to place them routinely in special classrooms where the work *is* appropriately challenging for them while excluding many other students from the opportunity to do that work if it would benefit the excluded students as well.

That calls on us not so much to be talent refiners as to be talent incubators and talent producers (Wiliam, 2011b). I believe we can largely accomplish that by teaching up effectively in "big tent classrooms" where the teacher is vigorously supported in learning how to teach up and in which he/she can partner with specialists in defensible teaching for advanced learners and specialists in other areas who can support teaching up for a wide range of learners. This is not a once-and-done proposition, but is absolutely doable with a vision-oriented, stepwise, sustained process of schoolwide growth and change (Tomlinson et al., 2008; Tomlinson & Murphy, 2015).

Just as there are some students whose learning challenges are too great to be addressed effectively in an inclusive classroom, there will be some students who are so far advanced in their development that a general education teacher, even teaming with a specialist in teaching advanced learners, cannot help them adequately to extend their development. In those instances, schools and/or districts can provide meaningful alternatives for those students in a variety of ways that have been used over many years.

TRAITS AND NEEDS OF STUDENTS THAT SHOULD BE ON OUR TEACHER RADAR

There are some traits that are generally ascribed to "gifted" learners that teachers should look for in and encourage in *all* students. Once we begin attending to these traits, we will likely see them both in students whom we decided early on were advanced learners and in students in whom we did not really expect to see them. When we observe the traits in any student, it is a cue to continue watching that student and, more importantly, to create learning opportunities that enable the student to focus on and develop those traits. More to the point, these traits should be in the forefront of our thinking as well our planning of curriculum and instruction to help refine, incubate, and produce the skills, attitudes, and habits of mind that stretch capacity in a broad spectrum of learners.

As is the case with every other "category" of learners, it is important for teachers to understand that there is no such thing as "*an* advanced" or "gifted" learner. They may show great promise in some subjects but not in others. They may be careful rule-followers or have considerable disdain for rules. They may be impressive with convergent tasks but do work that is mediocre or less than mediocre with divergent tasks (or vice versa). They may have attention spans that are remarkable for their age or find it quite difficult to pay attention in school. They may have well-developed and intuitive social skills or be quite awkward in that area. They may have a specific learning disorder or be on the autism spectrum and struggle mightily with reading, writing, or communication and yet have a great store of knowledge and insight in multiple areas. They may be socially and/or emotionally mature or immature in one or both of those areas. Their abilities may be masked as a result of grappling with gender identity, racism, trauma, or poverty. Here are a few traits ascribed to learners we think of as gifted. There should be no expectation that the list is complete, or even that the presence or absence of many of the traits is adequate to evidence that a learner has or lacks high ability.

The student:

- is an independent thinker;
- is an abstract thinker;
- is an original/creative thinker;
- likes producing original products;
- generates multiple solutions to problems;
- processes complex ideas and information;
- is observant;
- is inquisitive;
- is insightful;
- is excited about new ideas and eager to learn new things;
- takes intellectual risks;
- makes connections between ideas, across content area, and with his/her experiences;
- is idealistic and has high ethical standards;

- masters skills and knowledge quickly;
- memorizes easily;
- comprehends readily;
- has strong communication skills/advanced language skills;
- assumes responsibility;
- sees cause-and-effect relationships readily;
- has strong problem-solving skills;
- has high expectations for self and others;
- is persistent;
- has a large vocabulary and refined language development;
- has a keen sense of humor;
- pursues personal interests eagerly;
- is a self-starter;
- has a high energy level;
- is well-liked by peers; and
- challenges the thinking and ideas of peers and adults.

It is wise to think about how these traits might appear or be disguised in students who live with poverty, students from different cultures, students learning the language of the classroom, students who have a specific learning disorder, and so on. For example, an English learner may not have what we would think of as refined communication skills in English for her age group but is acquiring the skills of English much more rapidly than agemates who have been learning English for the same length of time or longer. A student of color who is impressive at solving interpersonal problems among peers may be less impressive in solving word problems in math, or vice versa. A student who experiences poverty may seem to have mediocre background knowledge about science, for example, when, in fact, the knowledge is remarkable given the student's limited opportunity to learn outside of school. A student with a specific learning disorder may struggle with reading and become easily frustrated with text and yet comprehend spoken text readily and with depth of understanding.

Further, *no* student exhibits all those traits (or even most of them), and certainly not all of the traits in all contexts. In addition, there are some traits of learners identified as gifted that can be problematic for that student or for others. They can be impatient, perfectionistic, too self-confident, lacking in interpersonal skills, and so on. The goal in a classroom with all students should be to help the learner develop and then refine positive attributes and habits of mind as well as better understand how to cope with or reduce the negative impact of less productive traits.

THINKING ABOUT REFINING, INCUBATING, AND PRODUCING TALENT (TEACHING UP)

Nearly a quarter-century ago, the National/State Leadership Training Institute for the Gifted and Talented (N-S/LTI) outlined criteria that should be used in developing curriculum for students identified as gifted. Appropriate curricula would

- focus on and be organized to include more elaborate, complex, and in-depth study of major ideas, problems, and themes that integrate knowledge within and across the disciplines;
- allow for developing and applying productive thinking skills that allow students to reconceptualize existing knowledge and to generate new knowledge;
- enable the learners to explore continually changing knowledge and information and understand the value of pursuing knowledge in an open world;
- encourage exposure to, selection of, and use of specialized and appropriate resources;
- promote self-initiated and self-directed learning and growth;
- support students' development of self-understanding and understanding of one's relationship to persons, societal institutions, nature, and culture; and
- evaluate their work with the curricula in light of these principles and stressing high-level skills, creativity, and excellence in performance and products. (Hertberg-Davis, 2018)

Those basic principles are still fundamental to most curricula developed for students identified as gifted. In the time span between when the N-S/LTI principles were developed and now, however, there has been considerable conversation and debate about whether those principles and resulting curricula should be largely the purview of learners identified as gifted or whether curricula for virtually all learners should be framed around the same principles. The general consensus is that all learners should have access to and support for curricula that encompass the N-S/LTI principles—that is, curriculum that is concept-based and principle-driven, requires development of complex thinking skills and an emphasis on understanding, focuses on real-world problems and development of products or performances that address those problems, reflects the nature of the disciplines, mentors students in developing the habits of mind and work of practicing professionals in a field of study, and teaches the skills of independence in learning (Hertberg-Davis, 2018).

Hopefully, you recognize those principles from reading the first section of the book, which addresses the foundational principles and practices of differentiation for all learners as well as from recommendations in the second section of the book for all "categories" of learners featured in that section. In 1979, when the N-S/LTI principles were published, the field of cognitive psychology was in its very early stages of evolution. The prevailing approach to psychology and learning at the time was rooted in behaviorism and commended drill, practice, and memorization as dominant pathways to learning. By contrast, research in cognitive psychology was revealing the importance of thinking, sense-making, application of knowledge and skill in meaningful contexts, and so on. The N-S/LTI principles reflect the early belief of that group that a cognitive approach to learning was more appropriate for advanced learners than the behavioristic approach. In time, cognitive psychology proved the more effective of the two models in creating durable and transferable learning in a great majority of students—the kind of learning that, in a new century, many educational leaders would commend for all learners in a more complex and uncertain world.

There are still aspects of learning, of course, that require drill, practice, and memorization, but cognitive psychology and neuroscience suggest that that knowledge and those skills should be used in meaningful, relevant contexts beyond those in the workbook or on worksheets. The principles and practices of cognitive psychology have proven more effective as a basis for designing curriculum and instruction, and in more recent years, the emerging field of neuroscience has demonstrated why and how the principles of cognitive psychology benefit learning as the field continues to learn more about how the brain works.

As it has become clearer that principles of curriculum design such as those proposed by the N-S/LTI should be applied to curricula for all learners, proponents of Gifted Education largely concur with the idea that all learners benefit from the kind of "rich" curriculum and instruction that were once reserved for students identified as gifted. They propose that what distinguishes curriculum for more advanced learners from curriculum that should be available to all learners are descriptors such as depth, complexity, pacing, and problem ambiguity (Hertberg-Davis, 2018).

That brings us back to Wiliam's (2011b) idea of talent refineries versus talent incubators—two possible ways to think about the role of teachers and schools in developing student capacity. Inclusion (and differentiation) are inclined to opt for the latter approach whenever possible. Whereas the talent refinery strives to find evident capacity that already exists and is at least reasonably well developed, talent incubators follow the logic that all students have capacity that is hidden from view. With the right support, schools and classrooms can enable that capacity not only to come into view but also to continue to expand its dimensions. Incubator classrooms also ensure that students who have visible or evident advanced capacity likewise continue to extend their capacity as well. An instructional-planning approach for accomplishing those goals is teaching up.

In short, that means creating and offering curriculum to all students that is rooted in principles such as those proposed by the N-S/LTI and proponents of "21st-century learning" and "deep learning." In other words, the curriculum expects all learners to be thinkers and problem solvers, to understand the concepts and principles (or big ideas) of the disciplines they study, to connect their learning with the real world in ways that are relevant to the learner's experience, and to learn the skills and habits of mind that undergird success (including those of independent learning, collaborative learning, and self-evaluation). All learners could be challenged and supported in continually moving forward in learning from their current points of development.

One mechanism that guides teachers in enabling all students to work with rich, complex curriculum at degrees of difficulty that are appropriately challenging for varied learners is shown in Figure 17.1. "The Equalizer" is a guide for thinking about varying the degree of difficulty of a task. A teacher can mentally "move the buttons" on The Equalizer to the left a smaller or greater amount to reduce the degree of difficulty of an assignment, or mentally move them toward the right to varying degrees to increase the degree of task difficulty. Planning with one or more of the buttons moved toward the right, a teacher can write the original "high expectations" assignment with degrees of depth, complexity, problem ambiguity, multifacetedness, and so on that tend to create more advanced challenges. By moving one or more of the buttons varying degrees to the left, the same "rich" assignment can be configured to varied challenge levels that are appropriate for the varied points of development of learners in the class.

The Equalizer is designed to look like the "tuners" on a piece of audio equipment with which users can adjust volume, tone, fade, pitch, and so on. That kind of equipment is called an equalizer and suggested the name of the more abstract piece of equipment displayed in Figure 17.1.

In terms of instructional planning, The Equalizer is a metaphor rather than a piece of hardware, of course, but it is useful in helping teachers understand what it means to calibrate the challenge level of a task that is already robust in what it asks of students. It is a way of thinking about and planning for equity of access to excellent learning opportunities for students with a great variety of backgrounds and experiences.

"Scaffolding" takes its name from supports constructed around a building until it is able to safely stand without the supporting structure. The term scaffolding encompasses a range of tools that make it possible to create learning experiences that are at varying degrees of difficulty, allowing many students to work at appropriate levels of challenge while still engaging in curriculum that

Figure 17.1. The Equalizer—A Tool for Designing Differentiated Lessons Based on Learner Readiness in a Lesson or Topic

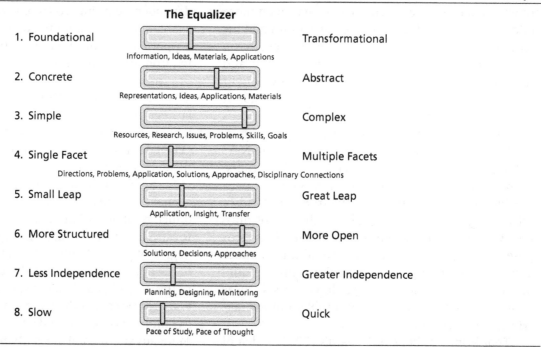

Source: Adapted from *How to Differentiate Instruction in Academically Diverse Classrooms* (3rd ed.), by C. A. Tomlinson, 2017, ASCD. Copyright © 2017 ASCD. Reprinted with permission.

is engaging, relevant, thought-provoking, and authentic. In teaching, scaffolding is support that enables a learner to grow stronger in one or more areas until that learner can work independently in those areas. There are many kinds of scaffolding that a teacher can use to enable a learner to access work that is a bit beyond his or her current reach. Figure 17.2 lists a few forms of scaffolding.

It is useful to understand that *any* student who is working at a challenge level a bit beyond his or her present comfort level, including those who are markedly advanced compared to most age-mates, will likely need scaffolding along the way. Making that stretch happen should be a primary goal in our instructional planning. That includes students who are working at a level that is markedly advanced when compared to most agemates.

In fact, a central goal in differentiated, Everybody Classrooms is for each student to work slightly beyond his or her comfort level or Zone of Proximal Development much of the time, with the teacher or peers providing support/scaffolding for the student to stretch and ultimately succeed with the work.

The next chapter provides two examples of assignments that teach up, with all students having access to learning experiences that meet the specifications for:

- appropriate curriculum and instruction for students identified as gifted (curriculum that we should see as the right of the vast majority of learners to access);
- fine-tuning or calibrating the assignment using the concepts on The Equalizer so the assignment is refined to be appropriately challenging for and accessible to the range of learners in a class;
- providing scaffolding that supports students in doing quality work with the assignment; and
- encouraging student choice and voice in suggesting/designing alternative options through which they will demonstrate the knowledge, understanding, and skills that are the learning targets for the assignment.

As you examine the examples and think about questions that point you back to ideas throughout

Figure 17.2. Examples of Scaffolding to Support Student Success When Assignments Are a Bit Beyond Their Current Reach

A Few Examples of Instructional Scaffolding

- Using recorded (or oral) vs. written directions for an assignment
- Writing the directions in simpler language
- Writing directions in bullet points rather than in paragraph form
- Asking a student to complete an assignment one step at a time rather than tackling all its parts at once
- Designating students to serve as "expert of the day" to assist with student questions about an assignment
- Providing resources in a learner's first language
- Providing clear criteria for success and ensuring that each student understands the criteria
- Providing models of quality student work at varied levels of complexity so that a student can look at effective work completed at about that student's challenge level
- Providing clear, actionable feedback on student work throughout a unit or inquiry
- Having students work in teams to support one another's work
- Encouraging a student to turn in work for teacher feedback several times prior to its due date
- Giving directions for work, or explaining complex ideas or skills required for the work, and posting the video on a class website or other locations so students can refer to the explanations as they work
- Making time for students to discuss their work and ask questions during direct instruction, small-group work, and student/teacher conferences
- Giving students a choice of the mode through which they will demonstrate what they have learned

the book, you should get a sense of what it means to create a classroom that is designed to address both the needs students have in common and those that are more particular to a single student or a small group of students. Both classrooms are built around the foundational ideas explored in the first part of the book. The architecture of that foundation makes it more natural to accommodate a broad range of academic, emotional, and social needs that learners bring to school each day.

NOTE

The following sources were consulted for this chapter. Full citations appear in the References section. Azano et al., 2018; Borland, 2003, 2018; Bryant et al., 2020; Callahan, 2018; Erickson et al., 2017; Fullan et al., 2018; Hertberg-Davis, 2018; Horn et al., 2021; Imbeau, 2020; S. Kaplan, 2018; National Research Council, 2000; Schlechty, 2011; Smith et al., 2020; Wiggins & McTighe, 2005.

CHAPTER 18

Two Examples From Everybody Classrooms

I remember a time when our class was analyzing lyrics from protest songs of the Viet Nam era. You walked around the room and sat with every group as we worked, asking us questions, prompting our thinking. At the time, I didn't realize that you had given different songs and directions to different groups based on our current needs and knowledge. I just knew that after the groups, we had a great whole-class discussion on our ideas. . . . I've only begun to understand how your teaching changed me as a learner and as a prospective teacher. You created perhaps the only truly nurturing class of my high school career. You knew me as an individual, not just as one blurry face among the scores of students who passed through your class each day.

—From a letter written to a former teacher by a preservice teacher at the University of Virginia

The examples that follow first present and describe learning sequences in a classroom, and then invite readers to think of themselves as clinical classroom observers and analyze the teaching examples as they relate to "teaching up" to enable a broad range of diverse learners to have equity of access to and support for succeeding at rich, complex work. The first example spans about half of a marking period in a middle school English class. The second example examines one math lesson in a 1st-grade class and is therefore more compact in its scope.

Example #1: Middle School English

As the third marking period of the school year begins, Ms. Ballard and her 7th-graders are about to begin literature circle discussions of novels. The example of her teaching featured here comes from her second-period class. Figure 18.1 provides the learning targets (KUDs) for the work these students will do with novels.

Ms. Ballard will show the class five student-developed trailers to introduce five novels, with brief discussions following each trailer. Students will then have several opportunities over the next three days to examine each of the five novels. Finally, Ms. Ballard asks students to give her the names of their top two individual choices for the novels they would most like to read. She meets separately with students who need some support in selecting a novel and discusses with some of them the option to use both written and spoken versions of the novel they choose. Two of the novels are available in Spanish.

Next, she assigns students to a literature circle in which all members selected the same novel. Her intent is to assign the groups based on students' first-choice novels unless she feels strongly that a student's first-choice book is so far above or below that student's readiness to read and respond to the book that the choice would not support student growth. In those instances, she talks with the student, and they decide together which option would be most likely to work well for the student. The five books, which vary in genre, cultural focus, reading level, and complexity of ideas, are:

A Place to Belong (Cynthia Kadohata)
The Westing Game (Ellen Raskin)
The Crossover (Kwame Alexander)
Touching Spirit Bear (Ben Mikaelsen)
The School for Good and Evil (Soman Chainani)

During the approximately 12–14-day span of the literature circles, Ms. Ballard assigns students to the traditional roles of:

Figure 18.1. KUDs Related to Student Work With Novels in Ms. Ballard's Second-Period Class

As a result of our exploration of novels and tools of novelists, students should:		
Know	Understand	Be Able to Do
Terms: fiction, novel, biography, autobiography, plot, setting, character, characterization, mood, tone, diction, analyze, supporting evidence	Good fiction is about the reader, too. Through good fiction, readers try on different lives to see how they fit.	Explain, with supporting evidence, how a writer makes characters come alive. Explain, with supporting evidence, how a writer uses elements of literature to create a theme (or "big idea" in a novel). Connect elements of fiction (including plot, setting, character, characterization, and theme) to your own lives.

Essential Question: How do good authors turn readers into thinkers?

- *Discussion Director.* Welcome the group; remind the group of the reading for the day; encourage group members to share something they liked, that puzzled them, or that they want to know more about; and so on. Call on students to play their role, taking care to support students as they speak. Develop 4–5 questions to pose to group members as the day's discussion continues. Keep time.
- *Literary Observer.* Find examples of literary devices such as metaphors, similes, onomatopoeia, alliteration, etc.; examples of passages that help build a theme; strong examples of characterization; etc.
- *Summarizer.* Prepare a brief summary of the day's reading and 4–5 key points or events to share with the group.
- *Illustrator.* Imagine or visualize something from the day's reading. Draw it. Add details in or around the drawing. Be prepared to explain the drawing and the details you added and why you did both as you did.
- *Vocabulary Detective.* Select 3–4 words in tomorrow's reading that you do not know the meaning of. Find out what they mean. Share the new words and their meanings with the group. Talk about why you think the author used each word as he or she did versus a synonym.
- *Connector.* Connect something—things, passages, people, ideas—in the reading with your experience, other books, movies, subjects, songs, and the world.

Ms. Ballard provides role cards that briefly explain the role and give examples of the kinds of things the student might focus on in preparation for a session. This is the third time this year that her students have been in literature circles, and so they understand the roles and discussion process well. The instructions in this cycle help student leaders focus on how an author uses characterization and setting to help readers think about possible messages, themes, or big ideas in the novel. Students generally keep their roles for 4 or 5 days in a cycle. In this round, Ms. Ballard assigns students to roles that are a good match for their strengths. At other times, students select roles or draw them randomly. Throughout the year, Ms. Ballard works with students on principles and practices related to successful collaboration, including respect for individual learning needs, individual perspectives, and supporting one another's growth.

When students have difficulty understanding or carrying out a role, Ms. Ballard may meet with them individually or in small groups to help them generate ideas. Sometimes she asks students who need extra support to connect with her in the evening for a brief Facetime chat or to email ideas to her so she can respond in time to be helpful. At other times, she asks a student who recently filled a role successfully to talk with a student who is now playing that role. In the back of the classroom is a small area that has a comfortable chair, a couple of bean bags, a shelf with a few books that change often, and a few tension-relieving "toys" where students sometimes sit as they read or write but that students can also use when they are feeling anxious or irritable to separate themselves from the group. This area is available to students who need to leave their circle for a bit or whom Ms. Ballard might invite to come there to talk with her for a bit.

While students are in the literature circles, Ms. Ballard visits each group, listening to their discussions, making notes on group function as well as individual contributions, and sometimes asking a few questions to prompt student thinking about the unit KUDs. During most class periods, Ms. Ballard reserves 10 minutes for one-on-one conversations with students. During those conversations, she works with students who have a variety of learning challenges. They may focus on skills that are problematic for a

student, behavioral or social challenges, goal-setting, or just talking about school or life in general. She finds these times to be quite valuable in helping her understand students so she can teach them more effectively and in establishing mutual trust. Sometimes these check-ins are valuable in providing a break for students who have difficulty with managing their emotions and behavior in groups.

During the last 10–12 minutes in a class period, she shares some of her observation notes, both pointing to specific strengths in what she saw (Glows) and making suggestions for next steps in their work with the process of group analysis and discussion (Grows). In addition, she poses one or two questions to the group for their consideration and response. The questions are applicable across novels rather than being book-specific. In this round of literature circles, her questions generally focus on qualities of compelling writing, how plot and character lead

THINKING ABOUT MS. BALLARD'S THINKING

Ms. Ballard's second-period class is an "umbrella classroom," with two students who have clear reading challenges, three students who are relatively new to English, two who have been in the United States for at least 5 years but who are still working toward English proficiency, one student with attention and behavioral challenges, a number of students who come from low-income families, and several students who are academically (though not always socially or emotionally) advanced. Several students of color in her class show some signs of struggling with issues related to equity and "fairness at school and beyond." She often says, however, "As nearly as I can tell, every one of my students has special needs. Every one of them needs my attention in ways that change over the year. My challenge to myself is to teach as though I have a room full of exceptional learners— exceptional in many ways." To analyze her work in the preceding example, use the following prompts:

- Use a highlighter or sticky notes to indicate elements in the description that suggest she is using a principle or practice you have learned about in this book that contributes to successful Everybody Classrooms. Jot an abbreviated version of the principle or practice in the book's margin near the highlight or on the sticky note.
- Look at Figure 5.3. Find indicators on the list that you have not already highlighted and mark those in the description of Ms. Ballard's work as well.
- Review the principles and practices section of one or more chapters in this book on students with EBD, ADHD, specific learning disorder, English learners, students of color, students who experience poverty, and students who are advanced academically (these are the categories Ms. Ballard says are represented in her second-period class and that are explored in the third section of this book).
- Which principles and practices in the list(s) at the end of the chapter(s) you selected do you see implemented in the portion of Ms. Ballard's work described previously?
- Which other principles in the list(s) you selected are not explicitly described in the overview of Ms. Ballard's class but that you might infer are present because the description of the nature of her practices suggests they could be a fit for her way of thinking about and teaching a wide spectrum of learners?

readers to understand a theme, and how elements in the novel relate to students' own experiences.

On some days, Ms. Ballard asks students to respond in writing or via recording to brief questions or prompts to provide formative evidence of student thinking and understanding related to an author's use of setting and character to develop themes. She uses student responses to help her know how to adjust whole class, small group, and individual assignments in the short term.

During the second segment of the quarter, Ms. Ballard and her students will continue their work with reading and analyzing novels, but will also use photography to study poetry, work with several strategies for vocabulary-building tailored to current needs of the diverse learners in the class, and write regularly with a focus on both whole-class and individual goals. In all these areas, there will be a balance of whole-class, small-group, and individual work time so students can share interesting and important investigations related to their work and also have time to focus on their own strengths and needs. As they read or work on writing individually, some students are likely to wear headphones to cancel sound, to visit the small "living room" in the rear of the classroom, or to work at one of three stand-up desks in the room. This segment of the quarter will last about 3 weeks.

As the second segment of the marking period begins, Ms. Ballard again asks students to select a novel they are interested in reading—this time from the classroom library or school library, both of which have large selections of novels that appeal to a wide variety of middle schoolers. Students can choose from any genre—mystery, science fiction, fantasy, animal tales, adventure, graphic novels, and so on. She even included biography and autobiography in the possibilities because, as she said, "Good biographies and autobiographies are inevitably *great* stories and provide prime opportunities for readers to try on lives of *real* people too." As students make their selections, she gives them a Think-Tac-Toe assignment that will serve as a performance assessment for this portion of the quarter (see Figure 18.2). In the assignment, students will select one challenge related to characterization, one related to setting, and one related to theme.

Each assignment asks students to demonstrate an understanding of how authors use characterization and setting to lead to a theme and to apply the unit's two understandings (big ideas, principles) in contexts that are different from work they have done in class.

In the figure, you will note that there are two versions of the assignment, labeled Version 1 and Version 2. Those labels do *not* appear on the students' copies of the Think Tac Toe. They are added in the figure to help readers understand the process the teacher used to create the two versions. You will also notice that both versions contain the same KUDs on the bottom of the page and both contain quality descriptors on the top of the page. The quality descriptors are slightly different on the two versions, with those on Version 1 at a higher degree of difficulty.

Students will do their work guided by a rubric that focuses on the elements of fiction that are spotlighted in this segment of the marking period as well as a category called "Quality of Work." They meet first in small groups and then with Ms. Ballard to develop descriptors of the qualities at the top of their Think Tac Toe assignment sheet (thoughtful, original, accurate, detailed, elegant in description, insightful) to be sure there is a shared understanding of the terms. Note that "thoughtful" and "original" are included on both versions of the assignment. Note also that three cells on Version 1 are also included on Version 2. Ms. Ballard included three of the less complex options from Version 1 on Version 2 because she felt some students would likely "straddle" the two versions. Including some of the same tasks on both versions could allow a smooth transition for those students. She also pointed out that for early adolescents, it sometimes feels important to do the same work your friend is doing. If two friends ended up with different versions of the Think Tac Toe, they could still decide to select the same tasks by choosing the three tasks that are on both versions.

Ms. Ballard created Version 1 with students who are very advanced readers and/or thinkers in mind. She then created Version 2, which other students in the class will use, by adjusting some of the continuums reflected on "The Equalizer" (for example, complexity, abstractness, leap in thinking and understanding) to reduce the degree of assignment

Figure 18.2. A Midpoint Performance (Summative) Assessment on Analyzing Novelists and Their Tools in Ms. Ballard's Second-Period English Class

Novel Think-Tac-Toe Assessment
Version 1

Directions: Select and complete one activity from each horizontal row to help you and others think about your novel. Remember to make your work thoughtful, original, insightful, and elegant in expression. Use our rubric to guide your work.

Character — Write an "I am from" poem about yourself and another about a main character in the book you selected so your readers see how you and the character are alike and different. Be sure to include the most important traits in each poem.	A character in the book is being written up in a news feature 20 years after the novel ends. Write the piece. Where has life taken him/her? Why? Now, do the same for yourself 20 years from now. Make sure both pieces are enlightening feature articles.	You're a "profiler." Write and illustrate a full and useful profile of an interesting character from the book with emphasis on personality traits and mode of operating. While you're at it, profile yourself, too.
Setting — Research a town/place you feel is equivalent to the one in which the novel is set. Use maps, sketches, population, and other demographic data to help you make comparisons and contrasts.	Make a model or a map of a key place in your life, and an important one in the novel. Find a way to help viewers understand both what the places are like and why they are important in your life and the characters'.	The time and place in which people find themselves and when events happen shape those people and events in important ways. Find a way to convincingly support that idea using the book you selected.
Theme — Find out about famous people in history or in current events whose experiences and lives reflect the essential themes of your novel. Show us what you've learned.	Create a multi-media presentation that fully explores a key theme from the novel. Use at least 3 media (for example painting, animation, music, poetry, photography, drama, dance, sculpture) in your exploration.	Find several songs you think reflect an important message from the book. Prepare an audio collage. Create an exhibit card that helps your listener understand how you think these songs express the book's meaning.

Know: theme, setting, characterization **Do:** Relate elements of fiction to a novel and to your own life.
Understand: Good fiction is often about the reader, too. Good fiction helps readers try on different lives.
Essential Question: How do good authors turn readers into thinkers?

Novel Think-Tac-Toe Assessment
Version 2

Directions: Select and complete one activity from each horizontal row to help you and others think about your novel. Remember to make your work thoughtful, original, accurate, and detailed. Use our rubric to guide your work.

Character — Create a pair of collages that compares you and a character from the book you selected. Compare and contrast physical and personality traits. Label your collages so viewers understand your thinking	Write a bio-poem about yourself and another about a main character in your book so your readers see how you and the characters are alike and different. Be sure to included the most important traits in each poem.	Write a recipe or set of directions for how you would solve a problem and another for how a main character in the book would solve the same problem. Your list should help us know you and the character from your think and solve problems.
Setting — Design and write a greeting card or e-greeting card that invites us into the scenery and mood of an important part of the book. Be sure the verse helps us understand what is important in the scene and why.	Make a model or map of a key place in your life, and an important one in the novel. Find a way to help viewers understand both what the places are like and why they are important in your life and the characters'.	Make 2 timelines. The first should illustrate and describe at least 6 shifts in settings in the book. The second should explain and illustrate how the mood changes with each change in the setting.
Theme — Using books or websites of proverbs and/or quotations, find at least 6–8 that you feel reflect what's important about the novel's theme. Find at least 6–8 that do the same for your life. Display them and explain your choices.	Interview a key character from the book to find out what lessons he/she thinks we should learn from events in the book. Use an interview format on a blog or website or in a magazine for format and style. Be sure the interview is thorough.	Find 3–4 songs you think reflect an important message from the book. Prepare an audio collage. Write an exhibit card that helps your listener understand how you think these songs express the book's meaning. Include in the exhibit 1 song you feel reflects a theme in your life and explain it, too.

Know: theme, setting, characterization **Do:** Relate the elements of fiction to your own life. Write for an audience.
Understand: Good fiction is often about the reader too. Good fiction helps readers try on different lives.
Essential Question: How do authors turn readers into thinkers?

difficulty in Version 2. In other words, she planned for "teaching up" by beginning with KUDs and expectations that call on all students to understand what they are learning and to be thinkers and creators. She then developed the Version 1 assignment that is relatively complex, multifaceted, abstract, open-ended, requiring significant leaps of insight, and so forth, so that it would be a bit daunting for students who are academically advanced in the areas of writing and comprehension and analysis of literature. Version 2 of the assignment maintains the same KUDs as well as the expectation that students will need to understand what they are reading, successfully analyze it, and transfer their knowledge and understanding to contexts that are unlike ones they have used in class during the novel study. However, the assignment components (except the ones shared by both versions) on Version 2 are generally a little further to the left on some of The Equalizer continuums than is the case for the same components on Version 1. Both versions offer students options that tap into varied student interests and preferences for sharing what they have learned.

Ms. Ballard will further scaffold Version 2 by hosting start-up conversations as students are deciding which three challenges they will decide to do; by providing planning grids on which students lay out their ideas, steps in their work, and timelines before they begin the work; having optional check-in dates that allow her to provide early feedback to students; having the assignment translated into

THINKING ABOUT MS. BALLARD'S USE OF TEACHING UP AND THE EQUALIZER

- Take a few minutes to examine the two versions of the Think-Tac-Toe assignment in Figure 18.2.
- Select one cell or component from the Setting row on each version (but not the cell that is in the Setting row of both versions).
- Compare the two cells you selected by using The Equalizer. Can you see one or more indicators on The Equalizer that seem further to the right (in other words, indicators in Version 1 that are pitched at a higher degree of difficulty than that same indicator on Version 2)?
- Now, select one cell in the Theme row from Version 1.
- Select one indicator from The Equalizer to use with your selection from Version 1. Think about the assignment in that cell. How might you tweak the assignment to make it more complex, abstract, open-ended, multifaceted, and so on than it now is?
- Select one cell from the Theme row in Version 2.
- Select one indicator from The Equalizer to use with your selection from Version 2. Examine the assignment in the cell you selected. How might you tweak the assignment to make it less complex, less abstract, have fewer facets, require a smaller leap of thought or transfer, and so on?
- What scaffolding is Ms. Ballard using to make student work on either or both versions of the Think-Tac-Toe task more doable for students?
- Think about a couple of students in one of your classes who have particular learning needs, emotional or social challenges, are quite advanced academically or highly creative, and so forth. Rewrite the assignment in one of the cells you selected with those students in mind, so it is in an appropriate "challenge zone" for that learner.
- Now, look at The Equalizer again. Which buttons were you adjusting when you modified the assignment (even if you were not looking at The Equalizer at the time)?

Remember that The Equalizer is a heuristic (guide), not an algorithm (recipe). It can point you in a reasonable direction—provide you with some vocabulary that is useful for your thinking and planning. The thinking itself, however, will still necessarily be yours.

Clear and high expectations + the Equalizer continuums + scaffolding = equity of access to high-quality, meaningful learning opportunities for a very broad spectrum of learners.

home languages of her English learners; using learning stations where students can find materials related to the various assignment components and work with those materials alone or with a partner; holding writing workshop sessions several times during the assignment's 3-week duration; and conferencing with students during class work time. In addition, she will use clips from movies and television shows with the whole class to discuss ideas like introducing, complicating, and solving a problem in a novel, television show, or movie; how music contributes to setting; and how students relate events in fiction (or biographies/autobiographies) to their own lives.

Students working with either version of the Think-Tac-Toe have access to art materials and supplies that are available in Ms. Ballard's room and in the art room. Students can check out laptops from Ms. Ballard. They can access apps that they often use in class on the laptops and through the class intranet site. These apps enable them to communicate their learning through many modes. Several apps allow students to collaborate with peers and to post their drafts for peer feedback.

Example #2: First-Grade Math

Mr. Minkel teaches 24 first-graders in a Title I school where about 80% of students are English learners and where most students qualify for the free and reduced lunch program. In addition to learning needs based on language, culture, and poverty, he teaches students who may have specific reading disorder and/or ADHD, as well as children who have experienced or are experiencing trauma. Several of his students, while new to English, are quick learners and fluid thinkers, particularly in math.

Two characteristics of this teacher's approach to teaching are evident as today's lesson begins. First, he has taught students a variety of classroom routines from the very earliest days of school so that when he signals time for a change of subject, assignment, or working arrangements, the students move seamlessly to what comes next. As this math lesson begins, he has just asked his students to move to the colorful rug along one side of the room. They sit attentively, looking at their teacher, who is sitting in front of the group in a swivel chair. Their comfort with the routines makes the day predictable and gives them a sense of agency in the environment.

A second characteristic is that the classroom environment is peaceful and feels safe. He speaks to the young learners as though they are comfortable with English, while still using many strategies to reinforce key vocabulary and modeling sentence structure both in the language itself and in math. Classroom walls contain word charts, student work, and reminders about traits of a growth mindset and how to talk with one another respectfully. He consistently teaches his students the skills they need to work together successfully and emphasizes that students can work in ways that grow their brains—that make them smarter. There is a sense that the teacher trusts the children and that they trust him.

In today's math lesson, he and the students are continuing their work with arrays and sets and will begin an exploration of multiplication as it relates to notation of arrays and sets. Figure 18.3 provides the KUDs for the lesson.

Mr. Minkel has planned today's lesson based on two pre-assessment observations. One is his purposeful observation of an activity from the previous week. The second is purposeful observation of a game the students play called Circles & Squares. Prior to today's lesson, students have had numerous previous experiences with equal sets and counting sets of things. As numbers in the arrays with which students are working get larger, he will introduce the concept of multiplication as repeated addition and as an efficient way of describing sets.

After he welcomes the students to today's math lesson, he points to the flip chart next to his chair and asks students to read the unit's "big question" with him. As he points to each word briefly, students read, "How do we compose sets into different arrays?"

Pointing to a grid that has 4 rows with 5 cells in the first 2 rows and 3 cells in the next 2, Mr. Minkel begins a brief review. "Who can tell me whether this is an array?" Most of the students either shake their heads or answer, "No!"

"Okay, take a look at this example," he says, pointing to another grid on the flip chart. "Is this an array?" This time students nod and/or say *yes* enthusiastically.

"Then how do we know whether something is an array or not? Turn to a friend and tell that person what you think."

Figure 18.3. KUDs for a Portion of a Unit That Focuses on Sets and Arrays in Mr. Minkel's 1st-Grade Class

As a result of their study of sets and arrays, students should:		
Know	Understand	Be Able to Do
Arrays are composed of rows and columns.	Numbers can be decomposed in different ways.	Arrange sets of objects in two or more different ways
Sets are groups of objects.	Quantities are not static.	Write notation for an array in three different ways
Equations describing sets can be written in three ways.	Mathematicians can decompose quantities in multiple ways.	

After a pause for those conversations, which he is monitoring carefully to see their interactions and responses, Mr. Minkel asks, "What makes this one an array?"

Students respond, "It has the same number of squares in the columns and the rows."

"Remind me with your hands what a column looks like."

All the students use both hands to make an up-and-down motion.

"Right," their teacher says. "Now remind me what a row looks like."

This time, the students use their hands to "draw" a horizontal space.

"Take a look at this array," he says, pointing to another grid on the flip chart. "Which of these ways of decomposing the array is correct?"

He reads and points to three notations one by one. "$5 + 5 + 5 = 15$. 3 sets of 5 is 15. $3 \times 5 = 15$."

After a pause for students to discuss with a partner which notation is correct, many of the students answer that all three ways are correct. Next, he asks students to decompose "a regular number" rather than an array, and they propose ways to decompose $8 + 4$.

"Look around our room and see if you can find an array."

In about 15 seconds, he asks students to tell a partner what they found. One student says the number chart on the wall is an array and explains why he thinks so. Another student points to the colorful geometric rug they are seated on. Mr. Minkel nods and smiles as he says to the students, "Did you know you were sitting on an array?!"

The students smile or giggle as they look down at the rug. He asks students to remind him which direction the columns go on the rug and then which way the rows go. Again, students "draw" the up-and-down and the left/right directions with their hands. Now that students have considered two correct examples of arrays in the room, he extends the time for them to find other arrays and then lets several students share their finds.

Every once in a while, as he watches the students closely, he says quietly, "Does that sound right, Miguel?" or "Are you thinking with us, Sofia?" The questions are so soft and seamless with the ideas he is sharing that only the student whose name is spoken seems to be aware that he has addressed them.

When the review is complete, he tells the students they will be working together today to decompose a set into an array. "You're going to magically be transformed into employees in a candy factory and you will need to figure out how to package the candies you make in an array."

He takes a heart-shaped box of chocolates out of his desk drawer, explaining that one of the students gave him the candy for Valentine's Day. Opening the box, he points out that the people in the candy factory where this box was made decided to pack the candies in the shape of a heart.

Drawing the heart-shape with his fingers so the students could see, he asks, "Did they pack the candies in an array?"

Students shake their heads, "No."

Mr. Minkel agrees.

"In your candy factory today, the designer wants to pack the chocolates in an array to save space so he can fit more chocolates into each box." Mr. Minkel points to spots in the heart-shaped box that could have been used to place chocolates if the designer there had wanted to use an array instead of a heart-shape.

He asks the students to magically transform themselves into employees of the candy factory. Instantly, they respond, "SHAZAM" as they use a common hand signal to make the magic happen.

After a brief explanation of the work students will do next and one more example of notation using a 4x4 array, Mr. Minkel asks them to join him in a fishbowl demonstration on the other side of the room. They move readily and gather around as he asks Kayla to be his partner in solving a problem. "My 1st-graders don't always pick up on directions when I just say them, but when they see something demonstrated, they are generally ready to go."

He gives Kayla a baggie with bright blue wooden tiles in it while he holds a grid that fills a sheet of paper with cells the size of the tiles. He says that Kayla will use the tiles to make an array that uses all the tiles in the baggie. When she finishes and they both think the design is really an array, Kayla will cut the shape of the array out of the large grid, and he will write the notation in three ways they agree are correct. Then, if they were doing the whole activity instead of just modeling part of it, they would trade roles and he would make another array that he would cut out and for which Kayla would write the notation they agree on. "It will take both of you to figure out all the parts," he points out.

Kayla thinks she has a good idea for an array, but it doesn't work. There are not enough tiles in the baggie to make the third column the right length. "Oh, that didn't work," Mr. Minkel says to the group. "Should I give up?"

Students vigorously shake their heads, "No!"

"That's right!" he says. "Mathematicians always persevere!"

After a couple of additional attempts, Kayla and Mr. Minkel create an array with Kayla cutting out the shape of the array and Mr. Minkel writing the notations to model that process for the class. Mr. Minkel groups and regroups students quite often. In a research project the students completed earlier, they were grouped by interests in a common topic. Sometimes in reading they are grouped by a particular need such as fluency or comprehension. In today's math lesson, they will work together based on various points of readiness that he noted in two observational assessments from the previous week during which he took careful notes as students worked. He passes out baggies of tiles to pairs of students, calling their names as he hands the baggies to each pair. The lesson today is a tiered lesson. While the task remains the same for all pairs, some groups have 12 tiles in their baggies, some have 18, and some have 24. For students who are still mastering addition, 12 tiles will be easier to count, to shape into an array, and to write correctly in notations.

Students move automatically to a section of the room where there are desks with plenty of surface to lay out the tiles. Grids and scissors are in the middle of each table as students move to their seats. They leave some space between pairs as they settle in and immediately begin work on their candy factory job. Mr. Minkel moves around the room, listening to conversations, making notes, and asking questions.

Periodically, he sits with a pair of students to coach them. Two boys are having difficulty figuring out how to make a correct array, so their teacher sits with them asking questions, providing plenty of wait time for them to consider next steps. After a good bit of time working with the pair, he removes a few of the tiles from their design and asks the boys to think about how they could position those tiles so there would be the same number in each row and each column. After a couple of additional tries, they get it, and as Mr. Minkel moves on to another pair of learners, the two boys are talking together about notation.

He sees that a pair of girls are able to create several arrays in quick order, but also sees that they are creating familiar patterns that provide little challenge for them. He talks with them about his observation that they seem ready to make arrays with larger numbers of tiles or in less familiar shapes. For several minutes, the two struggle to break set, but as Mr. Minkel comes back to their desk after another tour around the room, he sees the two grin broadly and give one another a high-five as they accomplish their challenge. The notation is yet another challenge, but they keep at it after their teacher says, "You accomplished your first goal. I believe you will figure this one out, too."

When it is time for Mr. Minkel to signal the 1st-graders to wrap up their work, he looks over a couple of pages of notes he has taken while the students work to decide on points he wants to bring up as the math lesson ends. Then, pointing to a chart above the whiteboard, he asks students to think about whether they have worked hard during all of the activity, during most of it, during some of it, or during little of it. All the students give a thumbs up for the first response.

"I agree," Mr. Minkel says. "Every single kid has been working hard today. So, does that mean you've gotten a lot smarter, some smarter, a little smarter, or no smarter today?"

The growth mindset continuum is familiar to the students, who all agree that they have gotten a lot smarter because of their hard work.

Next, the teacher asks the 1st-graders to take a gallery walk to look at the arrays their classmates have created as well as their notations. Then, with the students gathered together on the rug where the lesson began, he talks with them about positives he observed as they worked and ideas they would keep working on together to keep learning.

Ending the class with the earlier focus on multiplication as an efficient way to describe an array, he writes on the flip chart next to an array $3 + 3 + 3 + 3 + 3 + 3 = 18$. Beneath that, he writes $6 \times 3 = 18$. He asks his students to read the first response with him as he points to the numbers and reads the array slowly and with effort, saying, "Whew!" when they finish. "Is that a correct way to describe this array?"

The students all nod. "Yes, it *is* correct."

Then he asks them to read the second notation, which proceeded more swiftly. "Is *this* notation correct?" he asks.

The students nod again.

"Yes, you're correct again. Both answers are right. The second way is just so much faster. That's the way mathematicians would write the notation."

Pointing again to the first notation and then the longer one, Mr. Minkel asks the students which of the two answers ends up with a bigger number. Many of the students respond, "They are both the same."

"You're working hard and learning well," he says, smiling.

Then he asks them to let him know how comfortable they are with the ideas in today's lesson. "Thumbs up if you think you totally understand the ideas. Thumbs up if you pretty much understand but still need a little more work to be sure. Thumbs up if you are a little confused right now."

Different students hold up a thumb for different options.

"If you're a little confused, is that okay?" he asks.

Students say *yes* and nod.

"Sure it is," he replies. "I get confused all the time. I just keep on working and things get clearer."

As class ends, Mr. Minkel again asks his students to use their magic, this time to turn themselves back into being 1st-graders.

THINKING ABOUT MR. MINKEL'S MATH CLASS

- In what ways do you think Mr. Minkel teaches up to his students?
- What does he do during whole-class time (highway time) to support a wide variety of student needs in terms of content readiness, language, poverty, emotional need, and interests/strengths?
- What does he do during whole-class time (highway time) to address learner variance?
- In what ways do his beliefs and approaches to teaching and learning provide equity of access to complex and multifaceted learning opportunities that these students might not find in other contexts?
- What does he do during exit ramp time to address a range of student understanding related to sets, arrays, notation, and a basic understanding of multiplication?
- What is his approach to formative assessment? Why do you think he approaches it as he does?
- How does he gather data about student development? How does he use what he learns from the information?
- Thinking about The Equalizer, what does Mr. Minkel do to have all learners working with sets, arrays, and notation but at levels of challenge (degrees of difficulty) that are appropriate for their current points of development with this math content?
- What personal and professional traits do you think contribute to his success as a teacher and his students' success as learners?
- What question would you like to ask Mr. Minkel if you had the opportunity?

Conclusion

A doctoral student who was just completing her first year of study at the university where I taught said to me with a furrowed brow, "I feel like I keep reading the same ideas over and over, no matter what I'm reading about."

"Tell me a bit more about that," I said, uncertain of her meaning and of her evident dilemma.

"Well," she said after a generous pause, "when I read about curriculum, the ideas seem to be the same ones I find when I read about instruction." Pause. "And when I read about assessment, somehow the same ideas are there." Longer pause. "And when I read about differentiation, they are there all over again."

I understood exactly where she was in her thinking. I had been there myself not too many years before her. I knew which authors my doctoral student was reading and understood exactly the echoes she heard from one book to another. I also knew that she would make a discovery that I had ultimately made as I traveled a journey much like hers.

"I think you're on to something important," I said. "Keep reading and as you read, think about roots."

The root system that feeds (or should feed) our thinking, research, planning, and implementation in teaching has been soundly in place for nearly half a century. The roots have strengthened over time with the kinds of discoveries that evolve from ongoing inquiry in any field of scholarship—and from the relatively young field of educational neuroscience.

We know much, for example, about how people learn; about what the brain needs to learn durably; about the interdependence between affective development, social development, and academic or intellectual development; and about impediments to learning (both short- and long-term) and how to teach around those barriers. We know about the power of communities of learning to better the work of those who make up the communities and about the centrality of teacher/student trust and relationships in the success of learners. We know that without relevance, academic content has little chance of benefiting the fabric of a child's life.

So it should not have been a surprise to me that in the scores of books I revisited and consulted for the first time as I wrote this book, the recommendations for successfully teaching students who live with poverty are, in so many instances, the same as the recommendations for students who are learning English and students with specific reading disorder or ADHD or EBD. It should not have been worthy of note that experts on students who experience trauma are so similar to those for students who find that their race becomes a barrier to accessing excellent learning opportunities or for students whose cultures span the spectrum of non dominant cultures in the United States.

As I completed the first draft of this book and reviewed and revised it, then added to it and repeated the process, I realized again that quality teaching for any student has roots in what we know about quality teaching for all students. There are some themes that sound more loudly for one student than another, for one category of students than another (including the caution that there are no two learners who are just like any others and that one-size-fits-all teaching is not part of the canon of quality). My takeaway this time around is that students who are vulnerable in life for any number of reasons and for variable spans of time are the ones hurt most when the foundation of quality learning is shaky.

Viable inclusion begins not as classroom teachers become experts in a range of learning exceptionalities, but as those teachers are supported in "constructing" themselves, their trust of and respect for the learners they teach, flexible learning environments, their approaches to and uses of assessment, their modes of instruction, and their capacity to lead and inspire young learners. That root system draws on our profession's best knowledge about successful teaching and learning. That root system belongs to every learner, and it both invites and enables inclusion.

One book I revisited as I concluded my writing of this book was Alfred Tatum's (2005) *Teaching Reading to Black Adolescent Males*. My copy is full of underlines, highlighters, check marks, and boxes from rereadings over the last 15-plus years. The title sounds like it is written for teachers of a specialized group—adolescents, not all ages; males, not females; Black students, not students of other ethnicities. Indeed, that specialized focus *is* the intent of Tatum's book. Tatum knows experientially that the students about whom he writes are regularly diminished by both racism and ineffective teaching. He understands the students and the nature of instruction that is necessary to right their futures. He speaks in the book directly to those things on virtually every page, emphasizing both the primacy of and pathways to equity of access to excellent learning opportunities for Black adolescent males.

And still, because the book draws on the root systems of our knowledge about teaching that reaches students and supports their growth, it speaks on behalf of the great swath of learners in our schools. As Tatum describes the attributes of culturally responsive teachers, think about how many of the descriptors reflect guidance from the first section of *this* book as it talks about foundational teaching and learning. Then reflect on how many of the descriptors appear in the guidelines that constitute the majority of each of the chapters in Part II of the book as those chapters spotlight particular categories of student need. (I have paraphrased Tatum's words slightly and have omitted a few of the items on his list of 27 attributes.) Tatum uses the heading "Culturally responsive teachers" for his list.

With the few edits I have made in the list and based on the focus of this book, I will head the list that follows here with:

Responsive teachers

- know their students and the subject matter they teach.
- place learning in a meaningful context.
- help students understand more about themselves and more about the world.
- find ways to help students see the implications texts have for their lives, futures, and communities.
- provide instruction that gives shape and form to students' lives.
- use literature that is relevant and speaks to their students' experiences.
- help students define who they want to become, regardless of society's perception of who they are.
- avoid reducing learning to prescribed skills and information required by a test.
- establish classroom communities based on the concepts of care and respect for the learner and his/her culture.
- establish trusting relationships and feelings of kinship.
- address students' needs for academic, cultural, developmental, emotional, and social learning.
- understand the lived experiences of their students and how their students respond to these experiences.
- connect, as best they can, students' in-school lives with their out-of-school lives.
- understand their role as being much broader than helping students do well on tests.
- emphasize cooperation and collaboration over competition during instruction.
- carry the burden of success with their students, not assigning success or failure to the students only.
- plan instruction and assessments with a rich audit of who the students are.
- confront stereotypes in curriculum and in the instructional environment.

- understand that literacy and reasoned thinking are tools of resistance.
- resist curricula and orientations of curricula that are disempowering.
- seek ways to help students make connections—within subjects, across subjects, and with their lives.
- focus instruction on helping students develop strategies and hope for overcoming academic and societal barriers to success.

While I chose to modify "culturally responsive teachers" to "responsive teachers" in adapting Tatum's list, I could just as well have used Tatum's header. We are all shaped by a culture—or, rather, by cultures. We typically have a national culture that defines us in many ways, but we also carry the culture of a region, of being female, or of being male. We are part of the culture of sports or of poets or of musicians or of tribes or of twins or of only children. We reflect the culture of trauma or a non conforming sexual identity or poverty—of blindness, of autism, of high ability. And so we need teachers who, day by day, become more proficient in creating classrooms that are culturally responsive as well as academically responsive. Both kinds of responsiveness are rooted in quality teaching, a focus on the very individual learner, and ensuring that each learner has equity of access to the kind of learning opportunities that maximally extend his or her capacity to learn and to translate that learning into living.

Here is a final echo of what has long reverberated in my thinking and into this book. Grant Wiggins (1992), just about 3 decades ago, and drawing on the deep roots of the wisdom of educational practice, summed up both the challenge of the field of education and our challenge as individual educators.

We will not successfully restructure schools to be effective until we stop seeing diversity in students as a problem. Our challenge is not one of getting "special" students to better adjust to the usual. . . .The challenge remains . . . ensuring that all students receive their entitlement. They have the right to thought-provoking and enabling schoolwork, so they might use their minds well and discover the joy therein to willingly push themselves farther. They have the right to instruction that obligates the teacher, like the doctor, to change tactics when progress fails to occur. They have the right to assessment that provides students and teachers with insights into real-world standards, useable feedback, the opportunity to self-assess, and the chance to have dialogue with or even challenge, the assessor—a right in a democratic culture. Until such a time, we will have no insight into human potential. Until the challenge is met, schools will continue to reward the lucky or the already-equipped and weed out poor performers. (pp. xv–xvi)

I think my more seasoned doctoral student would now understand the echoes that reverberate in the work of Tatum and Wiggins and in this book and in the books listed in the references that follow this conclusion and in other books like them. I believe she would understand now that the authors of these sources draw from the hearty roots of our best knowledge—developed and developing—in the field of education. And I feel confident that she would understand that knowledge to be the key to teaching that opens equity of access to all learners.

These are the roots that run deep in Everybody Classrooms. They echo the sentiments of Harry Bosch, whose last name is the title of a television series. He is a crusader for justice—his edges both hardened and softened by the crusade. One of his guiding principles could well be the slogan for Everybody Classrooms: "Everybody matters or nobody matters."

Acknowledgments

This book is not the product of a grant or project or sustained work with a particular school where a team of individuals came together to address a need and to learn. In those contexts, it is generally straightforward to name those whose contributions shaped a publication.

This book is different. It has been shaped by a lifetime of educators and students who have contributed—often generously, sometimes unknowingly—to who I am and to what I understand about courageous and transformational teaching. Even if I thought it was within my reach to name the individuals in that long chain (it is not!), I would fear unintentionally leaving out the name of people who belong in the list or including individuals who would rather not be associated with me or with my work. Still, I am who I am and do what I do because of this legion of "teachers," and I feel a need to, in some way, acknowledge those influences.

I am a product of teachers throughout my school and university careers who saw hope in me when I saw none in myself—who took time to communicate caring, who went out of their way to find "projects" for me to do that might help me find myself: a 4th-grade teacher who asked me to walk to the entrance to the schoolyard to meet her young son when he arrived at the end of his school day and escort him back to our classroom; a middle school teacher who understood my delight in writing notebooks full of beautiful language that I found in all sorts of books I read in the public library as I waited for my mother to attend meetings there; a high school teacher who asked me be the student chair of a statewide language conference and then to join her as a summer teaching assistant at a university several hours away from my home; a high school teacher who wouldn't settle for my inclination to remain silent and unnoticed and who spent hours with me after school each week to help me find both voice and courage to use that voice; a high school teacher who asked me if I would like to design and carry out a study on the relationship between student access to a car and grades; a college professor who knew just the right setting for me when she sent everyone in our U.S. History class into the community for a year-long study of a group or organization whose history would parallel what we studied in class; a noted poet who taught my sophomore English class and who, just often enough, would write, "WOW!" beside something I had written and who also took care to give me sometimes uncomfortable feedback that pointed to the long path ahead. Those teachers, and more, engrained in me the power of a caring teacher to change the course of a life. I have tried to take that understanding into my own classrooms daily and to advocate the power of seeing, believing in, and caring for young people in my writing as well.

A piece of advice I received as a young teacher also shaped my trajectory. The advice was to find colleagues who were the best at what they do and to build partnerships with those individuals. That, the advisor said, would be a source of mentorship, collegiality, and aspiration. In my life, at least, he was correct. Sometimes I sought out those teachers. Sometimes we found one another by happenstance. Throughout my career as an educator, these were the people who invited me into their classrooms, the people with whom I built brick and board bookshelves in poorly furnished classrooms, the people with whom I sat or stood through countless formal and informal conversations as we developed brilliant and ill-fated plans and who shared with me and allowed me to share with them laughter, tears, humiliation, and joy. Some of them comprised the group of teachers who, over a period of about

15 years, developed and implemented and polished the seeds of what we now call differentiated instruction.

For over 4 decades, there have been authors and conference speakers who created in me a hunger to learn more about the profession we share, who challenged me to work from a solid belief system or philosophy, and who always made clear that the work of the teacher is enabling young people to build satisfying and productive lives.

And always, my best and most compelling teachers have been and are the students who came into the classrooms we shared and inevitably left me energized and better equipped to teach and to share ideas with other educators. They were triumphant and traumatized, frighteningly mature and frighteningly immature, well supported by wise parents and adrift in the world. They were (mostly) honest with me, and while that occasionally caused pain, it was a prime source of insights. They wanted learning to be joyful. They were nearly always up for a challenge. Every one of them needed teachers to see them as the individuals they are, to dream their dreams with them, and to be catalysts for accomplishing what they once believed was beyond their reach. They continue to shape me still through memories, visits, correspondence, and on social media. They are shop owners, teachers, lawyers, university professors, psychologists, laborers in hard and sweaty jobs, social workers, musicians, artists, authors, actors, a former pole dancer, and a wingwalker on classic airplanes. They are parents who experience the joys, weariness, and soul-eating tragedies that come with that role. They are everything. They are daily reminders that how we teach matters profoundly.

I am indebted to and filled with gratitude for all the lives that are mirrored in my life and work every day and whose presence is woven throughout this book as well.

References

11 facts about education and poverty in America. (n.d.). DoSomething. https://www.dosomething.org/us/facts/11-facts-about-education-and-poverty-america

American Psychological Association. (2017). *Ethnic and racial minorities and socioeconomic status.* https://www.apa.org/pi/ses/resources/publications/minorities

American University School of Education. (2020, August 26). Teaching culturally and linguistically diverse students. https://soeonline.american.edu/blog/culturally-and-linguistically-diverse-students#:~:text=%20Teaching%20culturally%20diverse%20students%20entails%20the%20following,diversity%20in%20teaching%20styles.%20Making%20an . . . %20More%20

Annie E. Casey Foundation. (2006). *Race matters: How race affects education opportunities.* https://www.aecf.org/resources/race-matters-how-race-affects-education-opportunities

Anti-Defamation League. (2021, April 27). *U.S. antisemitic incidents remained at historic high in 2020.* https://www.adl.org/news/press-releases/us-antisemitic-incidents-remained-at-historic-high-in-2020

Applied Behavior Analysis. (n.d.). *30 things all teachers should know about autism in the classroom.* https://www.appliedbehavioranalysisprograms.com/what-all-teachers-should-know-about-autism-in-the-classroom/

Azano, A., Missett, T., Tackett, M., & Callahan, C. (2018). The CLEAR Curriculum Model. In C. M. Callahan & H. L. Hertberg-Davis (Eds.), *Fundamentals of gifted education: Considering multiple perspectives* (2nd ed., pp. 293–309). Routledge.

Bailey, E. (2019, April 2). *Creating a dyslexia-friendly classroom.* ThoughtCo. https://www.thoughtco.com/creating-a-dyslexia-friendly-classroom-3111082

Barile, N. (2017, August 2). 5 things you can do to support your LGBTQ students. *Hey Teach!.* https://www.wgu.edu/heyteach/article/5-things-you-can-do-support-your-lgbtq-students1809.html

Berger, R., Rugen, L., & Woodfin, L. (2014). *Leaders of their own learning: Transforming schools through student-engaged assessment.* Jossey-Bass.

Borland, J. (2018). Problematizing gifted education: Thinking radically about our beliefs and practices. In C. M. Callahan & H. L. Hertberg-Davis (Eds.), *Fundamentals of gifted education: Considering multiple perspectives* (2nd ed., pp. 71–82). Routledge.

Borland, J. (Ed.). (2003). *Rethinking gifted education.* New York: Teachers College Press.

Boroson, B. (2020). *Decoding autism and leading the way to successful inclusion.* ASCD.

Brandt, R. (1993). On teaching for understanding: A conversation with Howard Gardner. *Educational Leadership, 50*(1), 4–7.

Breiseth, L. (n.d.). *Getting to know your ELLs: Six steps for success.* Colorín Colorado. https://www.colorincolorado.org/article/getting-know-your-ells-six-steps-success

Bryant, D., Bryant, B., & Smith, D. (2020). *Teaching students with special needs in inclusive classrooms* (2nd ed.). Thousand Oaks, CA: Sage.

Burnham, K. (2020, July 31). *5 culturally responsive teaching strategies.* Northeastern University Graduate Programs. https://www.northeastern.edu/graduate/blog/culturally-responsive-teaching-strategies/

Callahan, C. (2018). The characteristics of gifted and talented students. In C. M. Callahan & H. L. Hertberg-Davis (Eds.), *Fundamentals of gifted education: Considering multiple perspectives* (2nd ed., pp. 153–166). Routledge.

Callahan, G. (2020, October 26). *Teaching methods & strategies for students with autism.* https://www.rev.com/blog/instructional-teaching-strategies-for-students-with-autism

Centers for Disease Control and Prevention. (2019). *Attention deficit hyperactivity disorder.* https://www.cdc.gov/nchs/fastats/adhd.htm

Centers for Disease Control and Prevention. (2020a). *ADHD in the classroom: Helping children succeed in school.* https://www.cdc.gov/ncbddd/adhd/school-success.html

Centers for Disease Control and Prevention. (2020b). *Data and statistics on autism spectrum disorder.* https://www.cdc.gov/ncbddd/autism/data.html

Centers for Disease Control and Prevention. (2021). *Data and statistics on children's mental health.* https://www.cdc.gov/childrensmentalhealth/data.html

Chaltain, S. (2016, March 14). *Restorative justice: A better approach to school discipline.* GreatSchools. https://www.greatschools.org/gk/articles/discipline-in-schools-moves-toward-peacemaking/

Cochran-Smith, M. (1991). Learning to teach against the grain. *Harvard Education Review, 61*(3), 279–311.

Cohen, E., & Lotan, R. (2014). *Designing groupwork: Strategies for the heterogeneous classroom.* New York: Teachers College Press.

Cole, R. (Ed.). (1995). *Educating everybody's children: Diverse teaching strategies for diverse learners.* ASCD.

Collaborative Classroom. (n.d.). *Collaborative literacy: Comprehensive ELA curriculum reimagined.* https://www.collaborativeclassroom.org/programs/collaborative-literacy/

Collins, M. (1992). *Ordinary children, extraordinary teachers.* Hampton Roads Publishing.

Conn, A., Nelms, S., & Marsh, V. (2020). Creating a culture of care. *Educational Leadership, 78*(3), 58–63.

Cooper, T. (2016, August 10). *You can teach children living in poverty.* The Educator's Room. https://theeducatorsroom.com/teach-children-living-in-poverty/

Coulombe, M., & Marquez, K. (2020, December 2). *Supporting multilingual students in the early grades.* Edutopia. https://www.edutopia.org/article/supporting-multilingual-students-early-grades

Council for Exceptional Children & Council for Children with Behavior Disorders. (2020). *Information about emotional/behavioral disorders.* https://debh.exceptionalchildren.org/behavior-disorders-definitions-characteristics-related-information

Dack, H., & Tomlinson, C. (2015). Inviting all students to learn. *Educational Leadership, 72*(6), 10–15.

Desautels, L. (2017, April 26). *Reaching students with emotional disturbances.* Edutopia. https://www.edutopia.org/article/reaching-students-emotional-disturbances-lori-desautels

DiPietro, M. (2012). Association of American Colleges and Universities. *Applying the seven learning principles to creating LGBTQ-inclusive classrooms.* https://www.aacu.org/publications-research/periodicals/applying-seven-learning-principles-creating-lgbt-inclusive

Dyslexia Help. (2021). *10 helpful text-to-speech readers for back to school.* http://dyslexiahelp.umich.edu/tools/software-assistive-technology/text-to-speech-readers

The Dyslexia Resource. (2020, March 23). *Top teaching strategies for students with dyslexia.* https://dyslexiaresource.org/top-teaching-strategies-for-students-with-dyslexia/

Earl, L. (2013). *Assessment as learning: Using classroom assessment to maximize student learning* (2nd ed.). Corwin.

ED100. (n.d.). *Poverty and race: How do students' backgrounds affect their school performance?* https://ed100.org/lessons/poverty

Education and Behavior. (n.d.). *Try these 14 strategies to help children with ADHD improve focus and behavior.* https://educationandbehavior.com/strategies-for-children-with-adhd/

Eide, F. (n.d.). *How to help a dyslexic student in a general education classroom.* Dyslexic Advantage. https://www.dyslexicadvantage.org/how-to-help-a-dyslexic-student-in-a-general-education-classroom-part-i/

El-Mekki, S. (2017, April 14). 9 things every educator should know when teaching Black students. *Education Post.* https://educationpost.org/9-things-every-educator-should-know-when-teaching-black-students/

Erickson, H., Lanning, L., & French, R. (2017). *Concept-based curriculum and instruction for the thinking classroom* (2nd ed.). Corwin.

Ferlazzo, L. (2016, November 3). *Do's and don'ts for teaching English-language learners.* Edutopia. https://www.edutopia.org/blog/esl-ell-tips-ferlazzo-sypnieski

Ferlazzo, L. (2017, July 6). Author interview: "Culturally Sustaining Pedagogies." *Education Week.* https://www.edweek.org/teaching-learning/opinion-author-interview-culturally-sustaining-pedagogies/2017/07

Ferlazzo, L. (2020, Oct. 28). Raising "the bar" for ELL instruction. *Education Week.* https://www.edweek.org/teaching-learning/opinion-raising-the-bar-for-ell-instruction/2020/10

Ferlazzo, L. (2021a, February 14). Ten culturally responsive teaching strategies for the science classroom. *Education Week.* https://www.edweek.org/teaching-learning/opinion-ten-culturally-responsive-teaching-strategies-for-the-science-classroom/2021/02

Ferlazzo, L. (2021b, April 11). Strategies for supporting LGBTQ students. *Education Week.* https://www.edweek.org/leadership/opinion-strategies-for-supporting-lgbtq-students/2021/04

Ferlazzo, L., & Sypnieski, K. (2018). *The ELL teacher's toolbox: Hundreds of practical ideas to support your students.* Wiley.

Fisher, D. (1917). *Understood Betsy.* Henry Holt Publishers.

France, P. (2019, May 31). *Supporting LGBTQ students in elementary school.* Edutopia. https://www.edutopia.org/article/supporting-lgbtq-students-elementary-school

Fullan, M., Quinn, J., & McEachen, J. (2018). *Deep learning: Engage the world change the world*. Corwin.

Gay, G. (2018). *Culturally responsive teaching: Theory, research, and practice* (3rd ed.). Teachers College Press.

Gillis, M., & Kessler, E. (n.d.). *Treating dyslexia*. Smart Kids With Learning Disabilities. https://www.smartkids withld.org/getting-help/dyslexia/treating-dyslexia/

GLSEN. (n.d.). *Developing LGBTQ-inclusive classroom resources*. https://www.glsen.org/sites/default/files/201911/GLSEN_LGBTQ_Inclusive_Curriculum_Resource_2019_0.pdf

Gobir, N. (2021, May 25). How unconditional positive regard can help students feel cared for. *Mindshift*. https://www.kqed.org/mindshift/57646/how-unconditional-positive-regard-can-help-students-feel-cared-for

Gonzalez, J. (2017, Nov. 5). Making school a safe place for LGBTQ students. *Cult of Pedagogy*. https://www.cultofpedagogy.com/lgbtq-students

Gonzalez, J. (2014, December 11). 12 ways to support English learners in the mainstream classroom. *Cult of Pedagogy*. https://www.cultofpedagogy.com/supporting-esl-students-mainstream-classroom/

Gorski, P. (2018). *Reaching and teaching students in poverty* (2nd ed.). Teachers College Press.

Green, E. (2021, March 25). Shifting the climate for transgender and non-binary students. *ASCD*. .https://www.ascd.org/el/articles/shifting-the-climate-for-transgender-and-non-binary-students

Greene, R. (2014). *The explosive child* (5th ed.). Harper.

Greene, R. (2014). *Lost at school: Why our kids with behavioral problems are falling through the cracks and how we can help them*. Scribner.

Greene, R. (2016). *Lost & found: Helping behaviorally challenging students (and while you're at it, all the others)*. Jossey-Bass.

Guskey, T. (1994). Making the grade: What benefits students? *Educational Leadership, 52*(2), 14-20.

Guskey, T. (2000). Breaking up the grade. *Educational Leadership, 78*(1), 40–46.

Guskey, T. (2019). Grades vs. comments: Research on student feedback. *Phi Delta Kappan, 101*(3), 42–47.

Guskey, T. (2020). Breaking up the Grade. *Educational Leadership, 52*(2), 14–20.

Haap, J. (2020, April 9). The private logic behind a trauma-informed mindset. *ASCD*. https://www.ascd.org/el/articles/the-private-logic-behind-a-trauma-informed-mindset

Hammond, Z. (2015, April 15). 3 tips to make any lesson more culturally responsive. *Cult of Pedagogy*. https://www.cultofpedagogy.com/culturally-responsive-teaching-strategies/

Harmon, W. (2018). *5 concrete ways to help students living in poverty*. The Art of Education. https://theartof education.edu/2018/09/11/5-concrete-ways-to-help-students-living-in-poverty/

Hattie, J. (2012). *Visible learning for teachers: Maximizing impact on learning*. Routledge.

Hertberg-Davis, H. (2018). Defensible curriculum for gifted learners: Where the rubber hits the road. In C. M. Callahan & H. L. Hertberg-Davis (Eds.), *Fundamentals of gifted education: Considering multiple perspectives* (2nd ed., pp. 249–251). Routledge.

Horn, C., Little, C., Maloney, K., & McCullough, C. (2021). *Young scholars model: A comprehensive approach for developing talent and pursuing equity in gifted education*. Prufrock.

Hosier, D. (n.d.). *Twelve examples of traumatic childhood experiences*. Childhood Trauma Recovery. Retrieved December 19, 2021, from https://childhoodtraumarecovery.com/all-articles/twelve-examples-of-traumatic-childhood-experiences/

Imbeau, M. (2020). Teaching students with special gifts and talents. In E. Smith, E. Polloway, & T. Taber-Doughty, *Teaching students with special needs in inclusive classrooms* (8th ed., pp. 323–345). Pro-Ed.

Institute for Child and Family Well-Being. (n.d.). *Translating trauma-informed principles into trauma-responsive practices*. https://uwm.edu/icfw/translating-trauma-informed-principles-into-trauma-responsive-practices

International Dyslexia Association. (n.d.). Reading Rockets. *Accommodating students with dyslexia in all classroom settings*. https://www.readingrockets.org/article/accommodating-students-dyslexia-all-classroom-settings

Jensen, E. (2019). *The handbook for poor students, rich teaching*. Solution Tree.

Johns Hopkins Medicine. (n.d.). *Attention-deficit / hyperactivity disorder (ADHD) in children*. https://www.hopkinsmedicine.org/health/conditions-and-diseases/adhdadd

Johnson, C. (2013, November/December). Leading learning for children from poverty. *AMLE Magazine*. https://www.amle.org/leading-learning-for-children-from-poverty/

Kafele, B. (2021). *The equity and social justice education: 50 critical questions for improving opportunities and outcomes for Black students*. ASCD.

Kaplan, E. (2019, April 19). *6 essential strategies for teaching English language learners*. Edutopia. https://www.edutopia.org/article/6-essential-strategies-teaching-english-language-learners

Kaplan, S. (2018). Differentiating with depth and complexity. In C. M. Callahan & H. L. Hertberg-Davis (Eds.), *Fundamentals of gifted education: Considering multiple perspectives* (2nd ed., pp. 270–278). Routledge.

Kam, K. (2020). *Asian American students face bullying over COVID*. Web MD Health News. https://www.webmd.com/lung/news/20200820/asian-ameerican-students-face-bullying-over-covid

Karten, T. (2017). *Building on the strengths of students with special needs. How to move beyond labels in the classroom.* ASCD.

Kearney, M. (2021, February 5). Child poverty in the U.S. *Econofact.* https://econofact.org/child-poverty-in-the-u-s

Keels, M. (2020). Building racial equity through trauma-responsive discipline. *Educational Leadership, 78*(2), 40–45, 51.

Kelly, K. (n.d.). *The difference between dysgraphia and dyslexia.* Understood. https://www.understood.org/en/learning-thinking-differences/child-learning-disabilities/dysgraphia/the-difference-between-dysgraphia-and-dyslexia

Kids Together, Inc. (n.d.). *Benefits of inclusive education.* https://kidstogether.org/benefits-of-inclusive-ed/

Kiebel, M. (2017, December 18). Helping LGBTQ students thrive in school. *The Chalk Blog.* https://www.learnersedge.com/blog/helping-lgbtq-students-thrive

Kluth, P. (n.d.). *Supporting students with autism: 10 ideas for inclusive classrooms.* Reading Rockets. https://www.readingrockets.org/article/supporting-students-autism-10-ideas-inclusive-classrooms

Ladson-Billings, G. (1994). *The dreamkeepers: Successful teachers of African American children.* Jossey-Bass.

Learning for Justice Staff. (2017, August 2). *Six ways to stand behind your LGBT students.* https://www.learningforjustice.org/magazine/six-ways-to-stand-behind-your-lgbt-students

Lindsey, D., Thousand, J., Jew, C., & Piowlski, L. (2018). *Culturally proficient inclusive schools.* Corwin.

Love, B. (2019). *We want to do more than survive: Abolitionist teaching and the pursuit of educational freedom.* Beacon.

Loveless, B. (2021). *Emotional and behavioral disorders in the classroom.* Education Corner. https://www.educationcorner.com/behavioral-disorders-in-the-classroom.html

Low, K. (2020). *Teaching strategies for students with ADHD.* Verywellmind. https://www.verywellmind.com/teaching-strategies-for-students-with-adhd-20522

Lukowiak, T. (2010). Positive behavioral strategies for students with EBD and needed supports for teachers and paraprofessionals. *Journal of the American Academy of Special Education Professionals, Winter 2010,* 40–52. https://files.eric.ed.gov/fulltext/EJ1137055.pdf

McKibben, S. (2014, July 1). The two-minute relationship builder. *ASCD.* https://www.ascd.org/el/articles/the-two-minute-relationship-builder

McGraw Hill. (2019, April 24). *Supporting English learners with culturally responsive social and emotional learning: An interview with Aislinn Cunningham, ELA expert and manager of professional learning, StudySync.* Medium. https://medium.com/inspired-ideas-prek-12/supporting-english-learners-with-culturally-responsive-social-and-emotional-learning-7ed9d9f809a6

Mendler, A., & Curwin, R. (2007). *Discipline with dignity for challenging youth.* Solution Tree.

Merrill, S. (2020, Sept. 11). *Trauma is "written into our bodies"—but educators can help.* Edutopia. https://www.edutopia.org/article/trauma-written-our-bodies-educators-can-help

Mertz, J. (2016, April 19). *Why being a good observer matters.* https://www.thindifference.com/2016/04/good-observer-matters/

Miller, C. (n.d.). *What's ADHD (and what's not) in the classroom.* Child Mind Institute. https://childmind.org/article/whats-adhd-and-whats-not-in-the-classroom/

Miller, K. (2019, April 24). Culturally responsive and English learners. https://rpscurriculumandinstruction.weebly.com/tools-tips--tricks/culturally-responsive-and-english-learners

Milner, H. R., IV. (2006). *The promise of Black teachers' success with Black students.* https://files.eric.ed.gov/fulltext/EJ794734.pdf

Minahan, J. (2020). Maintaining relationships, reducing anxiety during remote learning. *Educational Leadership, 78*(2), 20–27.

Minkel, J. (2018, August 16). How can White teachers do right by students of color? *Education Week.* https://www.edweek.org/teaching-learning/opinion-how-can-white-teachers-do-right-by-students-of-color/2018/08

Mizerny, C. (2018, December 18). We can do lots more for students with dyslexia. *Middle Web Blog.* https://www.middleweb.com/39393/we-can-do-lots-more-for-students-with-dyslexia/

Namahoe, K. (2020, Dec. 2). *Natural-born hustlers: Combatting the school-to-prison pipeline through entrepreneurship education.* SmartBrief. https://www.smartbrief.com/original/2020/12/natural-born-hustlers-combating-school-prison-pipeline-through

National Association of Colleges and Employers. (2021). *Equity.* https://www.naceweb.org/about-us/equity-definition/

National Association of Secondary School Principals. (2019). *Poverty and its impact on students' education. https://www.nassp.org/poverty-and-its-impact-on-students-education/*

National Autistic Society UK. (n.d.). *What is autism?* https://www.autism.org.uk/advice-and-guidance/what-is-autism.

National Center for Education Statistics. (2018). *Number and percentage of public school students eligible for free and reduced-price lunch. Selected years 2000-01 through 2016-17.* https://nces.ed.gov/programs/digest/d18/tables/dt18_204.10.asp

National Center for Education Statistics. (2020). *Racial/ethnic enrollment in public school.* https://nces.ed.gov/programs/coe/indicator_cge.asp

National Child Traumatic Stress Network. (n.d.). *About child trauma.* https://www.nctsn.org/what-is-child-trauma/about-child-trauma

National Education Association. (2006). *Teaching students with autism in inclusive classrooms.* https://www.autism-society.org/wp-content/uploads/2014/04/Puzzle-of-Autism.pdf

National Research Council. (2000). *How people learn: Brain, mind, experience, and school* (Expanded ed.). National Academies Press.

National Science Teaching Association. (n.d.). *Behavioral disorders.* https://www.nsta.org/behavioral-disorders

New Brunswick Association for Community Living. (n.d.). *Inclusive education and its benefits.* https://nbacl.nb.ca/module-pages/inclusive-education-and-its-benefits/#:~:text=Inclusive%20education%20%28when%20practiced%20well%29%20is%20very%20important,other%20students%20their%20own%20age.%20More%20items%20...%20%20

Ottow, S. (2021, April 29). *What English learners need now.* Learning Forward. https://learningforward.org/2021/04/29/what-english-learners-need-now/

PACER's National Bullying Prevention Center. (2020). *Bullying statistics.* https://www.pacer.org/bullying/info/stats.asp

Paley, V. (1993). *You can't say you can't play.* Harvard University Press.

Parrett, W., & Budge, K. (2020). *Turning high-poverty schools into high-performing schools* (2nd ed.). ASCD.

Parrish, N. (2018, April 27). *Setting students with ADHD up for success.* Edutopia. https://www.edutopia.org/article/setting-students-adhd-success

Pate, A. (2020). *The innocent classroom: Dismantling racial bias to support students of color.* ASCD.

Pesce, A. (n.d.). Cultural diversity in the classroom: 5 useful tips on how to teach students from different cultures. *Busy Teacher.* https://busyteacher.org/17479-how-to-teach-students-different-countries-5.html

Peterson, M., & Hitte, M. (2005). *Inclusive teaching: Creating effective schools for all learners.* Allyn & Bacon.

Positive Action. (2021, February 26). *9 effective teaching strategies for students with emotional and behavioral disorders.* https://www.positiveaction.net/blog/teaching-strategies-for-emotional-and-behavioral-disorders

PsychGuides. (n.d.). *Behavioral disorder symptoms, causes, and effects.* https://www.psychguides.com/behavioral-disorders/

Public Schools First NC. (2020). *Facts on child poverty.* https://www.publicschoolsfirstnc.org/resources/fact-sheets/facts-on-child-poverty/

Randolph, D. (2021, April 15). Black lives ain't never gon' matter in the classroom until Black English does. *ASCD.* https://www.ascd.org/blogs/black-lives-aint-never-gon-matter-in-the-classroom-until-black-english-does

Rebora, A. (2020, October). Increasing awareness of student trauma in the COVID-19 era. *Educational Leadership, 78*(2), 10. http://www.ascd.org/publications/educational_leadership/oct20/vol78/num02/Increasing_Awareness_of_Student_Trauma_in_the_COVID-19_Era.aspx

Resilient Educator. (2018, May 30). *5 tips for handling EBD kids (Emotional Behavior Disorder) in an inclusive classroom.* https://resilienteducator.com/classroom-resources/5-tips-for-handling-ebd-kids-emotional-behavior-disorder-in-an-inclusive-classroom/

Riddell, L. (2020, July 2). *Three factors to focus on when teaching kids living in poverty.* Northwest Evaluation Association. https://www.nwea.org/blog/2020/3-factors-to-focus-on-when-teaching-kids-living-in-poverty/

Rojas, V. (2007). *Strategies for success with English language learners.* ASCD.

Russaw, J. (2019, October 16). Muslim students still almost twice as likely to face bullying at school despite "minimal improvement": Report. *Newsweek.* https://www.newsweek.com/cair-islamophobic-bullying-report-2019-1465490

Sandman-Hurley, K. (2014, Oct. 23). *Dyslexia in the general education classroom.* Edutopia. https://www.edutopia.org/blog/dyslexia-in-general-ed-classroom-kelli-sandman-hurley

Schlechty, P. (2011). *Engaging students: The next level of working on the work.* Wiley.

Scholastic. (n.d.). *10 common challenges and best practices for teaching students with ADHD.* https://www.scholastic.com/teachers/articles/teaching-content/10-common-challenges-and-best-practices-teaching-students-adhd/

Segal, J., & Smith, M. (2020). *Teaching students with ADHD.* https://www.helpguide.org/articles/add-adhd/teaching-students-with-adhd-attention-deficit-disorder.htm

Shaw, M., Hodgkins, P., Caci, H., & Young, S. (2012). A systematic review and analysis of long-term outcomes in attention deficit hyperactivity disorder: Effects of treatment and non-treatment. *BMC Med, 10,* 99. https://doi.org/10.1186/1741-7015-10-99

Smith, E., Polloway, E., & Taber-Doughty, T. (2020). *Teaching students with special needs in inclusive settings* (8th ed.). ProEd.

Smith, C. (2021, June 9). The benefits of speech-to-text technology in all classrooms. *MindShift.* https://www

.kqed.org/mindshift/57786/the-benefits-of-speech-to-text-technology-in-all-classrooms

Solar, E. (2011). *Emotional and behavioral disorders.* EBD for Everyone. https://ebdforeveryone.weebly.com/for-teachers.html

Sorrels, B. (2015). *Reaching and teaching children exposed to trauma.* Gryphon House.

Sousa, D., & Tomlinson, C. (2018). *Differentiation and the brain: How neuroscience supports the learner-friendly classroom* (2nd ed.). Solution Tree.

Star Autism Support. (n.d.). *Supporting students with ASD in general education.* https://starautismsupport.com/supporting-students-asd-general-education

Storti, C. (1999). *Figuring foreigners out.* Intercultural Press.

Tatum, A. (2005). *Teaching reading to Black adolescent males: Closing the achievement gap.* Stenhouse.

Teacher Vision. (n.d.). *Strategies for teaching culturally diverse students.* https://www.teachervision.com/teaching-strategies/strategies-for-teaching-culturally-diverse-students?

Thiers, N. (2020, October). Nadine Burke Harris on responding to human trauma. *Educational Leadership, 78*(2),12–13.

Thorne, G., Thomas, A., & Lawson, C. (n.d.). *15 strategies for managing attention problems.* Reading Rockets. https://www.readingrockets.org/article/15-strategies-managing-attention-problems

Tomlinson, C. (2017). *How to differentiate instruction in academically diverse classrooms* (3rd ed.). ASCD.

Tomlinson, C. (2021). *So each may soar: The principles and practices of learner-focused classrooms.* ASCD.

Tomlinson, C., Brimijoin, K., & Narvaez, L. (2008). *The differentiated school: Making revolutionary changes in teaching and learning.* ASCD.

Tomlinson, C., & Imbeau, M. (2010). *Leading and managing a differentiated classroom.* ASCD.

Tomlinson, C., & Javius, E. (2012, February). Teach up for excellence. *Educational Leadership, 65*(9), 28–33.

Tomlinson, C., & Murphy, M. (2015). *Leading for differentiation: Growing teachers who grow kids.* ASCD.

Tomlinson, C., & Sousa, D. (2020). The sciences of teaching. *Educational Leadership, 77*(8), 14–20.

The Trevor Project. (n.d.). *Estimating the number of LGBTQ youth seriously considering suicide.* https://www.thetrevorproject.org/trvr_press/national-estimate-of-lgbtq-youth-seriously-considering-suicide/

Tucker, M. (2019, December 5). *Child poverty and its impact on education in the United States.* National Center on Education and the Economy. https://ncee.org/2019/12/child-poverty-and-its-impact-on-education-in-the-u-s/

Understood.org. (2018). *Dyslexia fact sheet.* https://assets.ctfassets.net/p0qf7j048i0q/7gUDX1YFkaOHbBHiqylfli/4c5292b9283a2dc41f6b33a14dd867b4/Dyslexia_Fact_Sheet_Understood.pdf

Vygotsky, L. (1986). *Thought and language* (A. Kozulin, Ed. & Trans.). MIT Press. (Original work published in 1934)

Walkington, C., Milan, S., & Howell, E. (2014). What makes ideas stick? *The Mathematics Teacher, 108*(4), 272–279.

Waterford Foundation. (2014, March 11). *Dyslexia in schools: Understanding & teaching students with dyslexia.* https://www.waterford.org/education/dyslexia-in-schools/

Waterford Foundation. (2019a). *ADHD in the classroom: How to teach & support students with attention-deficit/hyperactivity disorder.* https://www.waterford.org/education/adhd-in-the-classroom/

Waterford Foundation. (2019b, March 26). *Information on supporting students with autism.* https://www.waterford.org/education/activities-for-children-with-autism/

Wiggins, G. (1992). Foreword. In R. Villa, J. Thousand, W. Stainback, & S. Stainback (Eds.), *Restructuring for a caring and effective education: An administrative guide to creating heterogeneous schools* (pp. xv–xvi). Paul H. Brookes.

Wiggins, G., & McTighe, J. (2005). *Understanding by design* (expanded 2nd ed.). ASCD.

Wiliam, D. (2011a). *Embedded formative assessment.* Solution Tree.

Wiliam, D. (2011b, September 16). *What assessment can—and cannot—do.* http://dylanwiliam.org/Dylan_Wiliams_website/Papers_files/Pedagogiska%20magasinet%20article.docx

Witt, D., & Soet, M. (2020, July 13). *5 effective modeling strategies for English learners.* Edutopia. https://www.edutopia.org/article/5-effective-modeling-strategies-english-learners

Wlodkowski, R., & Ginsberg, M. (1995, September 1). A framework for culturally responsive teaching. *Educational Leadership.* http://www.ascd.org/publications/educational-leadership/sept95/vol53/num01/A-Framework-for-Culturally-Responsive-Teaching.aspx

Woolf, N. (n.d.). *2 X 10 relationship building: How to do it (and why it works).* Panorama Education. https://www.panoramaed.com/blog/2x10-relationship-building-strategy

Worthington, B. (2021). *Dyslexia in the classroom.* Dyslexia Help. http://dyslexiahelp.umich.edu/parents/living-with-dyslexia/school/classroom

Zacarian, D., Alvarez-Ortiz, L., & Haynes, J. (2020, October). Meeting student trauma with an asset-based approach. *Educational Leadership, 78*(2), 69–73.

Zimmerman, K. (2017, July 12). *What is culture?* Live Science. www.livescience.com/21478-what-is-culture-definition-of-culture.html

Index

The letter *f* after a page number refers to a figure.

About the Author

Carol Ann Tomlinson is William Clay Parrish, Jr. Professor Emerita at the University of Virginia's School of Education and Human Development, where she served on the faculty for 29 years, including serving as Chair of Educational Leadership, Foundations, and Policy, and Co-Director of the University's Institutes on Academic Diversity. Prior to joining the faculty at UVA, she was a teacher in public schools for 21 years, during which she taught students in high school, preschool, and middle school and also administered programs for struggling and advanced learners. She was Virginia's Teacher of the Year in 1974.

Carol was named Outstanding Professor at UVA's School of Education and Human Development in 2004 and received an All-University Teaching Award in 2008. In 2022, she was ranked #12 in the *Education Week* Edu-Scholar Public Presence Rankings of the 200 "University-based academics who are contributing most substantially to public debates about schools and schooling," and as the #4 voice in Curriculum.

Carol is author of over 300 books, book chapters, articles, and other educational materials, including *How to Differentiate Instruction in Academically Diverse Classrooms* (3rd Ed.), *The Differentiated Classroom: Responding to the Needs of All Learners* (2nd Ed.), *and So Each May Soar: The Principles and Practices of Learner-Centered Classrooms*.

She works throughout the United States and internationally with educators who seek to create classrooms that are more effective with academically diverse student populations.